Aham: I

FOUNDATIONS OF PHILOSOPHY IN INDIA

GENERAL EDITORS
Ranjit Nair (Coordinator)
Arindam Chakrabarti
Mrinal Miri
J.N. Mohanty

The series FOUNDATIONS OF PHILOSOPHY IN INDIA, initiated by the Centre for Philosophy and Foundations of Science, New Delhi, aims to make available a critical reassessment of the philosophical achievement of the classical Indian tradition in such a way that it contributes to the dialogue between civilizations of the new century. Although a wealth of literature is already available in translation, it exists in scattered form and is primarily oriented towards philological rather than philosophical concerns. The series will, uniquely in the history of scholarship in this area, focus on concepts and theories, rather than the conventional schools. The objective in each case will be to provide a rigorous and analytical examination of key arguments and doctrines in a manner that makes them available for contemporary engagement and reflection.

Although there is an interest worldwide in Indian philosophy, the absence of a corpus of texts which presents the contents of the tradition in a scholarly, well-researched yet accessible format, has long been a handicap. The FOUNDATIONS OF PHILOSOPHY INDIA series will, it is hoped, fill this gap in a systematic and comprehensive manner.

Aham: I

The Enigma of I-consciousness

ANINDITA NIYOGI BALSLEV

OXFORD
UNIVERSITY PRESS

OXFORD
UNIVERSITY PRESS

Oxford University Press is a department of the University of Oxford.
It furthers the University's objective of excellence in research, scholarship,
and education by publishing worldwide. Oxford is a registered trademark of
Oxford University Press in the UK and in certain other countries

Published in India by
Oxford University Press
YMCA Library Building, 1 Jai Singh Road, New Delhi 110 001, India

ISBN-13: 978-0-19-808951-3
ISBN-10: 0-19-808951-1

Typeset in Minion Pro 10.5/13
by Alphæta Solutions, Puducherry, India 605 009
Printed in India at G.H. Prints Pvt Ltd, New Delhi 110 020

For Erik
who shares the inward journey

Contents

Preface

It was rather early in life, indeed long before my formal initiation as a student of philosophy, that I began wondering about the enigmatic character of I-consciousness. It is evidently indubitable, yet remains unfathomable. This is indeed a phenomenon that appears to resist all explanation but does not cease to challenge our understanding. What seemed then, as it also does now, to be especially intriguing is the remarkable manner in which this phenomenon sustains its identity in the midst of all kinds of change. It seems inevitable that any serious attempt to unravel I-consciousness is bound to assume in the long run the character of a quest that demands a readiness to walk on a 'razor's edge', as our ancients put it.

Subsequently, as I delved into the history of philosophy, both Indian and Western, it became clear that none of the contending schools of thought provided a definitive answer that is acceptable to all. Nevertheless, these attempts unmistakably show that a search in this direction has led the enquirers to devise a range of explanatory models that are of deep philosophical interest. Moreover, accounts of this intricate process of second-order reflection disclose to an enquirer the important differences between the phenomenon of I-consciousness and any other topic—however profound, complex, or abstract—that has been subjected to philosophical scrutiny. Perhaps this difference lies in the particular way the presence of I-consciousness manifests itself.

In contrast to any other mental episode where that which is apprehended has the status of not-I, the 'I' has the character of a subject and is never immediately encountered as an 'other' to or as an 'object' of consciousness—even if in some rare philosophical analysis it has been thus interpreted. This is also why an attempt to delineate I-consciousness invariably seems to demand much more than a purely cognitive probe in a discursive mode. In other words, if this is a phenomenon that simply cannot be formulated as a problem like any other phenomenon or subjected to similar sort of objective critical examination, it is precisely because of its very intimate and subjective character whose source and support remain beyond our cognitive grasp. We gaze at it with a sense of bewilderment, indeed, as the 'puzzle of all puzzles'.[1]

It is worth mentioning here that in the course of my reflections I was simply struck by the gradual unfolding of the multiple layers of subjectivity. The phenomenon of I-consciousness is not only absolutely central to all our cogitations on cognitions, emotions, and volitions, but is also invariably impregnated with deep existential concerns that have subtle moral as well as soteriological dimensions.

Remaining rooted in the very centre of our existence, this phenomenon is inextricably intertwined with the recurring states of sleep, dream, and wakefulness that encompass what each of us calls 'my life', demarcating it as distinct from the lives of others. To put it more poignantly, if I-consciousness, on the one hand, seems to be inseparably linked to our cherished sense of being here and now, on the other hand, it can hardly be disentangled from the weird sense of uncertainty arising from not knowing how it manifests itself. To make matters even worse, there is a feeling of dead-certainty that this 'I' is not here to stay, at least not in its present base. However, in all cases this awareness of 'I' involves a physical complex that I describe as 'my body', since along with I-consciousness there is always an entailed a feeling of intimacy with 'my body', where the line between a sense of identity and that of difference is blurred but not fully missing.[2]

Later on, during my studies, I was to gradually encounter a host of theories interpreting the dawning of 'the sense of self' in relation to this intimate yet ambivalent 'body-awareness', giving

1 William James, 1950 [1897], *The Principles of Psychology* (New York: Courier Dover Publications); see essay 'On Consciousness of Self'.

2 Gabriel Marcel, in his well-known book, *L'Etre et L'Avoir* observed: 'The primary object with which I identify myself, but which still eludes me, is my own body. We may well think that we are here at the very heart of the mystery, in the very deepest of having'.

rise to such competing theoretical claims, as dualism and monism. Each of these positions comes in several versions within which in turn there are subtle internal divergences. The former philosophical stance clearly acknowledges the reality of both, leading to what has been designated as the 'mind–body problem'. The latter may assume the form of one of the several versions of physicalism, or the other extreme of affirming the sole ontological reality of consciousness, accounting for the first person in each case variously. Indeed, there are various designations that bear witness to the intricacies that theory-makers introduce while weaving theories about the status of I-consciousness—a phenomenon that otherwise no one doubts or denies.

It is not surprising to find that this topic of I-consciousness has called for an intellectual exploration of an incredibly wide range of interconnected issues in the historical context of cross-cultural philosophical enquiries. There are ample records that testify to diverse theoretical interpretations of I-consciousness along with a large number of questions and concerns which touch upon this central theme of human existence, ranging from birth to death. As is to be expected, these questions have psychological, epistemological, metaphysical, ethical, and even religious dimensions. Viewed holistically, all these concerns are significant parts of such an investigation. However, given the existing disciplinary boundaries in academia at present, the focus is on specific aspects of this theme in particular disciplines. A comprehensive undertaking calls for collaborative work, which is still missing. Nevertheless, one comes across imaginative speculations that have ensued from various quarters in the course of exploration of what lies at the core of I-consciousness.

There are narratives—philosophical, religious, and mythological—which describe the phenomenon either in a similar or in an opposed fashion. Some, for example, speak of its ultimate imperishable character and others, on the contrary, of its inevitable dissolution and eventual passing into nothingness. A variety of stories and accounts exist concerning the emergence of this phenomenon, in terms of its creation, its embodiment, or its embrainment. In some of those that are available from cross-cultural sources, the I-consciousness of the present life is depicted as unique, whereas others maintain the possibility of its continuation through many lives, often situating the accounts within specific soteriological frameworks. Indeed, the diverse renditions of these views that are naturally at variance depend not only upon the genre of texts one is consulting—ancient or modern—but also on the convictions of the narrators themselves about the source of the sense of I. Reference will be made later on in this monograph to these debates that are not merely of historical interest but are relevant even today with regard to such issues as whether the phenomenon can be said to arise and to exist exclusively within or only in close association with the physical and the neuro-biological processes, or whether its source must be sought elsewhere. In other words, just as there are some who claim that the first person features are entirely embedded in physiological processes, there are others who reject such a theoretical rendition, holding the view instead that this phenomenon is an expression of an irreducible, non-physical principle. Consequently, documents also disclose a host of speculations concerning the status of the first person in the context of death and hereafter. According to some, the sense of 'I' is eventually destined to dissolve into nothingness at death. Again, there are others who claim that death is nothing but a casting off of the mortal frame, that is, the physical garb with which the sense of self is provisionally associated at present. There are many reordered statements about the possibilities of pre-natal as well as post-mortem existence. All cultures are storehouses of such stories.

In philosophical literature 'I-consciousness' is accounted for with or without reference to a metaphysical entity called the self or *atman*. Mythologically, the self is often treated as the emblem of immortality. Many thinkers across cultures are even persuaded to ponder over, among various other concerns, the soteriological significance of the phenomenon. Consequently, advocates of some traditions not only pronounce that a notion of a metaphysical self is to be assumed in order to explain I-consciousness, they even boldly declare that 'knowledge of the self' is the same as salvatory or liberating[3] knowledge. However, it is remarkable that even

---

3 As in the Upanisads: '*atmavidya hi parama vidya*', that is, knowledge of the self is the highest knowledge.

among philosophers of such persuasions there are widespread controversies regarding the very idea of self. A survey of the Upanisadic tradition provides us with classical examples of how, despite the common tenet of the ontological reality of atman, many subtle differences nevertheless arise in the elaboration of the notion of self. The philosophical implications of these notions of self in their rich variety are discussed in this monograph.

Indeed, an amazing vista of interpretations lies before an investigator who is prepared to examine relevant documents from cross-cultural sources. This monograph especially seeks to deal with a few carefully chosen views extracted from the Indian and Western sources with the specific intent of bringing them within a common frame of enquiry. In this process, one encounters strictly naturalistic explanations which in certain cases assume a pronounced form of metaphysical nihilism (*ucchedavada*). In contrast to these, one comes across readings that altogether repudiate a naturalistic explanation of I-consciousness, while adopting a metaphysical notion of self that emphasizes the religious idea of transcending death.

This latter reading with all its variations opens up before us a realm of understanding in which the status of I-consciousness is not merely that of a natural phenomenon but has a distinct facet that soteriologies across cultures emphatically seek to reveal. In this connection, it is also interesting to note that even when cognitive enterprises in a given phase of history of philosophy have not been particularly concerned with the theme of consciousness as exemplified in the case of Western philosophy during the heyday of behaviourism, the topic remained at the core of various forms of soteriological quests usually associated with the different world-religions. These reflections have important bearings on the crucial questions of consciousness, self, and I-consciousness which are not usually highlighted in academic philosophical textbooks. However, there is no need to camouflage such concerns, since, these arise in the course of inquiry into the multidimensional, multilayered theme of I-consciousness. Evidently, the precise relevance and degree of importance attached to such reflections largely depend on their respective contexts. Generally there are well-defined motivations that shape the framework of such undertakings right from the start. It often seems that the disciplinary frame itself determines which sets of issues come to the forefront of intellectual focus as matters of deep concern and which, in turn, are simply played down as irrelevant in a given discourse. The diverse observations that have been made with regard to this topic show the specific kinds of doubts and convictions that investigators operate with, none of which are shared unanimously.

At any rate, it is likely that the questions that baffled me then and still continue to do so to this day also dawn in the minds of many readers of this monograph. Even though only a few across cultures actually engage in the task of weaving or unmaking theories about I-consciousness, philosophical reflections on this theme continue especially in response to questions asked at various levels of enquiry. Indeed, the strength of this enterprise seems to have only increased in our time as is witnessed by the enormity of publications on topics related to this subject. Consequently, an abundance of ideas has accumulated concerning this enigmatic phenomenon. The present venture has been to put in relief that the phenomenon of I-consciousness is neither simply to be considered as being too mysterious to deserve serious intellectual attention nor to be sidetracked as being beyond the scope of any cognitive enquiry. Indeed, a cross-cultural survey of philosophical discourses displays before us the fascinating array of arguments and counter-arguments used by the advocates of opposed camps concerning the status of the 'I' as an enjoyer (*bhokta*), as an agent (*karta*) or as a cognizer (*jnata*). The intricacies and challenges that are embedded in such a philosophical project become evident as one witnesses the series of attempts that have been made to unravel I-consciousness.

A perusal of relevant literature from cross-cultural philosophical sources shows how an exploration of consciousness has given rise to a plethora of views. Note that whereas religious discourses on this theme have had a sway from time immemorial on the minds of people in the past, nowadays, it is particularly the scientific investigations that are amply influencing the conceptualization process by providing a basis for interpretive strategies for comprehending this phenomenon in the physical universe. However, it is noteworthy that there are prevalent intellectual forces which operate in support of as well as against the naturalistic interpretations. In the contemporary West, especially with the progress in the areas of neuro- and life-sciences, an array of naturalistic views has appeared in the domain often described as neurophilosophy. Intense focus on this theme is also unmistakable in various efforts to promote the science–religion dialogue at present. It is indeed time to carry out the bridge-building task within the academia, transcending the existing disciplinary boundaries among philosophy, science, and religion. In the process, the philosophical insights available from appropriate sources, cutting across the boundaries of cultures, need to be carefully considered.

Over the years, I have kept on reading with great interest accounts of diverse views and varied analyses, primarily from Indian and Western sources that touch upon the multiple facets of this fundamental question. Although unanimity among philosophers with regard to the indubitable presence of I-consciousness as the nucleus of our mental life is readily obtainable, explanatory narratives follow divergent routes. We find that though philosophical argumentations cannot decisively resolve, the problem, these can effectively highlight in what consists the ultimate mystery of I-consciousness. Although I never quite expected that a purely cognitive probe could ever unveil that deep mystery, there is no doubt that sharing that inward journey—which thinkers across cultures have undertaken—has been an enriching experience. It is an amazing fact that the urge to unravel the phenomenon has even led some philosophers of great intellectual merit to consider making a conceptual distinction between the self and I-sense. Equally remarkable are the records of those who proceeded to devise methods of enquiry for withdrawing from the overpowering presence of all that is external to I-consciousness. By 'external' is implied anything whatsoever that is presented to the I as not-I. It is this contemplative process that led to the startling interpretation of I-consciousness as being composite in character or as being 'constituted'. Some even went to the length to characterize the 'I' as 'not-self', in a similar vein as the body or the mind are depicted by some thinkers as an 'other' to the self. It is evident that in certain cases the innovation of meditative practices has eventually informed the theorization process, as exemplified so markedly in the Indian traditions. As a phenomenon I-consciousness seems inscrutable, yet its indubitable and intimate presence is universally witnessed.

While exploring the complex conceptual scenarios in Indian and Western intellectual traditions, I found it fascinating to come across theories or theory-making efforts that are similar to each other just as there are those that are radically opposed in approaches and interpretations. Some of these cogitations about several identical concerns in relation to various sub-themes that are integral parts of that inquiry made me appreciate the stupendous difficulties embedded in the question of I-consciousness. Let me insert a word of caution here. Sometimes one encounters in the current literature on consciousness studies carefully crafted positions where lack of substance in thinking are camouflaged by the use of certain technical jargons such as by listing certain views under the caption 'scientific', while rejecting and describing other accounts simply as 'unscientific' or at best as 'pre-scientific'. Philosophical antennas—I feel—must remain on alert while considering such claims.

The accounts of 'self' and 'I-consciousness' that form a significant part of the history of philosophies of India and that of the West make one aware of some of the elemental but open-ended questions that are bound to give rise to lively debates and elaborate controversies. Indeed, I have gradually become familiar with the battle of ideas that has been waged over centuries with regard to a large number of issues that are unavoidable in a study of I-consciousness. What has been of crucial interest to me is not whether or not there is any final outcome to these debates but the opportunity to share the passion of these philosophers who have helped to keep alive the undaunted spirit of human enquiry about who we are. Cognitively speaking, the phenomenon seems to remain by and large a terra incognita. What is known seems insignificant when compared to what remains to be known.

An intriguing feature of I-consciousness is the sentiment of sameness that it carries despite the perceived differences all around it. How is this sense of identity to be explained in the midst of a stream of inner and outer changes? A scrutiny of the phenomenon of change involves views about time. Interestingly, the theme of time and consciousness had captured my attention when I researched and reflected on a variety of views on time in Indian and Western philosophical traditions. While I was engaged in writing a monograph on that topic,[4] I had indeed noticed the impact of the different theoretical moves accounting for time-experience on the setting up of various conceptual models regarding 'self' and 'consciousness'. The records of theory-making endeavours seem to show that all these issues have a special bearing on each other. To some extent this is surely due to the fact that these themes resist any clear-cut comprehension of whether they need to be considered manifestly as a part of nature or as cultural construals. Time, as has been observed by Charles Sherover,[5] is central to our thinking no matter if we are reflecting on the 'nature of nature or nature of the self'. However, according to certain philosophers no metaphysical implications need to be drawn from these notions but these are to be treated only as sociolinguistic conventions or, at best, as diverse modes of conceptual constructions. Nevertheless, there are many philosophers who totally reject such readings and keep endeavouring to disclose their ontological status.

Importantly, it is in that process of intellectual venture that I have learnt to appreciate the complexities that are entailed in the many facets of these large themes and how to recognize the distinct configurations of these ideas as hallmarks of major traditions of thinking. It is worth mentioning here that it was indeed during such reflections that I became acutely aware of exactly how in an intercultural context traditions are played against each other in the pursuit of politics of knowledge[6] and how conceptual differences

4 cf. my monograph, 2009, *A Study of Time in Indian Philosophy*, 3rd ed. (New Delhi: Motilal Banarsidas Publishers).

5 Charles Sherover, 1975, *The Human Experience of Time* (New York: New York University Press).

6 cf. my essay, 1993, 'Time and the Hindu Experience', *Religion and Time*, ed. Anindita Niyogi Balslev and Jitendranath Mohanty (The Netherlands: E.J. Brill). I discuss in this essay the sources and consequences of such misleading metaphorical usages as Indian conception of time is cyclic as opposed to the Judeo-Christian understanding of linear time.

are blown up out of proportion in order to construe cultural otherness.

Leaving aside other aspects of the long story of deep fascination and involvement with this question of I-consciousness, what is of interest here is that it eventually led to my noting how these themes are treated from the phenomenological, metaphysical, or from ethico-religious and linguistic standpoints. Reflections on some of these readings gave rise to the publication of several papers over the years. I thought of writing a small monograph on the subject not with the view of either solving or dissolving the problem of I-consciousness but as a contribution toward enlarging the conceptual space where notable strands of philosophical thinking from the East and West are brought together within a common framework. This requires shedding some of the existing inhibitions in the field of cross-cultural studies, especially in the area of philosophy, in order to tap freely from the intellectual resources of India and the West. This work is neither an attempt to compile an anthology with reference to either the Indian or Western philosophical tradition, nor to comply with any standard model of what is called 'comparative philosophy'.

The material used in this monograph is a part of the sustained research-work that has gone on over the years. Let me take this opportunity to acknowledge the support that I received from the Danish Government's initiative (FREJA), thanks to the laudable effort made by the then education minister, Jytte Hilden, allowing me to spend a period of three years at the University of Copenhagen. As can be seen in the list of contents of this monograph, although my major focus is on Indian philosophy, I have discussed some of the significant contributions from Western philosophy regarding ideas of self, no-self, and I-consciousness.

Let me conclude this by noting that the effort to acquaint myself with various philosophical endeavours to unravel the phenomenon of I-consciousness has been a rewarding experience. I always dreaded lengthy books and so decided to sort out only a portion of the collected material from Indian and Western sources in a modest, manageable volume. It will be indeed gratifying if this work stimulates further pursuits toward constructing a common frame of enquiry for exploring ideas from diverse philosophical traditions across cultures. On my part, I constantly remain aware of the importance of promoting 'cross-cultural conversation'. I initiated such a forum precisely in order to serve this task of bridging the gaps between traditions and cultures.[7]

7 cf. Anindita Niyogi Balslev (ed.), 1995, *Cross Cultural Conversation* (USA: Oxford University Press); 2000, *Cultural Otherness*, 2nd edn (USA: Oxford University Press); Balslev and Dirk Evers (eds), 2010, *Compassion in the Religions of the World* (Germany: Udo Keller Stiftung Forum Humanum and Cross Cultural Conversation).

Introduction

A SEARCH FOR THE SOURCE OF I-CONSCIOUSNESS

This study aims at creating an appreciation for the many facets of the question of I-consciousness, primarily focusing on Indian sources, but also referring to Western philosophy. Cross-cultural conceptual resources can indeed inform us about the divergent perspectives and the philosophical intricacies with regard to this fascinating theme. A philosophical probe into this phenomenon opens up a very complex area of investigation where notions of change and permanence, identity and difference remain locked in a perplexing manner. Indeed, attempts to unveil I-consciousness have incited diverse methods of enquiry, leading to different conceptual approaches. Even a cursory glance at a global history of ideas pertaining to this theme amply demonstrates that these inquiries have proceeded on the basis of varied assumptions; consequently, the enquirers have often reached dissimilar conclusions. Remarkably diverse conceptual hues are visible in the records of speculations covering an array of interpretive strategies that range from firmly naturalistic stances to those that are almost on the verge of the esoteric. The general feeling, nevertheless, is that none of the theoretical moves has the kind of explanatory power that is needed in order to provide a completely coherent picture to the satisfaction of all enquirers coming from diverse disciplinary and cultural backgrounds. Perhaps, it is only when we hear the stories that are woven around this fundamental theme, told in different tongues and in different voices, that we will be able to adequately situate the queries within a common frame of enquiry and take stock of the pertinent issues concerning I-consciousness. We can then appreciate the arguments and motivations that prompt critical thinking within various intellectual traditions on this topic and understand why despite the common existential core the theoretical narratives deviate.

To start with, I-consciousness seems to form a stable nucleus of our incessantly changing mental life. However, reflection lays bare the intricacies that are inherent in the theme intertwined with a broad spectrum of concerns. Following the customary academic disciplinary labelling practices, these are often discerned and categorized as epistemological, linguistic, psychological, ethical, metaphysical, and religious concerns. A few representative samples from Indian and Western philosophical sources that will be discussed in what follows demonstrate the form and content of such analyses.

What is remarkable is that although the presence of I-consciousness is commonly acknowledged as being of central importance, the phenomenon itself seems to remain inscrutable defying any close examination. What makes I-consciousness especially difficult to unveil is the fact that it is never encountered in our experience in an isolated fashion. In other words, we simply cannot capture in abstraction the 'I-phenomenon' all by itself for a philosophical inspection. No matter how carefully one proceeds to examine by going deep into the inner recesses of experience in order to grasp the 'I' as a solitary phenomenon in its transparency, it resists disclosure. It remains constantly and continuously intermingled with some other component, which is other than the 'I'. This becomes clear as one attempts to withdraw from everything else in order to clasp it existentially or seeks for the exact referent or even for a sense of what is linguistically expressed by the pronoun in first person singular number. It can hardly be entirely disentangled from the not-I. This feature has been observed by certain philosophers both in India and in the West.

Consequently, we find that some philosophers highlight an unshakeable conviction about the irreducibility of I-consciousness. They are prone to consider, as their analyses show, an identical, abiding 'selfhood' as its basis, and attribute to the phenomenon a set of metaphysical characteristics. On the other hand, there are philosophers who outright question its seeming unity, its homogeneity, and make those characterizations that are favoured by the advocates of the former camp look dubious. Moreover, what is especially worth noticing is that none of these contending paradigmatic models—that is, those that generally operate with the idea of self as well as those which do not—come in just one standardized, uniform formulation. In other words, striking internal differences abound in both camps while their respective proponents project and justify their own interpretations. Thus, as relevant literature discloses, a firm affirmation of the idea of the indubitable presence of a self as the basis of I-consciousness can go hand in hand with different notions about the self. Likewise, one also encounters varied lines of interpretation from those quarters where the thinkers altogether deny the former position, advocating instead the view that there can be found no abiding self at all. In other words, there are alternative versions of both paradigms. The point worth noting is, in short, that although the sense of indispensability and indubitability of I-consciousness has not been seriously questioned by philosophers in general, this does not entail that the idea of an 'abiding self' has been unanimously accepted as a necessary implication of that universal experience (*sarvanubhava-siddha*) of I-consciousness. On the other hand, literary records show that there is a variety of interpretations—both from secular and religious standpoints—where the no-self position has been defended while accounting for the phenomenon of I-consciousness. Reference will be made to such views later on in this work. Interestingly, there are also some theoreticians who even claim the 'I' to be no more than a conventional, socially constituted linguistic entity.

Thus, while focusing on the central theme of I-consciousness, one comes across an entire gamut of metaphysical views concerning what the 'first person' is all about. This is a quest which has been present from time immemorial in religious discourses. Moreover, various mythologies across cultures seem to have been equally probing to find an answer. Currently, scientific research in the domain of neuro-physiology and brain-research has provided a rich resource for further investigation in this direction. Philosophical renditions based on these neuro-physiological studies are now part of the global history of ideas and surely many more theories about consciousness are in the process of construal at present.

The available material is indeed vast, especially in a cross-cultural philosophical setting. Precisely this wide canvas is needed as that alone enables an investigator to appreciate the subtle challenges that confront the theoreticians and lead them to hold contending views about I-consciousness. One of the goals of this study has been to draw attention to some of these varied readings from different sources and exemplify in the process how answers to the same or similar questions can sometimes converge and at other times be at variance with one another. To be sure, a project of this sort also demonstrates that not all questions are necessarily asked everywhere, at least not with the same rigor and emphasis. Interpretive strategies differ while engaging in the common cognitive pursuit regarding the theme of I-consciousness, since specific investigators have diverse points of departure. Moreover, the conceptual gaps between the philosophical awareness of the theoretical bearing of a first person account of subjectivity and of the limitation of a third person account of the 'I' are also striking. An overall review of such a seemingly simple phenomenon calls for a cautious study not only of various expository material but also of the recorded debates and controversies centring on a variety of crucial issues related to the theme of I-consciousness. A close inspection of the relevant literature concerning the question of subjectivity discloses, as mentioned before, various dimensions of this investigation and brings out the psychological, epistemological, metaphysical, linguistic, ethical, and even religious implications of a given stand. This monograph focuses on some of the fundamental issues and questions that keep reappearing in a cross-cultural philosophical context, while drawing from some select works by a few distinguished philosophers representing different thought-traditions.

Given the indubitability of I-consciousness, the philosophical search has been to detect its source. It is noteworthy in this connection that although in the history of Indian and Western thought one comes across diverse conceptual moves that are employed for studying the theme of I-consciousness, the predominant paradigms nevertheless seem by and large to be based on two distinctly different moulds of explanation. These primary lines of interpretation are formulated either by affirming or by negating the notion of an identical self. Indeed, these philosophical views are often informed by religious concerns and scientific findings. The main concern of this study is to highlight some of the predominant views of philosophers from the Indian sources belonging to the Upanisadic as well as the Buddhist traditions. These views will be discussed especially with reference to carefully selected expository as well as polemical material that has profound bearing on the central concern of this monograph. To mention some Western philosophers whose significant contributions will be referred to are Descartes, Locke, Hume, Kant, Husserl, and Sartre as well as contemporary scholars such as Strawson, Parfit, Nozick, and a host of naturalistic thinkers like Nagel, Curchland, Searle, etc. Although Hegel, Freud, Piaget, and Mead are known for their respective contributions toward exposing various aspects of this complex theme, reference to their concerns calls for a wider framework than that of this monograph.

In the section below, a brief account is attempted as a way of introducing the reader to the nature of the speculation in the early Upanisadic tradition that preceded the emergence of specific schools of philosophy.

UPANISADIC TRADITION: EARLY REFLECTIONS ON SUBJECTIVITY

Given the enormous amount of available documents across cultures with regard to an enquiry into the question of subjectivity, the allusions here are intended to highlight only certain phases of an ancient discourse that is alive in the Indian subcontinent. While making this brief review of early Upanisadic reflections on subjectivity, I have therefore consciously avoided any reference to the rich and sophisticated analysis of this theme found in the Western thought. This enables us to recapitulate the various steps of enquiry in the Indian philosophical discourse where the exposition and analysis are exclusively based on records of reflection that belongs to an epoch of history when the world of Indian philosophy did not define itself either as similar to or as different from any such intellectual adventure in the West.[1]

Effort is made here to acquaint the reader with the Indian conceptual world with the hope that deeper acquaintance with these ideas would lead to fresh and more substantial cross-cultural exchanges. Note, when later on in this work reference is made to Western philosophy, it is not done in accordance with the standard form of 'comparative studies' of Indian and Western discourses as is prevalent in recent times. The attempt is to dispose of the attitude that creates hindrances for an appreciation of philosophical readings by signalling that no communication is possible between different conceptual worlds across cultures.

Reflections on subjectivity—a feature attributed only to consciousness—dates back so early in time in the Indian conceptual world that it defies any strict chronological retelling. Classical Indian philosophy encompasses several distinct traditions—the Upanisadic, the Buddhist, and the Jaina being the principal ones among them. This distinctness is amply exemplified in the way in which the advocates of the principal schools of philosophy belonging to these traditions have construed conceptual strategies in order to explore this theme. Anyone acquainted with the history of classical Indian thought cannot but notice a spectrum of views concerning the large theme of consciousness in these traditions. Moreover, there are also records of many illuminating exchanges and debates among the adherents of various schools of Indian philosophy with regard to a wide range of issues that are pertinent to a study of I-consciousness. As has been mentioned earlier, the concern for the central theme of consciousness in

1 Subsequently and understandably this mode of presentation has become a common practice among all those who deal with Indian thought since the last two hundred years. However, the Indian intellectual traditions have not as yet received adequate representation in the curriculum of the departments of philosophy in the universities in the West. cf. my essay, 1997, 'Philosophy and Cross Cultural Conversation: Some Comments on the Project of Comparative Philosophy', *Metaphilosophy*, Vol. 28, No. 4, pp. 359–70.

Indian thought has proceeded with as well as without the postulation of an idea of an enduring self—paradigms which can later be seen at play in the thought traditions of other cultural soils as well. This seems to be the case, regardless of whether the outcome of a philosophical investigation of a school is realistic or idealistic or absolutistic in character in their respective epistemological and ontological preferences. It is noteworthy that both of these paradigms have been ingeniously employed and in some cases creatively combined in philosophical thinking in India as in the West. These views appear and reappear in various versions.

Prior to considering the diverse views advocated by the proponents of the various schools of philosophy that emerged later in the course of history within the Upanisadic tradition, let me highlight a few early but nevertheless key ideas that have been retained in the course of centuries. While considering the import of these ideas that constitute salient features of the Upanisadic tradition, which to this day is the predominant tradition of India, it may be briefly observed that the oft-repeated phrase of 'mind–body problem' in the Western discourse at first sounds a bit awkward for reasons stated below. Even if this expression may well be considered to be a matter of choice, the ambiguities in the use of philosophical vocabulary in different contexts need to be gradually removed, at least to the extent that is feasible in order to avoid misunderstanding.[2] Anyway, it is noteworthy that in the case of the Upanisads, the word '*manas*' or '*antahkarana*', generally translated as mind, can hardly be considered to be a substitute for the notion of self or *atman*. Already in the early Upanisadic texts which date back to third century B.C., very likely even prior to that, and undoubtedly long before the rise of the distinct philosophical schools in the Indian context, there are records which suggest quite clearly the conceptual differences among the notions of mind (manas), body (*sarira/deha*) and sense-organs (*indriya*) just as those between the mind and the self (manas/antahkarana and atman). Again, especially in order to emphasize the view

2 To give an example, notice how in certain renderings of Cartesian view, the words 'mind' and 'soul' are used interchangeably.

that the mind is an indispensable instrument that is required for any cognition, there are such utterances as: 'it is by mind that one sees or hears'.[3] The point of this utterance is to stress the fact that even if conjunction of objects with external sense organs is present, cognition does not automatically arise without the instrumentality of the mind. In support of this reading, the *Brhadaranyaka Upanisad* refers to everyday experiences and utterances as expressed in statements such as 'I was absent-minded, therefore I could not see or I could not hear', etc., demonstrating thereby the role of the mind as an inner organ (hence, also called antahkarana). From this, one primary line of interpretation has kept on projecting the idea of mind as an instrument (*karana*), and also often as an internal sense organ (*antarendriya*) in contrast to the external sense organs. An interesting implication that follows from this is that if the mind is to be regarded as an instrument, it must be different from the agent who uses it.

Thus, in a knowledge-situation, the mind is never the knower (*jnata*) but an instrument (karana) of knowledge. The knower is the self (atman).

In this connection an intriguing reading that needs to be especially taken note of is the one that the mind belongs to the natural order, which in some cases is intended to emphasize the idea of its material character and in some other cases as indicative of its essentially biological character. This interpretation is very much in vogue in current philosophical discussions especially among the naturalist thinkers in the West. As it happens, these are not startlingly new conceptual readings that are unknown to the Indian conceptual world. It is a matter of historical fact that every school belonging to the Upanisadic tradition holds it to be so. Indeed, there are certain pronounced naturalistic trends even in the mainstream Indian thought but ultimately there is no succumbing to naturalism. Their main philosophical difference from the naturalists who are pushing such a point of view in contemporary West—with great deal of sophistication, drawing support from the neuro-sciences—consists essentially in their interpretation

---

3 'manasa hyeva pasyati', 'manasa srnoti', etc.

of the phenomenon of consciousness and in their understanding of the notion of self. Eventually, the naturalistic explanations of consciousness in the Indian context were discerned to be utterly inadequate by traditional thinkers—Upanisadic, Buddhist, and Jaina alike. The rampant view among the Upanisadic thinkers was that similar to the external sense organs, the mind—often viewed as an internal sense organ—cannot be regarded to be intrinsically conscious. Thus, what can be said to belong to the natural order or what cannot be so designated and for what reasons are among some of those subtle questions that gradually crystallized into important topics for debate in the Indian context.

Note that the all-important question of self (atman) rests at the very heart of the Upanisadic tradition; hence this predominant tradition of India is designated as *Atmavada*. However, the notion of self has been subjected to intense critical scrutiny by the philosophers of the different schools that developed within the fold of the Upanisadic tradition itself. This deserves special mention since the issues that are carefully discussed in this connection are also central to the philosophical exploration of the theme of consciousness in general and that of I-consciousness in particular.

Prior to plunging into the large question regarding how the distinct philosophical positions with regard to the phenomenon of I-consciousness actually differed, it is important to review the fundamental convictions contained in the exegetical texts of the Upanisads that deeply influenced the development of the schools that gradually emerged within this tradition. Although it is not possible to give a detailed account here, it is however indispensable for the present study to recount a few essential ideas.

One of the central insights elaborated in the Upanisads concerning the idea of self entails the notions of unsublatability and indestructibility of the atman. Note that this is not only a notion of an enduring self, understood as a psycho-physical complex persisting in the backdrop of a finite temporal stretch, but that here one encounters a firm assertion of its ultimate timeless character, its ontological reality. The theoretical renditions with regard to the idea of self offered by the advocates of different schools vary but this core insight is retained all throughout. As one reviews the scene, one begins to appreciate the different ways in which the various theoreticians come to treat the epistemological, psychological, and metaphysical dimensions of the problem of I-consciousness as well as how debates related to these issues ensue among themselves and also with the Buddhists and the Jaina thinkers.

As the philosophical scrutiny proceeds, what is indeed noteworthy is the way these philosophers fearlessly respond to the soteriological concern when it gradually presses for attention in the process of this cognitive undertaking. It is obvious that all the three traditions—the Upanisadic, the Buddhist and the Jaina—despite their distinctly different interpretations of I-consciousness, have without exception highlighted the soteriological dimension of this quest. In their ultimate analysis, this latter concern comes to occupy a major place in their cognitive traditions. Thus these became integral to Hinduism, Buddhism, and Jainism as world-religions. It is in this sense that there are no clear-cut boundaries between philosophy and religion in the Indian conceptual world and that is no detriment to the philosophical enterprise.

While pursuing the study of the phenomenon of I-consciousness, it is tempting to observe the way in which contemporary naturalists with atheistic leanings are exploiting the findings of neurobiology in support of naturalism as a philosophical stand. If modern researchers in the field of consciousness-studies would explore with equal zeal the deep insights that are embedded in the religious discourses across cultures about these issues—a field which is generally ignored by contemporary mainstream philosophers—it may well open doors to new ideas and understanding on this topic. All these could especially benefit those involved in 'science–religion' dialogue. The Indian discourse has important resources that deserve to be adequately explored in this context.

Documents are available which show that each of the diverse interpretations of I-consciousness within the Upanisadic tradition has been a topic for philosophical debates and disputes not only among the thinkers of different schools belonging to this tradition itself but have also led to prolonged and lively controversies with the advocates of the Naturalistic, the Buddhist, and the Jaina traditions. The disagreements among these philosophers in the Indian conceptual scene about the notion of I, its status and how it is cognized are intimately related to their respective stand vis-à-vis the idea of self. The Upanisadic thinkers, despite their variations in the perception and evaluation of the idea of the atman or self never lost sight of the central tenet, viz. that the atman remains ever-identical, abiding, and indestructible. It is also interesting to observe in this connection that although the Upanisadic philosophers—all without exception—held on to the conceptual pattern of conceiving the self as unchanging and unchangeable in the midst of change, there have been, nonetheless, many philosophical controversies among them with regard to the status of the phenomenon of change. Some grant it an ontological status whereas others only empirical. As is to be expected, there are various views about time that were propounded by various schools. This is why for a deeper comprehension of these various modes of thinking, it is useful to take note of the treatment of the problem of time in each case and its philosophical implication for the notion of the immutable self or the atman, the prime concern of the Upaniṣadic tradition. Evidently, no matter whether the metaphysical scheme of a given school is committed to a form of non-dualism, dualism or pluralism, all the schools belonging to this tradition steadfastly hold on to the view that the self is immutable and that it can never be reduced to the changing states of consciousness. The core perception of the self as ever-constant and irreducible is clearly reflected in the well-known metaphorical expression of Vacaspati Misra: 'that which is constant in whatever is variable is different from the latter as the thread in a garland is different from the flowers'.[4] I have discussed this question elsewhere in detail.[5]

---

4 Vacaspati Misra says in *Bhamati*: 'Yesy vyavartamanesu yad anuvartate tat tebhya bhinnam yatha kusumebhya sutram', trans. by T.M.P Mahadevan in 1938, *The Philosophy of Advaita* (London: Luzac & Co).

5 cf. my paper, 1987, 'Time, Self and Consciousness: Some Conceptual Patterns in the Context of Indian Thought', *Journal of Indian Council of Philosophical Research*, Vol. 5, No. 1, pp. 111–119.

What is fascinating to observe is that despite the fact that the philosophical schemes of diverse Upanisadic schools operate with diverse views of time, one finds that nevertheless there is invariably a conceptual space in every scheme for a category which is outside the influence of time (*kalaprabhava-mukta*). In other words, there is always room for an abiding self. It is amazing to watch how this idea has been philosophically defended over the centuries. This is one of the major components in their thinking that made them totally reluctant to accept the position of the Indian naturalists and materialists in the course of their exploration of subjectivity or even to validate a no-self stand. These questions will be discussed in subsequent chapters.

However, it is worth recalling that in spite of a lot of overlaps in their readings and convictions, one comes across significant internal differences in the philosophical accounts of various schools belonging to the Upanisadic tradition regarding the notion of self and concerning the question of I-consciousness. These are all documented in the literature. Moreover, a review of the controversies, firstly among the Upanisadic philosophers themselves, then with them and the ancient Indian naturalists, and finally, with the Buddhist and the Jaina philosophers, is philosophically intriguing and enriching. Some of these anticipate many of the contemporary debates on this subject.

CROSS-CULTURAL PHILOSOPHICAL EXPLORATION: ITS AIM

It seems to me that a true creative participation in cross-cultural philosophical thinking—valuable and urgent as it is for obtaining deeper insights—is possible only when the authentic sources of the traditions are fully explored without any bias. This study aspires to proceed in the direction of gradually establishing a common framework.

Comparative studies, based on secondary sources alone, often tend to overlook some of the subtleties of the questions formulated within a specific philosophical discourse since in that way the content and context of a thought tradition cannot be adequately appreciated related. In order to bring together the philosophical traditions of various cultures, there is need for more translation works from the original sources along with critical expositions by authors who are well-acquainted with such traditions. In some cases, good translations of original texts are already available whereas others are yet to be done. Since I do not share the untranslatability thesis of radical cultural relativists, I would like to emphasize that the important point is to create the conditions so that the interested 'outsiders' must be able to plunge into the historical process of interpretation of texts, etc., carried out by the community of 'insiders'. To understand and appreciate American pragmatism, French existentialism, or Indian Vedanta one does not necessarily need to be born into those countries but be exposed to these traditions of thought. Today, this is neither an impossible nor a far-fetched task to attempt.

It is clear that the toil of philosophical endeavour across cultures has given rise to a vast literature with regard to the problem of consciousness in general and that of the theme of I-consciousness in particular. I strongly feel that at present, a study of these fundamental questions in an academic context can hardly limit itself only within the boundaries of a given cultural tradition by ignoring the intellectual resources and challenges that are obtainable from different sources. Looking at available documents, whether from ancient India or from the contemporary West or from sources from the centuries in-between, it is mind-boggling to see how a range of issues has received variegated treatment in the hands of thinkers across traditions and cultures. Even scanty information from a brief survey and re-telling of such philosophical speculations in a cross cultural context makes one aware of an array of concerns that have repeatedly surfaced and whose relevance can hardly be questioned.

A review of philosophical stands in Indian as well as in Western thought with regard to the subtle question of I-consciousness, for example, show that there are views in favour of, as well as against, naturalism. It is interesting to find how an affirmation of the idea of an abiding self as in Cartesian or in Vaisesika thought can go hand in hand with limited use of naturalistic thinking. Again, one finds that whereas both the Carvakas and the Buddhists can deny the notion of atman but can disagree vehemently regarding whether consciousness is a natural phenomenon or not. These representative examples will be discussed in this monograph. While dealing with naturalism in the West, references are mostly made to modern exponents of this view, whereas in the Indian part, ancient Carvaka philosophy plays a vital role. Original texts as well as secondary sources have been used while exposing views belonging to the rationalist, empiricist, phenomenological, and existentialistic thought. Various discussions and debates in the context of Indian thought are mostly based on some of the major Sanskrit texts comprised of the aphorisms (*sutras*), commentaries (*bhasyas*), glosses (*tika, varttika*) by reputed authors belonging to diverse schools of Indian philosophy. Some important secondary sources and translations are also used where the specific concerns of this work have been accentuated. This vast literature bears witness to the arduous process of the conceptual exploration of I-consciousness.

In the course of the following pages a range of views will be gradually taken up for examination, occasionally highlighting, as mentioned before, the linguistic, the epistemological, and the metaphysical dimensions of the intricate problem of I-consciousness. However, no attempt will be made to organize such immense material in any chronological order. The point is essentially to underscore the varied philosophical treatment that the phenomenon of I-consciousness has received at the hands of Indian philosophers and to appreciate the significance of the internal variations that are there in the context of discerning the overlaps and differences in interpretations in representative examples from Western thought.

Interestingly, these records of centuries of reflections also unfailingly show that many thinkers have wondered about the question whether I-consciousness can be said to be restricted only to the human context. An observation recorded in the Indian philosophical sources says emphatically that the I-sense (consequently, also the sense of my-ness) occurs in all living beings, not merely in humans.[6] Note that according to this latter reading,

---

6 In his *Bhamati*, Vacaspati Misra puts it in strong terms claiming that from insects (patanga) to gods and Rishis (devarshivya), all have I-sense.

I-sense and self-consciousness do not necessarily go together, it is claimed that self-consciousness is an episode that happens only in humans.

Even while restricting the enquiry to the topic of human consciousness, records reveal that no unanimous or definitive conclusion has been reached with regard to ascertaining its ultimate status in the natural world. Intellectual efforts have not yet culminated in any universally acceptable view. There is no unanimity among thinkers regarding how to construe the basis of I-consciousness or how the 'I' is known. All these only bear witness to the subtle intricacies that are ingrained in the topic under discussion, marking these questions intermittently either as problems that can in principle be resolved or even as mysteries that are beyond our capacity to unveil. Nevertheless, repeated attempts have been made to obtain a comprehensive understanding of a range of issues that is entailed in this explorative process.

Today, the subject matter of consciousness is no longer exclusively a concern for professional philosophers dealing with metaphysics or philosophy of religion. Indeed, an overview of the contemporary conceptual scene exhibits amazingly diverse directions of enquiry that highlight this multi-layered theme as a concern for a number of disciplines in humanistic as well as in natural sciences.

It is indeed a hopeful sign that now there is a clear recognition among thinkers that any attempt to comprehend our role and our place in nature demands a discernment of what consciousness is all about. The longstanding metaphysical questions whether body is conscious or whether consciousness is embodied have not vanished with the accumulation of results from cutting edge research in the domains of neuro-biology, neuro-physiology, and brain research. It is worthwhile recalling in this connection that some of these controversies have a long documented history, although the evidence offered in support of specific views has changed. Although the present-day advocates of physicalism come up with divergent and contending accounts, each of them demands legitimacy for a specific reading by referring to results from the neuro-sciences. What is interesting to observe is that despite the common claim that these views are based on scientific data, philosophically the advocates of these naturalistic theories clearly part company. Note, for example, that if some of those philosophers who advocate naturalism come to propose reductionism, others prefer non-reductionistic readings of the scientific data. In other words, despite the fact that data are derived from neuro-biological sources, the contending interpretations show the obvious conceptual differences in the making of theories. These differences are philosophically significant. As I said before, these readings arrived at via interpretations of scientific data have led to philosophical disputes that remind of old documented controversies. Thus, prior to endorsing or discarding any of these present-day, theory-making efforts, it would be worthwhile to argue in favour of obtaining at least a minimal knowledge of philosophical traditions in a cross-cultural context. This enables us to discern once again for what reasons philosophers keep struggling with the same or similar issues for or against naturalism as well as within the cognitive frame of naturalism itself over the centuries. However, to say this is not to underplay the fact that much of the current naturalistic readings are born of knowledge of neuro-biology and not merely of theoretical speculations based on epistemological and linguistic analyses which often was unquestionably the case in bygone eras. Undoubtedly, contemporary science has informed and sharpened our understanding of the physical body. Let us bear in mind the significance of the way in which some contemporary philosophers depict the differences between the Cartesian notion of the body as *res machina* and the complex understanding of the living body based on current neuro-biological findings.[7]

A fresh assessment of all these issues within a cross-cultural framework of philosophical enquiry brings once again to the forefront of academic discussions the need for critically assessing such positions as epiphenomenalism, psychophysical parallelism, mind–body interactionism, etc.—positions that have been philosophically defended as well as questioned earlier. If none of these seem to yield a completely satisfactory account of the origin, function, and status of consciousness, it only bears witness to the

7 John R. Searle, 1992, *The Rediscovery of the Mind* (Cambridge: MIT Press).

enormous complexity of this multifaceted question. The search can surely be expected to go on.

As a background for this study, it is noteworthy that the drift in contemporary interest towards the theme of consciousness is remarkably strong in the West today—especially since the demise of behaviourism—that the topic of consciousness is no more regarded as redundant or as a matter of purely antiquarian interest for recapitulating a chapter of bygone history of ideas. Given the prevailing mood of the investigators in the present scenario, it seems to me to be an opportune moment to share the outcomes of the widely divergent quests concerning consciousness across the boundaries of disciplines and cultures. Today it is possible to appropriately engage in the bridge-building task by bringing an array of views that have been already explored over the centuries regarding this theme together with various contemporary readings on this topic from various disciplines. Moreover, while dealing with specific philosophical issues from cross cultural sources one has to seriously confront the intellectual challenges and evaluate the strength of the arguments. This is precisely an undertaking which is quite different from treating these aforesaid discussions as merely a program for so-called standardized comparative philosophy or simply as a part of historical study of the unfolding of given traditions. The aim of philosophical endeavour in a cross-cultural context is not only to observe the similarities and differences that are there between two or more sets of what is regarded by the advocates as 'established thesis' (*siddhanta*) but it calls for a careful assessment of the ratiocination process, a comprehension of the nature of the evidence and even better, a detection of the assumptions underlying these modes of reflection.[8]

Considering that the dominant tendency in contemporary Western philosophical investigations pertaining to the topic of consciousness has given rise to a number of theoretical moves in support of various forms of naturalistic thinking, it is worthwhile recalling that the basic principles and assumptions of naturalism as a philosophical stance were well known in ancient India. However, the novelty of current Western versions of theories of

8 cf. my paper, 'Philosophy and Cross Cultural Conversation'.

consciousness is that these draw from a number of special sciences such as biology, physics, neuro-physiology as well as from computer science, artificial intelligence, etc. These surely add a distinct flavour to the cross-disciplinary probes into these ancient questions and concerns. Many of the readings that are subject-matters of current debates are not entirely unlike the accounts of disputes that are well-documented in the history of ideas entailing the old philosophical controversies about monism and dualism, about notions of non-material and material principles, etc. Despite the increasingly complex formulations that often surface at present with a considerable amount of sophistication in support of physicalism as a theoretical stance, conceptual parallels to many of these can indeed be traced back to ancient Indian philosophical texts showing the perennial character of these concerns.

In this connection, it is also to be noted that the on-going philosophical debates in the West are not exclusively among the advocates of naturalism of various sorts. The wider scenario includes participants who represent one or another school of classical Western thought that discard naturalism. To repeat once more, what now seems to me to be of crucial importance is the setting up of a frame of inquiry where a cross-cultural exploration of ideas can be gradually recognized as an important tool for identifying the central issues, some of which seem to remain as fresh since they were first formulated and recorded. As we grope for greater self-understanding, all these diverse accounts can eventually be expected to be perceived as important parts of an open-ended, ongoing intellectual investigation into this many-sided question.

Let me now turn to the Indian conceptual world. However, prior to introducing Indian ideas, it is important to note that there are many relevant words in Sanskrit such as *cit, caitanya, sambit, bodha, vijnana, jnana*, etc., similar to a range of terms with or without overlapping contents expressed in such English words as consciousness, awareness, cognition, knowledge, etc. It is obvious to any interested reader that all these words are not always consistently or uniformly used—neither in the Western nor in Indian philosophical literature. It calls for a careful scrutiny to discern the varied nuances of how these are actually employed in particular traditions or used by specific philosophers in a variety of contexts.

Given the large canvas of Indian thought, the difficult question that arises is how does one even begin to sketch a broad outline of the cognitive preoccupation with this complex question in the Indian philosophical scene? A good starting point, so it seems to me, is to recapitulate a recorded discussion that is absolutely relevant for this undertaking. This is documented in the literature under the caption 'darkness of the world'.[9] This is a conversation where the focus lies on the question of how we can draw a clear line of distinction between a 'simple awareness of something' and 'knowledge of something'. Granted the fact that an assertion of 'knowledge of something' has a truth-claim attached to it, such claims must be supported by evidence (*pramana*). The discernment generally agreed upon among the ancient Indian philosophers is that evidence is needed to constitute what can be termed as knowledge. This notion of pramana has been the basis for elaborate debates and discussions in Indian thought. Although I will not get into any detail here regarding this large question, I mention it in order to draw attention to the fact that a range of well-articulated views can be encountered in the Indian philosophical literature arguing for what can and cannot be said to be constitutive of evidence. The query into the idea of evidence is especially significant for understanding the long debate with regard to the theme of consciousness. How this particular concern is closely associated with the exploration of the idea of the epistemic primacy of consciousness will be discussed in the next chapter.

In this connection, it is worthwhile repeating that deeper reflections in the Indian context did actually lead to the key controversies about whether consciousness can be reduced to the natural order or not. In other words, the intense focus on the crucial question regarding what can be tacitly claimed to belong to the natural order and what cannot be so designated and why so, gradually crystallized into important topics for debates and deliberations over centuries. It seems to me to be of great philosophical interest to incorporate those ideas from the Indian sources into the contemporary discussions on the subject. Time is ripe for a

9 See Chapter 1.

fresh cross-cultural philosophical appraisal of the many facets of this fundamental theme.

In the on-going contemporary discussion on consciousness in the West, the notion of 'qualia' has received much attention. This especially points to the phenomenon of subjectivity, which is rightly recognized to be a feature that can be attributed to consciousness alone. This question of subjectivity is very complex and is evidently intimately related to that of I-consciousness. Consequently, many questions arise in this connection. Among those that can be listed as being central to this study, one could consider the following: Is the ecological structure integral to consciousness or not? No matter which of the alternative positions one seeks to support, an explanation is needed regarding the status of I-consciousness. Apart from these, there are a number of other issues that have been repeatedly discussed in the philosophical circles, such as whether all consciousness is intentional—that is—whether it is necessarily consciousness of something or is consciousness in essence non-intentional? Again, how to account for consciousness of consciousness? Is a state of consciousness self-revealing or must it be revealed by a subsequent state? Is consciousness a substance, a quality, or a function, and many others issues. These form a common pool of concerns and questions. However, as is to be expected, not all of these are answered in the same vein by the advocates of various schools.

Given the cross-cultural character of this present study, it is fascinating to watch the nature of the overlaps in the modes of enquiries. The way emphasis is laid in various conceptual formulations touching upon a variety of issues pertaining to the analysis of 'self' and 'consciousness' exemplify this. Apart from the list of questions mentioned earlier, the notions of permanence and identity as well as those of continuity, change, and difference are inescapable while dealing with these topics. Again, given the indexical character of 'I', philosophers have tried to analyze its significance by noting the differences between first-person sentences and third-person sentences in a discourse. Can any objective description of the world or the self make the inalienable subjective perspective redundant? It has been asked whether this so-called objective description, as if a 'view from nowhere' is any more than a myth?

Further, a host of statements can be cited which tell the readers why some philosophers think that the 'I' does not stand for the body or even the mind whereas others deny that; or why for some naturalism has been found to be questionable and even unacceptable as a philosophical stance for explaining consciousness. It is indeed an intellectual adventure in the cross-cultural context to try to comprehend why do some philosophers think that the 'I' refers to an identical self while others blatantly deny that possibility and thereby draw entirely different pictures of our mental life? How does one arrive at such notions as that of 'empirical self', 'transcendental self' or even arrive at the idea of 'no-self'? What are the epistemological stances regarding the question of self-awareness? Some of these questions are raised and discussed in this monograph.

It seems to me that to be acquainted with the distinctly different conceptual strategies dealing with various aspects of this large theme, based on material that is available both from ancient and modern philosophy, will enable us not only to identify the core issues succinctly but will help us to contemplate on these in a more cogent manner. To be wakeful to some of the important configuration of ideas from the Indian and Western sources, even though these may at first appear to be inextricably dependent on their specific cultural frameworks, may well open before us an expanded philosophical vista and deepen our philosophical sensitivity. On the one hand, the question of I-consciousness is particularly perplexing since no one doubts or denies its presence in our mental life and on the other hand, as documents show, there is no unanimity among philosophers with regard to what constitutes the basis of I-consciousness.

CHAPTER ONE

Consciousness as the 'Light of all Lights'

THE IDEA OF THE EPISTEMIC PRIMACY OF CONSCIOUSNESS

In our everyday experience we are not in general cognitively preoccupied with the phenomenon of subjectivity or for that matter with any of those features that are attributed to consciousness only upon critical, second-order reflection. We are, on the contrary, largely engaged with different things which are in and of the world that are presented to our consciousness. In other words, our attention is directed towards what we are conscious of but not toward consciousness itself. The fact that object-directedness is a prominent function and a dominant feature of consciousness has indeed been noted by philosophers in India as well as in the West, regardless of the fact that these thinkers may otherwise be affiliated with different schools or traditions of interpretation. A study of consciousness, therefore, demands a suspension of this natural attitude. The investigator must withdraw from the natural, outward-going attitude towards the world and be prepared to undertake an inward journey, directing the philosophical gaze on consciousness itself. This is a quest for a disclosure which, in the face of it, almost sounds like a paradox. The quintessence of this apparently paradoxical search has been powerfully expressed in the Upanisads with the help of a rhetorical question: 'That by means of which we know all, by means of what will we know that'?[1]

As one keeps turning the pages of numerous philosophical texts and comes across depictions of various conceptual scenarios, one discovers how the philosophical accounts—regarding not only

---

1 *Brhadaranyaka Upanisad*, any edition.

the status of objects but of consciousness itself—vary from system to system, and from tradition to tradition. It is precisely these internal divergences that are of great interest to any investigator of the multi-layered theme of consciousness in general and that of I-consciousness in particular. Embarking on an intellectual adventure such as the present one is indeed an opportunity to scrutinize the alternative networks of ideas, each of which alleges to provide explanations for this little understood phenomenon. As one begins to examine a series of questions specifically concerning the first person and attempts to follow closely the trajectories that have already been tried out, one's own critical gaze gradually leads one to an unexplored territory that happens to coincide with that mysterious region at the heart of one's own being. While probing into the records of the available answers to a range of queries on the topic of I-consciousness in a cross-cultural context, one finds oneself in the midst of a wilderness of views and ideas that various philosophical investigations have yielded. One important part of the challenge of this endeavour seems to consist in the discernment of a common point of departure with regard to which there is a general consensus. It is rewarding to watch carefully from that point onwards how and why differences arise that are emphatically noted in the formulations of alternative theories.

With the intent of sorting out a few focal points in the various charts of this inward journey, let us turn to the Indian conceptual world. Here one comes across a discussion documented in the literature highlighting an illuminating argument under the caption 'darkness of the world'.[2] This is a deliberation where the participants seem to have pondered over and reached the following conclusion, viz. that prior to any debate concerning various aspects of this multi-faceted problem, the idea of the epistemic primacy of consciousness has to be granted legitimacy. This reading provides a good starting point for sketching a broad outline of how some of the fundamental questions regarding consciousness and the 'I' came to be raised in the different phases of unfoldment of the Indian conceptual history. Interestingly such a study makes

2 'jagadandhya-prasanga', see Sankara's commentary on the *Brahma Sutra*.

it evident that arguments and reasoning in support of alternative viewpoints emerge in a distinctive manner only when the proponents of specific philosophical schools engage in a vigorous defense of their own views and oppose the counter-arguments presented by their opponents.

It is, therefore, critically important to follow that process of exchange of views, firstly in order to identify the point of agreement and then to notice when they begin to part company. In the Indian philosophical context that common point of agreement may well be said to lie in the shared discernment of this important idea of the epistemic primacy of consciousness. The underlying core argument runs thus: No pronouncement about whether anything exists or not is viable or feasible unless being witnessed and testified by consciousness. Hence, a denial of the idea of the epistemic primacy of consciousness will invariably lead to an absurd situation. A common acceptance of the epistemic primacy is an acknowledgement of this predicament.

Here, it is worthwhile noticing that there is pronounced diversity among the Indian philosophers with regard to the philosophical treatment of a wide range of questions and issues pertaining to the large theme of consciousness. The common point of departure, as is evident in the record of the deliberations prevalent in ancient Indian philosophical circles, also highlights that to accept the idea of epistemic primacy of consciousness is quite different from endorsing the idea of its ontological primacy. As the discussion unfolds, relevant documents show that there was indeed no unanimity among the classical Indian philosophers with regard to the idea of the ontological primacy of consciousness or even concerning the status of I-consciousness. These topics have been subjects of much philosophical controversy for centuries and the advocates of different schools of Indian philosophy did propose their own distinct theories. On the contrary, the idea of the epistemic primacy of consciousness was generally accepted and can hardly be said to be controversial.

A careful assessment of the idea of the epistemic primacy of consciousness receives further support when the relevant texts vividly elaborate on the subtle distinction between a case of a 'simple awareness' of something and 'knowledge' of something.

These are not identical episodes precisely because 'knowledge of something' has always a truth-claim attached to it. Consequently, philosophers come to agree that in the case of a statement where there is a claim of knowledge, evidence (*pramana*) is required in support of such an assertion. However, the difference between any such claims from that of 'simple awareness' consists primarily in the fact that no evidence can be provided without basing it on the latter. In other words, without the presupposition of something being presented to consciousness, it is not even possible to make an assertion that 'a thing is thus and not thus'. This is precisely why to question or challenge the idea of the epistemic primacy of consciousness is to be regarded as absurd.

Thus, this issue, as has been mentioned before, is quite different from the concern about the ontological primacy of consciousness. In the Indian conceptual context, one comes across several examples of philosophical views that vouch for the ontological primacy of consciousness. These can be found both within the Upanisadic (especially in Sankhya, Yoga, and Vedanta) and the Buddhist traditions (as in the Yogacara Vijnanavada philosophy).

Later on, it will be discussed more fully how the idea of the ontological reality of consciousness comes to play a crucial role especially with reference to the philosophy of Advaita Vedanta. The philosophers belonging to this school have vehemently engaged in debates with the opponents of this idea. Thus, while replying to the Buddhist thinkers belonging to the Madhyamika School, according to whom no independent existence of consciousness could be ascertained, Vacaspati Misra retorted on behalf of Advaita Vedanta by saying that even if one claims that the whole world is void, that too presupposes the witness consciousness (*sunyasya'pi saksitvat*).

Again, it may be briefly observed here that in order to retrace the march of ideas exposing the Advaitic notion of the ontological reality of consciousness, one has to relate it to the thesis of the eventual 'unknowability' (*avedyatva*) of consciousness. This adds another layer of complexity to the debate especially with those who treat the phenomenon of consciousness as a 'knowable' (*vedya, jneya*). The Advaitins claim that in the ultimate analysis consciousness can never be treated as an object (that is, as a knowable). This is a crucial issue which has been discussed in a subsequent chapter.

Anyhow, what is worth mentioning in this connection is that the question of pramana plays a central role in Indian philosophical discussions both for ascertaining what can be treated as a legitimate source of knowledge as well as for discerning the criterion for establishing the validity of what is claimed as 'knowledge'. A careful appraisal of these ideas deepens one's understanding with regard to the thesis of epistemic primacy of consciousness as well. In the course of these discussions, it has been said over and over again, using the metaphor of light, that consciousness reveals, manifests, and illuminates. Furthermore, it has been firmly maintained that all evidences—be these perceptual, inferential, verbal, or any other (no matter whichever of these are considered to be legitimate by any given school)—presuppose the testimony of consciousness. This is a minimal claim about which there is almost a total unanimity among the philosophers. Thus, to reiterate once more, the epistemic primacy of consciousness is to be granted since without it no debate can even ensue regarding whether 'a thing is thus or not thus'. This why it is said that 'darkness of the world' will prevail without this basic assumption of the epistemic primacy of consciousness. Consciousness is therefore regarded as the ultimate source of evidence and described as the 'light of all lights' (*jyotisam jyotih*).[3]

Consequently, critical deliberations began to take place regarding the question of what sort of evidence can actually be said to constitute knowledge. On this issue, important differences arose among the schools. Note that it is only on the ground of this commonly accepted premise of the epistemic priority of consciousness that the issue of what kind of evidence can or cannot be eventually accepted for legitimizing any knowledge-claim becomes a matter of debate and reflection. In this connection, it is also interesting to mention that the philosophers belonging to the school of Advaita Vedanta drew all the possible implications of this idea by further stressing that whereas the existence of all other objects require

3 Mundaka Upanisad, any edition.

evidence, consciousness is presupposed by all proof or disproof. They propagated the view that no pramana is needed in order to establish consciousness; since it is self-established (*svayamsiddha*). In other words, given that all forms of evidence pre-suppose the testimony of consciousness, it is pointless to demand that consciousness be established by any evidence at all. Consciousness is therefore said to be self-evident. It will be gradually seen how various aspects of the question of subjectivity are closely intertwined with this reading.

Indeed, in the course of history advocates of various schools of philosophy that emerged within the Upanisadic, the Buddhist, and the Jaina traditions came to hold different philosophical positions while answering questions that pertain to multiple aspects of the large theme of consciousness. Records are available of a wide variety of issues around which lively controversies arose. Some of these issues are as follows: Is consciousness a substance, a quality, or an action/function? Is it always intentional or directed towards an object or can it be ascertained that ultimately it is non-intentional in character? Is consciousness temporal or ultimately timeless? Is it self-revealing or not? Does consciousness belong to a subject or self or is this notion of a self merely a conceptual construction? It must also be mentioned here that the ancient Indian philosophers were equally concerned with the questions of the status of consciousness and self not only in the context of the waking state but also in the state of dream and in that of dreamless sleep. Consequently, as can be expected, all these led to vigorous philosophical exchanges among the participants.

There are indeed documents of controversies over similar issues in the course of the historical unfoldment of philosophy in the West. Current literature on the subject shows that some of these debates are still going on today. A few examples of such deliberations in the Indian and Western discourses will be recapitulated in the course of this study, making it apparent to the readers how reflections on these questions come to entail many of the same concerns. One can then appreciate why a common philosophical frame of enquiry is useful for treating all these questions from cross cultural sources.

ON THE INDUBITABILITY OF I-CONSCIOUSNESS

Given our deep sense of familiarity with I-consciousness which occupies a central place in our mental life, it is not really easy at the outset to figure out what kind of philosophical questions can at all be raised with regard to this phenomenon. History of ideas, however, shows that it is not at all unusual to encounter topics that were at first seen as problem-free and subsequently became subjects for systematic philosophical reflections. It is indeed amazing that such topics entailing various concepts and words, perhaps because of their regular conventional usages with seemingly standard implications do not immediately appear to be open to interpretation. However, relevant documents disclose how these, nevertheless, come to provoke thinkers across the boundaries of cultures to ponder over.

Leaving aside the word 'I' for the moment whose special characteristics will be noted shortly, consider for example the way words like 'God' or 'time' are used conventionally. Despite the fact that almost everybody uses the word 'time', critical reflections or thought-experiments and empirical investigations on this theme over the centuries expose the intricacies giving rise to numerous views and many readings. Look at the extensive records of debates in the history of philosophy, Western as well as Indian, regarding whether time is an objective reality or it is subjective, whether it is to be considered as an ontological category or simply as a conceptual construal, etc.

Again, consider the example of 'God' as a concept and as a word as used in our conventional language. Some may be fully convinced that there is a referent to this word, holding otherwise different views on the subject, whereas others may consider it to be entirely fictitious, at best to be an idea invented by the priestly class—as the ancient Indian Carvakas did. Also, it is significant to recall here that the idea of God has been questioned not only within materialistic or naturalistic frameworks; there are traditions of thinking in which there are unmistakably projects for attaining Freedom/Nirvana, may nevertheless still prefer to retain a non-theistic character. Consider the case of Buddhism where there is no room for any notion of a personal God but which champions the notion of Nirvana and is yet recognized as one of our world-religions.

In order to appreciate the complexity and profundity of the conceptual situation, one has to peruse the existing literature that not only demonstrate the different interpretive strategies and a wide range of views on these subjects, but also highlight the radical questions that have been raised about whether these are at all to be deemed as integral features of what is called 'Reality' or to be treated merely as conceptual constructions. In other words, we learn from these critical queries that not only alternative views are possible with regard to their nature and function but also that there are readings that poignantly shed doubt about the claims of their very existence. Note that in both these cases—God or time—there are not only examples of distinct views on these but also recorded instances of outright disavowals about the claim of their very existence.

These above observations are explicitly made in order to draw attention to a unique characteristic that the phenomenon of I-consciousness exhibits, viz. that no one questions or denies the presence of this phenomenon. As has been just discussed, there is conceptual room for doubting whether there is God or not, whether there is time or not but no one asks the absurd question 'whether I am or not'. Rather, it is acknowledged that even if there can be misgivings with regard to a range of other phenomena, there is hardly any room for doubt in this specific case. There are unequivocal statements by many philosophers across cultures expressing the conviction that this is a phenomenon which is beyond the scope of that ardent philosophical scepticism which can call into question the claim of existence of just about anything else—God, time, reality of the external world, etc.

The indomitable presence of I-consciousness in our experience is of such magnitude that one is tempted to say that its existence is incontestable. Indeed, it has seemed so to philosophers across cultures, who have otherwise interpreted the phenomenon diversely. Recall the well-known statement of Vacaspati Misra, who while elaborating on Sankara's famous commentary on the *Brahma Sutra*, observes: 'No one doubts whether I am or not, nor does anyone maintain the contrary of I am'.[4] He further remarked that I-sense is not a matter of mediate knowledge, but that it is 'immediate, hence unquestioned'.[5] Cross-culturally viewed, it can be said that there is unanimity among philosophers concerning the thesis that *I-consciousness is indubitable*. An over-view of the history of Indian and Western philosophy, generally speaking, lends support to the comment cited above, just as it does to the reading of the existentialist philosopher Jean Paul Sartre, who puts it in his characteristic manner : 'No one says, perhaps I have an ego' (emphasis added).[6]

To be sure, many similar remarks and statements by different philosophers from both hemispheres could be quoted in support of the idea of the indubitability of I-consciousness. However, this observation is not intended by any means to augment any expectation that in the long run philosophical accounts and analyses of the phenomenon of I-consciousness are likely to converge or to follow the same interpretive strategy that can give rise to a common explanatory model. As has been mentioned before, it is in a way indeed astonishing that there can at all be room for such a range of conceptual possibilities for interpreting the simple, indisputable phenomenon that I-consciousness seems to be at first sight. However, the fact is that philosophers in the past as in the present and that too across the boundaries of cultures seem to be fully aware of the perplexities that are entailed in I-consciousness. It is worthwhile listening to their careful articulations as they indulge in the process of discerning the status and the constitution of this apparently simple phenomenon. Indeed, a sense of awe can be seen expressed even in the case of such philosophers who steadfastly claim the phenomenon to be indubitable, as did Descartes in his famous statement *'cogito ergo sum'*. Listen to him carefully as he wonders: 'I know that I exist; the question is, what is this 'I' that I know'?[7] For a study of the theme

---

4 Bhamati: *'Na hi jatu kascidatra sandigdhe aham va naham veti'*.

5 *'Aparaksanubhavasiddha iti na jijnasaspadam'*.

6 cf., Jean-Paul Sartre, 1960 [1957], *The Transcendence of the Ego* (New York: Farrar, Straus and Giroux).

7 René Descartes, 1993 [1641], *Meditations on First Philosophy*, 3rd edn, trans. Donald A. Cress (Indianapolis: Hackett).

of I-consciousness, it seems to me, that this itself is the crucial question. It opens up the possibility of a philosophical exploration of the diverse dimensions of the phenomenon and makes room for alternative modes of interpreting I-consciousness. The issue of I-consciousness, not unlike many major philosophical problems, has different aspects that can be treated from a linguistic, phenomenological, metaphysical, and epistemological points of view. Indeed, a careful consideration of the various ways in which the word 'I' is used in everyday language and its sense is deciphered[8] already begin to disclose the complexities that call for explanation. Linguistic investigation itself gives rise to a range of questions. One important question for which it is difficult to get a clear-cut answer concerns the referent of the pronoun in the first person, singular number. Again, there are also other intriguing questions pertaining to I-consciousness that know not only of epistemological, metaphysical, but also of ethical and even soteriological dimensions. To try to obtain a comprehensive view of this intricate situation in order to adequately deal with some or all of these divergent aspects in a coherent manner is by no means an easy task. This also explains why there are so many contending viewpoints on the theory-making front. Nevertheless, the fact remains that whatever may be the genre of philosophy and however varied are the accounts concerning the phenomenon of I-consciousness, its presence as an integral component of all our experience hardly provokes any misgiving. In fact, a study of the multiple stands in a cross-cultural philosophical context is all the more perplexing precisely because no one questions whether or not there is an I-sense. However, despite all the agreement concerning its indubitability that the history of philosophy amply demonstrates, the mystery of I-sense has not as yet ceased to continue to baffle thinkers.

While exploring the theme of I-consciousness in a cross-cultural philosophical context, it is important to take note that neither the fact that there is such an awareness (*pratiti*), nor that it is expressible via a linguistic entity such as the word 'I'

---

8 For more on these issues, cf. Chapter 5 in this volume.

(*asmad-sabda*)—the latter being a pronoun in first person singular number that constitutes an essential component of conventional language—are matters of any controversy. Philosophical disagreements become pronounced only when one attempts to account for the source, the nature, and structure of the phenomenon such as when one specifically investigates into what forms the basis of I-consciousness or what the word 'I' actually refers to. The many inherent difficulties of such an enquiry become explicit only in this process of intellection (*manana*). Consequently, alternative answers to various queries gradually emerge and different paradigms steadily develop. History of ideas shows that some of these paradigms are of naturalistic moulds displaying various forms of physicalism (*dehatmavada*) whereas there are others which seek to avoid that orientation. Interestingly, while reviewing theories about I-consciousness in a cross-cultural setting, it becomes evident that there are two dominant paradigms—one unmistakably highlights the idea of self as a distinct principle or as a substance whereas the other categorically denies such a claim while attempting to explain the phenomenon of I-consciousness. Each of these comes in various versions but these basic standpoints are maintained. However, in all cases the question 'do I exist or not' is held to be redundant.

In this study references are made to some of these paradigmatic positions from Indian and Western thought. It is noted in that process, on the one hand, the kind of arguments and reasons that have been actually offered in support of these views and on the other hand, on what grounds these interpretations have been challenged by their opponents. Thus, given the idea of the indubitability of I-consciousness as a common point of departure, an important part of comprehending the philosophical trajectory consists in unravelling why and how differences arise as the investigations proceed.

In what follows an attempt will be made to focus on a few representative examples, selected from a host of views that are vying with each other to draw our attention to demonstrate that many of the questions and concerns are not confined exclusively to any specific tradition. However, even if some of the issues that have been taken up by philosophers across cultural boundaries do overlap, it is no simple undertaking to detect the assumptions and motivations that actually prompt the way these questions come to be raised in the course of reflection—be that in the Indian or in the Western context. It is tempting to hope that if these oft-repeated questions and problems are reviewed and analysed in a more comprehensive cross-cultural philosophical context, it would not only enable us to grasp the overlaps and differences in the queries and responses but would also help us eventually to gain insights into the hitherto unexplored conceptual possibilities. It seems to me that this kind of bold engagement with documented stories of reflections on some of the fundamental themes and sub-themes may not only engender a deeper appreciation of the intellectual traditions across cultures, but would also save the fruitless efforts of trying to conceive strategies over and over again that have been already tried and tested elsewhere.

Speaking of a construal of a common framework of enquiry for exploring this fundamental question of I-consciousness, it is pertinent to observe that the cross-cultural philosophical investigations of the large theme of consciousness and the discernment of its place in the physical world is of capital importance. For this latter purpose an over-all understanding of the subtle intricacies of this topic is needed. It is likely to be quite fruitful, for example, to put together the classical debates between the naturalistic philosophers and those who resist this mode of interpretation in Indian and Western thought. This also makes it possible to observe how philosophical stands obstruct or pave the way towards a religious quest. Note that the classical Indian philosophers devoted considerable intellectual energy reflecting upon the theme of I-consciousness not only in order to obtain a deeper understanding of our place in nature but also because it was considered to be an indispensable part of the quest for Freedom (mokṣa). No religious discourse in the Indian cultural soil could proceed without philosophy. Readers who are interested in the debates touching upon the naturalistic as well as religious dimensions of the enquiry into I-consciousness may note that such polemics among philosophers of different persuasions were rampant. Indeed, it is a stimulating exercise to explore in this connection the atheistic dimension that is integral to much of present-day Western naturalism, and compare this with the enthusiasm of the Indian philosophers of a purely naturalistic temperament who also vehemently opposed any non-naturalistic or religious reading of the phenomenon of I-consciousness. The naturalists offered explanations in consonance with their own philosophical convictions. All these form quite a significant part of the unfoldment of the history of ideas in the Indian context where we find that neither the naturalists were side-tracked nor the soteriological enterprise ignored in the over-all records of debates. In such a venture, the polemical exchanges between the philosophers of opposed camps become a matter of profound interest to which reference is made in this monograph.

This is indeed a vast subject-matter about which the theoreticians, both Indian and Western, have quite different stories to tell based on widely divergent philosophical premises as is documented in the literature—ancient and modern, original and secondary. As is to be expected, the Indian intellectual soil, not unlike the Western, has given rise to a host of competing theories while dealing with subtle complexities of the phenomenon. Thus, just as there are several versions of naturalistic and purely materialistic views about what I-consciousness entails, there are also views that interpret the phenomenon in terms of a non-material, non-physical principle. A review also shows that there are also readings where the phenomenon of I-consciousness is not simply analysed by referring to a simple, homogenous principle or entity but on the contention that it is composite in character. Besides these, there are also thinkers who hold that selfhood and I-ness are not identical. In the Indian context there are even explanatory models where I-consciousness is seen as arising from a confusion[9] of two distinct principles—one unchanging, the other dynamic. However, there are subtle differences among the advocates of this view, even though both regard these two principles to be primordial and pre-empirical. Some maintain that both of these principles are ontologically real, whereas others insist on reducing

---

9 Notions of '*viparyaya*' in Sankhya, '*Klesa*' in Yoga, and '*Adhyasa*' in Advaita Vedanta are pertinent in this connection.

the principle of change to the phenomenal level and highlight the unchanging principle alone as having ontological status. All these theories are elaborated in this monograph.

Given the complexities of such a fundamental philosophical enquiry, it is inevitable that many kinds of disputes and controversies manifest themselves, as evidenced in an extensive historical record. However, prior to alluding to any polemical literature, it may be helpful to discern whether any radically sceptical question can be raised precisely in order to challenge the thesis of the indubitability of I-consciousness. As mentioned earlier, I have not come across any document claiming that there is no I-sense at all in our experience. However, to say that there is no such prima facie claim does not imply that none—while speculating about the reference of the word 'I'—has reached a judgment where the 'I' is seen as no more than a 'dummy grammatical subject'.[10] Even such a linguistic analysis of the first person pronoun in the singular number cannot be taken as a denial of the phenomenon of I-consciousness as an everyday empirical experience. Certainly, 'no-self' theories abound which refute any interpretation of I-consciousness as entailing an abiding selfhood. However, even in no-self theories where the self is depicted as fictitious and devoid of any ontological reality, a denial of I-sense as a psychological datum is not possible or plausible. Recourse is to be taken by projecting an alternative theory for explaining this undeniable phenomenon. Thus, the thesis of indubitability of I-consciousness may well be taken at least as a common point of departure, in tune with common sense experience involving the everyday usage of conventional language that entails the pronoun in first person, singular number.

Indeed, one comes across a series of questions which have been asked both in the Indian as well as the Western philosophical traditions regarding I-consciousness. As the enquiry proceeds, one begins to perceive the many aspects of this multifaceted theme. There are, as mentioned before, psychological, epistemological, linguistic, metaphysical, ethical, and soteriological dimensions of these investigations. Documents show that there is a long range

10 See Anscombe's view in Chapter 5 in this volume.

of questions that philosophers keep asking. To mention a few examples: What is exactly designated by 'I', i.e. what is the designatum of the word 'I'? In every day usage, one comes across statements like 'I am sad', 'I am deaf', or 'I am fat'; do these imply that in fact there is no single entity that is referred to by the word 'I'; is it so that its meaning varies from context to context? In other words, the possibility of multiple references comes in. Again, when we attribute or ascribe various states of consciousness to the 'I' (such as in the statement 'I am happy' etc.), are these states related to the 'I' as a quality to a substance, or are these states to be understood as modifications of the same substance or as actions ascribed to an agent etc.? Moreover, how do I know this 'I'? Does this involve similar or different procedures than when we say 'this is a pot'—granted that the latter is an object of an external sense-perception; does one need to accept an internal sense-organ? Or, is there a non-discursive mode of knowing where the question of a subject–object distinction does not arise? As we will see, multifarious answers are available to these queries. What is philosophically intriguing is that although no one doubts I-consciousness, nevertheless there is no unanimous, definitive answer to any of these questions.

Attempt will be made in the following pages to focus on a few representative positions from a vast collection of ideas that I compiled in the course of time from Indian and Western sources. The intent is to examine this rich assortment of readings in a manner that would enable one to glimpse some of the most pertinent and predominant lines of thinking on I-consciousness. It is evident that Western as well as Indian philosophical literature contain important examples of interesting variations of hardcore materialism, naturalism, realism, idealism, as well as of absolutistic trends, giving rise to major and conflicting schools for interpreting this fundamental topic. What is remarkable is that a careful consideration of this plethora of views in the cross-cultural philosophical setting gradually reveals not only the profound insights into this central question but also divulges the limits that are embedded in these investigations, inevitably persuading us to recognize before our own critical gaze the obscurity and mystery of our own being. It is in fact like finding oneself in the midst of, what can essentially be described as an unknown territory, while listening to the echo of the startling question documented in the Upanisads: 'That by means of which we know all, by means of what can we know that'?[11]

---

11 *Brhadaranyaka Upanisad* 4.5.5: '*Yena sarvam vijanati tam kena vijaniyat*'

CHAPTER TWO

Facets of Naturalism

Consciousness is an overwhelmingly large and complex theme that can be studied from multiple perspectives. A perusal of Indian and Western philosophical literature makes it evident that repeated attempts to explore this challenging topic have given rise to a multitude of contending theories. The focus on the phenomenon of I-consciousness is an indispensable and integral part of that endeavour. Deep reflections and critical discussions abound in this intriguing cross-cultural philosophical scenario. An overall view of these theories that are historically documented leads one to think that all these can perhaps be classified under two broad categories. The central difference among these theories is that one adopts and the other rejects the naturalistic standpoint as a philosophical strategy for explaining consciousness.

A close look at a general compilation of such readings shows that naturalism and non-naturalism are the two predominant paradigms that are conspicuously opposed to one another. Their main difference lies in the philosophical assessment of the source and status of consciousness in determining whether it is to be regarded as a natural phenomenon or not. One finds that some naturalists show preference for viewing consciousness simply as being on a par with any other natural phenomenon, whereas others belonging to the same camp are ready to grant that although consciousness is a 'natural phenomenon', it has features that can mark it as being distinctly different from all other phenomena in nature. As opposed to these views, there are the non-naturalist philosophers who offer a counter paradigm insisting that consciousness is not at all to be considered as a 'natural phenomenon' but must be seen as a distinct principle. In short, these are the two major camps, each of which knows of internal variations.

The focus of this chapter is on naturalism which, no doubt, stands out as a major explanatory model in the history of philosophical elucidation of the theme of consciousness. I also intend to underscore the philosophical controversies between the advocates of 'naturalistic' and the 'Non-naturalistic' theories of consciousness, using examples of these philosophical trends of thinking from both Indian and Western philosophical traditions. These enable us to perceive the nature of reasoning and arguments in ancient and in modern times offered by theoreticians who vigorously seek to offer a naturalistic interpretation of consciousness and those who vehemently oppose that style of elucidation and explanation. Given that various forms of naturalism have been known in India and in the West and that these philosophical strategies have been employed for exploring consciousness, it is interesting to notice the kind of intellectual resistance that have been offered by the non-naturalists. Some of the concerns inherent in this continuing debate until today show how thought-traditions across cultures have coped with the challenges that were presented by the naturalists which by no means have been meagre.[1]

While proceeding to unravel the naturalistic line of thinking touching upon a range of relevant issues, it is to be noted that the advocates of various schools of naturalism in India and in the West exhibit a great deal of diversity with regard to approaches in the discernment of how consciousness emerges and is to be accounted for in terms of its possible constitution and function. It is evident that naturalism as a philosophical stance is certainly not monolithic. Some of the naturalists are advocates of epiphenomenalism; some propose reductionism whereas others prefer non-reductionistic moves. It is noteworthy that despite these differences there are certain basic common features that run through these diverse versions. For example, all naturalists,[2] without any exception, refuse to commit themselves to any form of substance—dualism which is a philosophical consequence of the view that consciousness is nothing but a natural phenomenon.

---

1 See section on 'Cross-cultural Philsophical Exploration: Its Aim' in the Introduction.
2 In Sanskrit, '*svabhavavadins*'.

They unanimously maintain that no second principle or category needs to be postulated as an explanatory tool. Interestingly, a review of the diverse accounts that are documented in the history of ideas cross-culturally, regarding the theme of consciousness in general and that of I-consciousness in particular, disclose that advocates of naturalism have unquestionably posed a considerable cognitive challenge to those who propose a non-naturalistic conceptual move as an interpretive strategy. A few examples of naturalistic accounts will be considered below.

Prior to embarking on various subtleties of this discussion, notice at the outset that there is an upsurge of naturalism in contemporary West. There has been a massive intellectual investment in recent times in the theory-making efforts that entail naturalistic approaches and contentions. Perhaps at no time in the documented history of ideas has one seen such a gamut of naturalistic theories regarding consciousness as are available today in the West. We need to take note of the multiple facets of naturalism both in order to appreciate why and how differences arise among the naturalists themselves and how in spite of their differences they retain a common ground and a shared conviction that distinguish them from the proponents of other schools of philosophy that present an altogether different picture with regard to this phenomenon, while repudiating naturalism. It is also interesting that these attempts are often perceived to be important parts of what is professed as the emerging 'science of consciousness' project. In this connection, it may be observed that although one often encounters such claims that these theoretical renderings are entirely derived from scientific investigations into the phenomenon of consciousness; nevertheless the fact remains that as a philosophical stand, naturalism is no new invention. Both ancient India and ancient Greece know of naturalistic conceptual frameworks. From those ancient accounts, one can perceive quite clearly some of the most significant theoretical as well as practical implications of such a standpoint for a study of consciousness.

However, the contemporary zeal in consciousness studies in the West has no doubt brought forth newer forms of naturalism based on advanced brain-research and neuro-biology in an impressive manner. It seems to me that there is no reason to underplay the fact that renewed intellectual vigour in consciousness studies in the West today owes much to the contributions of neuro-philosophers who actually profess one or another version of naturalism. What is also interesting—as will be seen shortly—is that the arguments offered by these contemporary Western thinkers in support of naturalism are different from those of ancient naturalists. Although there is undoubtedly a sharing of a common philosophical conviction with their ancient counterparts, today the naturalists claim legitimacy for their respective philosophical interpretations of the large theme of consciousness as being scientifically grounded since these are based on experimental and clinical data from physics, biology, and neuro-sciences. In other words, these latter sources are used as evidence for validating the theoretical claims of modern-day naturalism.

However, granted that the situation in the contemporary West is one in which several major but conflicting schools of consciousness-studies are vying for attention, one needs to note that many of the advocates are essentially interpreting naturalism in divergent ways. Newer versions of theoretical models appear in support of naturalism as soon as critical challenges are forwarded against an already existing model.[3] A cross-cultural philosophical review of the many facets of naturalism is fruitful for comprehending the internal struggle within the movement itself and also for appreciating the philosophical difficulties in exploring consciousness from a purely naturalistic standpoint. As has been mentioned, no naturalist is a dualist. However, not all naturalists for that matter are necessarily dedicated to materialistic or reductionistic thinking. These internal divergences in the theory-making venture are to be taken into account for any critical assessment of the movement.

In this chapter, besides considering the various faces of ancient Indian naturalism, some of the contemporary theories in the West have also been discussed. This review seeks to detect, on the one hand, the subtle variations in the philosophical assumptions

---

3 For a summary of an earlier report of these different approaches, cf. Ken Wilber, 1997, 'An Integral Theory of Consciousness', *Journal of Consciousness Studies*, Vol. 4, No. 1, pp. 71–92.

that these theoreticians operate with and, on the other hand, to review from a comparative perspective the common philosophical premise that they share with the ancient naturalists in the Indian context. A careful examination of some of the challenging interpretations offered by the ancient Indian philosophers as well as contemporary Western naturalistic philosophers allows one to assess the overall philosophical situation with regard to the study of consciousness from the naturalistic standpoint.

NATURALISM IN ANCIENT INDIA: THE CARVAKAS

Let me begin by recapitulating briefly the view that the Carvaka philosophers were propounding in the Indian philosophical scene. These ancient philosophers were precisely advocating '*svabhavavada*', literally naturalism. Their position—which knows of various versions—is of course not an example of what is today described as 'neuro-philosophy'. Unlike the present forms of naturalism emerging from the West that draw support from the neurosciences, the Carvaka philosophical readings are largely reflections based on observations of everyday experience and analysis of conventional language. It is therefore interesting to notice in what way their core perception and philosophical premise may still be said to remain pretty much the same as in the case of their modern counterparts in the West who vigilantly advocate a naturalistic view of consciousness. Notably, all naturalists, whether these advocates are ancient or modern, share a common tenet that there is nothing beyond nature; hence, they assert that the story of the emergence of consciousness cannot be told in any other manner than as a natural phenomenon, allowing of course room for different theoretical renditions that are in consonance with naturalism.

While dealing with the Carvaka theoretical accounts for the emergence of consciousness, it can be observed here that despite the paucity of material at our disposal,[4] it is clear—even from

4 Among the significant texts that are available, mention may be made of the following: *Brhaspati Sutra*, Madhavacarya's *Sarvadarsana*

the literature of their opponents—that the challenge of the Carvaka naturalists has not been by any means an insignificant one. References to the views that were advocated by the Carvaka philosophers can be found in the Upanisads as well as in Buddhist and several pre-Buddhist texts; all these bear witness to the fact that this line of interpretive thinking is indeed very old. Relevant documents show not only the differences among the advocates of the Carvaka school, who differed among themselves despite their common naturalistic bias, but also that there were lively debates among them and the opponents of the Carvaka school of philosophy. The implications of these exchanges are significant for a critical study of theory-making endeavours with regard to consciousness.

One could say that in certain ways, this old Carvaka school was, like logical positivism, anti-metaphysical in character. Their philosophy was geared to free enquiry and against traditional, established views. They accepted only perceptual evidence to be legitimate. Consequently, they made a critique of causality and denied any legitimacy to inference.[5] They held that no occurrence of an event can be attributed to any invariable cause as they did not admit of the possibility of establishing any 'necessary relation' between cause and effect. They argued this on the ground that no perceptual evidence can be provided in support of such a universal statement. Their critical analysis was aimed at demonstrating the untenability of what is traditionally regarded as legitimate sources of knowledge or counted as evidence (*pramana*), except perception. They were revolting against the religious cum moral beliefs and the ecclesiastical practices of the age. In some records, the Carvaka philosophy is described as '*lokayata darsana*', i.e. the philosophy of the common or the unsophisticated man. Sometimes 'lokayata' is interpreted as philosophy of 'this-worldliness' as

---

Samgraha, Jayarasi's *Tattvopaplava Simha*. For secondary sources, cf. D.P. Chattopadhya 1973 [1959], *Lokayata: A Study in Ancient Indian Materialism* (New Delhi: People's Publishing House).

5 In Jayarashi's well-known work, *Tattvopaplava Simha*, one comes across a powerful attack on the notion of evidence (pramana). The goal of this offensive is to show that empirical activity is possible without pramanas whereas no determination of the real is conceivable.

some of the Carvaka philosophers professed hedonistic ethics in consonance with their materialistic metaphysics. They advocated a view of life where nothing but pleasure should be seen as the *summum bonum* of human life. Since this life is the only life, they argued, pleasure is the highest good worth striving for. They were criticized by their opponents for promoting self-indulgence and for denying the notion of moral retribution. The Carvaka philosophers unhesitatingly rejected the possibility of existence of the 'other world' and decried any notion of metempsychosis or that of a soul, God, or salvation. They attributed all these ideas to be inventions of the members of a clever priestly class, who devised these ideas as a means of livelihood. It is evident from the records of the controversies documented in some of the well-known texts of the Upanisadic, Buddhist, and Jaina traditions that these views were taken quite seriously in philosophical circles and that they became subjects of lengthy debates prior to the mainstream traditions' rejection of these readings. Since these naturalist philosophers generally held perception to be the only legitimate source of knowledge, their opponents made efforts to critically expose the inadequacies of these naturalistic theories accounting for experience (without taking recourse to inference, etc.).

This is a broad description outlining their philosophical temper and attitude as a background for a study of their specific view of consciousness. To which extent modern day naturalists in the West share these attitudes can make an interesting subject for research.

Now leaving out the other philosophical concerns of the Carvaka school belonging to ancient India, let us focus here only on those specific ideas that have direct bearing on our present study. Although the Carvaka views come in diverse versions, nevertheless, all of them without exception claim that consciousness is *not* a distinct principle, it is not sui generis. Some proclaim that consciousness occurs as a result of a fortuitous combination of the elements. However, the significant variations in their theoretical accounts become evident as they respond to the query of what exactly must be considered to be the base of consciousness. Some of them claim that to be the body, others point more specifically to the sense-organs, still others to the mind (described as an internal sense-organ)—all of these are conceived in physicalist terms. In other words, though sense-organs and the mind are acknowledged to be distinct, the latter is not regarded as an independent, separate substance of non-physical nature. The elaboration of their respective versions of naturalistic theories of consciousness discloses specifically the internal differences regarding what they take to be the seat/source of consciousness. Some of these naturalists are pronouncedly epiphenomenalists, some are reductionists, and some others are materialists whereas there are still others who search for a conceptual space between materialism and dualism.

For some of the philosophers of the Carvaka school who vigorously propagated the idea that the 'gross body is the self' (*dehatmavada*), no notion of the self (*Atman*) apart from the living body was acceptable. Convinced of the fact that perception is the only acceptable valid means of cognition, they claimed that the elements[6] alone are the sources of all that there is. Any existent—be that animate or inanimate—is due to a combination of the physical elements. Some of these thinkers propounded the idea that consciousness is nothing but a by-product of matter. They held that when certain ingredients combine, new properties emerge; the arising of consciousness from physical processes is to be explained in the same way. An oft-used analogy is that just as fermented yeast, which is by itself not intoxicating, gives rise to the intoxicating quality in the wine, so does consciousness emerge from that peculiar combination of the elements that form the living body. Consciousness, they emphasized, is not a distinct principle independent of physical processes but is an epiphenomenon. Furthermore, they said that consciousness manifests itself only in a living body and disappears when that body disintegrates. Insisting on the fact that consciousness is always seen to be associated with a living body, they argued that it is pointless to attribute any separate existence to it. Carvakas opposed substance dualism.

One comes across the objections raised from the quarters of their opponents saying that our inability to cognize consciousness apart

6 For the Carvakas, these elements are earth, water, fire, and air. cf. Daksinaranjan Shastri, 1982, *Charvaka Darshana* (Calcutta: Rajya Pustak Parsat).

from the living body does not demonstrate that consciousness is a property of the body. If consciousness were a property, they asked, is it an essential or accidental property? The case of swoon and the state of dreamless sleep are cited to show that it cannot be considered to be essential. However, if it were accidental, they ask, which factors other than the physical process is required in that case for its emergence? Again, the question is posed that if consciousness were a property of the body, how can there be consciousness of the body? The argument seeks to stress that it can be said to be a property of that which is conscious and not of that of which one is conscious.[7] Finally, those opponents who accept the idea of Atman bring the charge of indemonstrability of the claim that these two—body and the Atman—are *not* distinct or different.[8]

One of the principal goals among the ancient Indian naturalists, who propagated various forms of naturalism, was to strive to disclose the seat of the sense of selfhood and identify it as a natural phenomenon. The various shades of naturalistic interpretations in their theoretical accounts bear witness to the presence of both a materialistic metaphysical bias as well as a proneness to explain the phenomenon in physicalistic or biological terms. As a consequence of these attempts, there emerged a series of alternative theories to the previous stance, mentioned earlier, that identified the self with the gross body. These are those that identified the seat of selfhood with the sense-organs or even with the mind or with the entire aggregate composed of all these factors.[9] In each case, however, the advocates see the body, the sense organs, and the mind to be no more than a part of the physical universe, belonging to the natural order. However, despite the fact that there are these internal differences within the naturalistic movement, they all seem to agree in maintaining the thesis that consciousness is

7 See Madhavacarya 1924 [1904], *Sarvadarsanasamgraha*, Gaekwad Oriental series, trans. E.F. Cowell & E.E. Gough (London).

8 cf. Parthasarathi Misra, 1915, *Sastradipika* (Bombay: Nirnayasagar Press).

9 These views, in Sanskrit, are called *dehatmavada, indriyatmavada, manatmavada* and *sanghatavada*.

not a separate and a distinct principle but unquestionably to be a derived one. It is seen as a by-product, as an emergent quality of the physical processes. In other words, there is no room for a metaphysical dualism in any of these versions of svabhavavada. The advocates of this school in the Indian context remain consistent with its premise that there is nothing beyond nature. However, records show that certain strands of Carvaka naturalism were regarded with more respect in the philosophical circles than others. Reference can be found to both the sly (*dhurta*) and the sophisticated (*susiksita*) Carvakas.

The Carvaka philosophers propounded different versions of naturalistic views regarding what forms the basis of I-consciousness.[10] The records of their debates with their opponents clearly demonstrate that they were keenly aware of the prevailing dominant theories and their implications. The Carvakas who advocated the living body to be the seat of selfhood polemized against those philosophers who held consciousness to be a quality of the self and thought of the self as something distinct from the body since they regarded that reading as being entirely misleading. The Carvaka physicalists (*dehatmavadins*) asked in a sarcastic mode that who has, after all, ever observed consciousness outside of a living body? Thus, the self is, according to them, not different from the living body.

Evidently, different shades of physicalism were present. Thus, apart from those who identified the gross body to be the self, there were also some naturalistic thinkers who held the sense-organs (*indriya*), and still others the mind (*manas*) to be the seat of selfhood. Note that the sense-organs or the mind are all understood in physical terms. This may indicate that perhaps some of these naturalists were seeking a more subtle version of physicalism than others. It is in a sense not rash to conclude from the kind of analogies they used to make their point that among these Carvaka philosophers were those who were propounding and anticipating more sophisticated forms of physicalism, epiphenomenalism, reductionism, and perhaps even non-reductive naturalism. It is evident that those who propounded that the mind is the self

10 For a summary, see Sadananda's *Vedantasara*.

(*manatmavada*), did not advocate any gross form of physicalism. This latter position knows of several modern versions in more refined forms.

Each of these naturalistic positions despite their differences in the discernment of where lies the base of consciousness has provoked strong responses from philosophers who questioned the explanatory power of naturalism as a whole. These opponents, belonging to the schools of philosophy within the Upanisadic, Buddhist, and the Jaina traditions, squarely challenged the Carvaka interpretations. Anyway despite their internal differences, the Carvakas agreed that consciousness is not to be taken as a principle per se. The abode of consciousness is to be found in the living body/ sense-organ/mind—either in each or in a conglomeration of all these. One comes across debates centred on the question regarding the discernment of the I-sense. The theories that emerged from the quarters of the Carvaka philosophers also draw from the everyday linguistic expressions of the personal pronoun in the first person. While answering the question what can be taken as referent of the indexical I, they answered by pointing to such conventional linguistic usages as 'I am thin' (Aham *krsa*), 'I am deaf' (Aham *badhira*), or 'I am happy' (Aham *sukhi*). In other words, to the question what constitutes the basis of I-sense, their answer remains the body, the sense organs, and mind respectively. As can be expected, these naturalistic views provoked counter-attacks from their opponents, demonstrating the inherent weaknesses of these positions.[11]

In this short summary, the point to note is that the Carvakas evidently sought to give a blow to the philosophical endeavours in which consciousness is not treated in naturalistic terms. They were vehemently opposed to the idea of consciousness as sui generis, which happens to play an important role in various forms of metaphysics as well as in soteriology. The Carvaka reading insisted upon the idea that 'I-consciousness' need not be accounted for with reference to any other principle besides this mortal frame (since there is nothing else besides that). Note that the consequence of such a position can be seen not only in the projection of a materialistic metaphysical view or for the sake of championing the cause

---

11 For refutation of the Carvaka view, see Chapter 3 in this volume.

for physicalism in one of its various forms but that this also has profound bearing on ethical and religious dimensions of human existence. The ideas of the self as corporeal and temporal, and as that which lives and dies with the body, made soteriological pursuits seem like a farce. The Carvakas attempted to expose the network of ideas that seek to project a notion of self as non-physical to be nothing more than a baseless conjecture, at best a clever manoeuvre of the priestly class, as mentioned before. They jeered at the notion of salvation or ultimate freedom (*mukti/apavarga*), while mockingly observing that 'death is salvation' (*marana eva apavarga*). Undoubtedly, the view, viz. that this life is the only life and that death is the extinction of all consciousness, is directly linked with their advocacy of a hedonistic ethics. There is a saying in ancient philosophical circles that the Carvaka motto was: 'live happily as long as you live, borrow money, but take clarified butter'.[12] However, some scholars are of opinion that this saying was actually conjured up by their adversaries in order to ridicule the Carvaka view. Be that as it may, the Carvakas did recommend a hedonistic approach to life, as was the case with the Greek epicureans. A pronounced materialistic approach ensued with regard to the status of consciousness. Their utter rejection of the mainstream ethical and religious views provoked critical thinking. Consequently, as documents show, there was a surge of philosophical rebuttal of these naturalistic readings.

In any case, a study of all these interconnected issues shows that how we conceive the notions of self and consciousness are matters that are not just of purely theoretical concern. These are not only abstract academic questions relevant for weaving pure theories, they do have deep impact on various sorts of practical concerns that have bearing on norms and values that guide our lives.

NATURALISM IN THE CONTEMPORARY WEST

Let me now focus on the modern West in order to assess why and to which extent naturalism today is regarded by many to be

---

12 *'Yavat jivet sukham jivet, rnam krtva ghrtam pivet'*

able to provide a satisfactory frame for understanding the large theme of consciousness. A survey of these modern theories is also interesting in order to figure out why despite their basic common and shared assumptions, the advocates of this philosophy split their paths, and some even go so far as to begin to show eventual distrust in our ability to at all fathom this mystery via the naturalistic program.

In contemporary West, one finds various versions of naturalism that are attracting much attention in the field of consciousness-studies. These contending naturalistic theories have assumed a more bold and sophisticated expression drawing support from the neuro-sciences. The following outline focuses on only a few of the diverse interpretations of naturalism that are available today. A probe into these representative examples of present-day naturalistic positions can eventually throw light on certain assumptions and attitudes that influence this specific mode of theorizing which seem questionable not only to the adversaries of naturalism as an explanatory model but can even show the disagreements among those who are proponents of naturalism yet prefer to weave their own theories differently. It is indeed illuminating to go through the literature that shows why exactly some of the participants of the movement raise objections to specific claims made by other co-participants.

In the very first line of the preface of his interesting book, Owen Flanagan writes: 'Naturalism is the view that the mind-brain relation is a natural one. Mental processes just are brain processes'.[13] He then begins to delineate how a number of views that have come forth which are born out of a 'gnawing suspicion' of a prevalent view that projects a 'picture of the mind as a sophisticated information processor'.[14] Indeed, this suspicion and distrust of a computational view of mind and philosophical speculations drawing support from the neuro-sciences have led to intense discussions regarding what consciousness is all about. The effort

13 cf. Owen Flanagan, 1993, *Consciousness Reconsidered* (Cambridge: MIT Press).

14 *Ibid.*

invested in the theory-making front has brought about important differences among the naturalists themselves, even though they otherwise agree in claiming that consciousness is nothing but a natural phenomenon. Flanagan describes his own view as 'constructive naturalism'. His labelling, based on an overview of various types of naturalistic theories, are insightful. He exposes his stand not only by contrasting it to 'non-naturalism' of the sort that seeks to understand consciousness in terms of a non-physical substance or principle, such as the views of Popper and Eccles, but also by showing how his own position differs from other naturalistic positions as that of Thomas Nagel's dual-aspect theory which Flanagan describes as 'principled agnosticism', that of Collin McGinn's 'anticonstructive naturalism', of Churchland's 'eliminativist naturalism', etc. While looking at these various naturalistic interpretations and commenting on them, I will also briefly refer to the view of John Searle who dubs his own position 'biological naturalism'.

A thorough critical examination of all these readings by the naturalist philosophers, as listed above, could possibly show how in each case a specific view contains important and helpful insights and yet why none can be said to be fully cogent and satisfactory. Although a detailed analysis of these views cannot be undertaken here, it is important to underscore the kind of difficulties that prevent theoreticians to reach a consensus. This is interesting because there is a common philosophical conviction and a sharing of a very down to earth common premise urging them to unanimously hold consciousness to be a natural phenomenon. Indeed, from a survey of these positions it seems that it is easier for the naturalistic thinkers to agree to disavow the so-called 'supernatural', the 'miraculous' interpretive stances and to discard the non-naturalistic readings about consciousness as inadequate than it is to explain the phenomenon in terms of known natural laws and weave theories that can meet with their peers' approval. It seems to be a comparatively facile task to condemn non-naturalistic conceptual moves to be unduly treating the phenomenon of consciousness as something 'mysterious' than to come up with an adequate explanatory model within the naturalistic framework itself and to theorize about the complex and subtle phenomenon of consciousness in a consistent manner. Indeed, responses to a premise like 'brains subserve minds' seem questionable on many fronts once the theory-making process begins to unfold, not only to those who decry naturalistic explanation, but sometimes even to the naturalists themselves as will be exemplified below. One could ask why in their theory-making effort, the naturalistic philosophers cannot see eye to eye while providing a general account regarding consciousness, despite their constant focus on the idea that there is a causal nexus between the brain states and consciousness?

Indeed, as one takes an overview of the current theories one begins to wonder why for these neuro-philosophers, who are openly devoted to the project of removing the sense of deep mystery from the 'mind-body' problem, the task seems to be proving to be far from simple. Are these difficulties indicative of certain basic limitations and drawbacks that are inherent in naturalistic thinking, ancient or modern, that show up whenever efforts have been made to offer a naturalistic explanation of the phenomenon of consciousness? A critical examination of naturalistic theories show time and again that no theory has succeeded so far in demonstrating the validity of their common assumption in a convincing manner or in accounting for the range of experience that calls for explanation. None has met with unanimous approval even from those who proclaim consciousness to be a natural phenomenon. In this connection, it is helpful to take note of the insights of the non-naturalists and note on what grounds these non-naturalists—cross-culturally—have firmly declined to consider consciousness to be no more than a natural phenomenon. For a deeper comprehension of these issues and concerns, a brief review of a few theories prevalent in the contemporary West is useful. This enables one to obtain a clearer picture for assessing the soundness of the project of the naturalists.

As an example, let us consider the view of Collin McGinn.[15] He seems quite emphatic about the soundness of the naturalistic venture. This is an enterprise, to put it in his own words, 'to take the magic out of the link between consciousness and the brain'.[16]

---

15 Collin McGinn, 1991, *The Problem of Consciousness* (Oxford: Blackwell).

However, soon enough the reader finds him wondering loudly: 'How can technicolor phenomenology arise from soggy gray matter? How could the aggregation of millions of insentient neurons generate subjective awareness'?[17] After a long discussion, McGinn comes to the conclusion, again to use his own words, that 'total cognitive openness is not guaranteed for human beings'.[18] The inherent strain of this line of thinking becomes evident when he tries to hold on desperately to his point of departure and observes that 'there is nothing inherently eerie or bizarre about this embodiment' and then declares, almost helplessly, that in fact 'we do not have access to the nature of the link' which, by his own admission, is crucial for solving the mind-body problem.[19] To openly admit as he does, that 'total cognitive openness is not guaranteed for human beings and it should not be expected',[20] is like confessing that a naturalistic explanation is doomed to fail. When he still tries to keep intact the naturalistic premise and backs up the claim of its soundness, it seems more like a matter of 'blind faith' than as a piece of scientifically grounded sound reasoning. This is far from providing a solid foundation for an explanatory theory. The vulnerability of the situation becomes tacitly clear when he finally observes that 'a deep fact about our own nature as a form of embodied consciousness is...necessarily hidden from us',[21] while insisting nevertheless upon the credence that this inability also has a neuro-biological ground. The kind of theoretical analysis and rendition that could really make up for a justifiable philosophical argument for validating his project seems to be missing.

Incidentally, McGinn's elucidation has met with criticisms not only from those belonging to the non-naturalistic camp, but it has not met with approval from other staunch naturalists as well. Patricia Churchland, for example, a naturalist philosopher holding

16 *Ibid.*
17 *Ibid.*
18 *Ibid.*
19 *Ibid.*
20 *Ibid.*
21 *Ibid.*

a reductionistic stand, seems to be convinced of the positive prospects of a neurobiological undertaking. Her response to McGinn's open acknowledgement with regard to the limitations inherent in the human neurobiological situation for cracking this tough problem is that such a reading is nothing more than 'a powerful prediction based not on solid evidence, but on profound ignorance'.[22]

It seems to me that only neuro-biologists, who are involved in empirical work, are genuinely sensitive to philosophical argumentations and who can assess what amount of 'knowledge' or 'ignorance' is present in Mcginn's insight and for that matter can equally discern really how much evidence is actually obtainable from current research in the field of neurobiology may salvage Patricia Churchland's own optimistic readings concerning this fundamental question. To be hopeful of a certain direction of enquiry, pronounced in the name of science, cannot itself be taken as a convincing philosophical argument for validating her reading nor can it be taken as a refutation of McGinn's position that openly declines such a possibility. In order to make a convincing case in favour of Patricia Churchland's claim, empirical demonstration will be called for since only that can conclusively lay bare the nature of the 'link' between brain and consciousness. However, the question for now remains whether that is possible. This is not a matter that can be established purely on theoretical speculation. Note that in the same paper Churchland has also raised objections against John Searle's anti-reductionistic stand, a view discussed below. There too her objections are also along the same lines, that is, raised more in the name of scientificity than assuming the form of a full-fledged philosophical argument.[23]

For a discussion on naturalism versus dualism, Thomas Nagel's view can be referred to as a fine example for demonstrating what is at stake. He proposes a dual aspect theory. Granted that the 'connection between the mental life and the body is very close', his concern in how to understand the presence of mind in the

22 Patricia Churchland, 1994, *Can Neurobiology Teach Us Anything about Consciousness?* (Lancaster: Lancaster Press).

23 cf. *ibid.*

physical universe to which belongs our bodies along with the central nervous system and the brain. His attitude to dualism is that as a philosophical stand it is 'conceivable', yet he finds it to be 'implausible'. His objection against dualism is that the latter postulates an additional non-physical substance without explaining how it can account for subjective mental state, which the brain is not supposed to be able to.[24]

However, Nagel seems to be quite aware of the philosophical complexities that are embedded in the position that he is proposing. This is exemplified when he first states that the 'mind is a biological product', and then begins to wonder about 'how can experience inhere in something that has physical parts'? Finally, he openly acknowledges that there is 'difficulty to make sense of the assignment of essentially subjective states to something which belongs to the objective order'. Consequently, his conceptual move goes definitely against reductionism, arguing that subjective reality cannot be reduced to the physical conception of reality, reminding the reader that 'reality is not just objective reality... independent of everything else'. He nevertheless keeps on returning to his foregone conclusion that 'reduction is not the only form of connection, and some of the things that make it appear that the mental is independent of every thing else are illusions'.[25] Despite his rejection of all forms of psycho-physical reductionism, he does not seem to substantiate adequately and appropriately this conclusion.

The conceptualization of this dual aspect theory is clearly motivated, as he puts it 'by the desire for an integrated conception of a single reality in which the mental and the physical are located in a clear relation to one another'. At the same time he seems to be aware of the fact that what hinders intelligibility of such a philosophical position is that 'one thing can have two sets of mutually irreducible essential properties, mental and physical'. In other words, he seems to hold the opinion that the relation between brain and consciousness cannot really be understood in naturalistic terms as no objective account of subjectivity can be obtained on the basis of

24 All citations are from Thomas Nagel, 1989, *The View from Nowhere* (USA: Oxford University Press).

25 *Ibid.*

present-day knowledge.[26] These conflicting perceptions, although surely worthwhile pondering over, do not seem to me to have been reconciled in his deservingly well-known work entitled, *The View from Nowhere*.

While describing the various twists and turns in the theory-making endeavour with regard to the mind-body problem, Jerry A. Ford has succinctly commented on the kind of tension that is there between the dualists and those who oppose this viewpoint as being incompatible with current findings. [27] One important objection that can be raised against dualism, as he puts it, is expressed in the question 'how can the non-physical give rise to the physical without violating the laws of the conservation of mass, of energy and of momentum'?[28]

What is interesting to watch in these debates is the inherent difficulty in seeking, on the one hand, to account for subjectivity on the basis of current knowledge of neuron-biology and on the other hand, to explain the interaction with the physical on a dualistic assumption.

While dwelling on various present-day renditions of naturalistic explanation as a scientifically supported philosophical theory regarding consciousness, it is indeed interesting to examine the views of John Searle. A review of the contemporary research on consciousness shows how Searle strives to obtain further insights into this complex question. He plays a significant role within the analytical tradition and at the same time seeks to create bridges between philosophical thinking and scientific findings in domain of physics, neuro-physiology, and biology. His refutations of the computational theories of the mind, especially what he describes as strong Artificial Intelligence, and his critical awareness of the *limitations* of different reductionistic theories based on metaphysical materialism, have indeed led Searle to adopt an interesting philosophical strategy. He seeks to carve out a conceptual space between dualism and materialism. Searle's view merits serious

26 *Ibid.*

27 cf. his essay in Richard Warner and Tadeusz Szubka (eds), 1994, *The Mind-Body Problem: A Guide to the Current Debate* (USA: Blackwell).

28 *Ibid.*

attention primarily because of this interesting conceptual strategy that he has adopted by denying both dualism and materialism. Against materialism, he has insisted upon the idea of irreducibility of consciousness; against dualism, he has argued that all states of consciousness are caused by brain-processes. Consequently, he comes to hold that consciousness is a part of the natural world and repeatedly claims that it 'is a biological phenomenon as any other'. This is a very brief rendition of what lies at the core of his biological naturalism.[29]

Searle seems to me to be making a strong claim that not only needs to be philosophically defended against metaphysical dualism but also against all those views that support the ontological primacy of consciousness—positions that have long been held in the Indian as well as Western philosophical traditions. Moreover, to my knowledge adequate substantiation from empirical investigations concerning neurophysiology of the brain is not available, at least not as yet, in support of the proposed position. It is therefore difficult to share his optimism that by simply adopting a conceptual strategy that 'consciousness is a higher level feature of the brain' will provide a 'simple solution' to the traditional mind–body problem—a problem that is anything but simple.[30]

In brief, as an advocate of biological naturalism, Searle maintains that since brain processes cause conscious states, the problem of consciousness is surely to be treated in terms of neuro-biology. In his effort to turn the mystery of consciousness into the problem of consciousness, Searle tries to substantiate his claims over and over again by making assumptions about the causal power of the brain processes which, in his own admittance, are still largely unknown. I am not as much persuaded by his arguments in favour of this position as by his refutation of materialism or criticism of various reductionistic theories. Sometimes his case against dualism takes a form that cannot necessarily be taken as a convincing philosophical argument. Consider, for example, his following comment: 'To accept dualism is to deny the scientific world-view

29 *Ibid.*
30 *Ibid.*

that we have painfully achieved over the past several centuries'.[31] As I have observed earlier, often naturalistic philosophers demonstrate this kind of bias in trying to legitimize a view by describing it as 'scientific'—as if that by itself conclusively validates the philosophical claim embedded in their theories.

It is encouraging that there seems to be an ongoing quest today where investigators seem to aspire for a larger framework for a study of consciousness cutting across disciplinary boundaries. It may be remarked in this connection that due to the rise of the prestige of science, a number of contemporary philosophers look into the domain of scientific research in search of new insights into this multifaceted topic but in this effort to combine knowledge from various disciplines they seem to ignore the cognitive traditions associated with various world-religions that also have a long history of preoccupation with this theme. This latter domain remains largely unexplored, being branded as esoteric and unscientific.

It may be worthwhile recalling here that William James is a significant exception in that regard. While surveying relevant material in the history of ideas precisely in order to make a philosophical assessment of views, he was open to both scientific and religious ideas. We find in his writings testimony of his boundless curiosity that led him to take into consideration the scientific findings of his time while also exploring the conceptual resources of religious and philosophical traditions as a fruitful context for understanding the questions and concerns in this area of investigation. Many contemporary philosophers often demonstrate a lack of neutrality in this respect. John Searle's overall framework of research, not unlike several other naturalists, seems to exclude outright the ideas and concerns embedded in religious traditions. These latter ideas, Searle openly brands as 'opinions (that) cannot be taken seriously'.[32]

Yet Searle is fully aware of the position taken by the neurosurgeon Penfield regarding this very issue of dualism. Penfield, who had most direct experience with a range of issues concerning

31 John Searle, 1997, *The Mystery of Consciousness* (New York: New York Review Books).

32 John Searle, 1992, *The Rediscovery of the Mind* (USA: MIT Press).

brain and consciousness, observes that 'after a professional life-time spent in trying to discover how the brain accounts for the mind, it comes as a surprise now to discover, during the final examination of the evidence, that the dualist hypothesis seems the more reasonable of the two possible explanations'. [33]

It is certainly not from the vantage point of a dualist but as one not much convinced by the present state of naturalistic interpretations, I sometimes wonder as an involved onlooker of the ancient as well as the ongoing debates whether this issue can at all be settled by further empirical investigation or is it our predicament that pure philosophical speculations will keep these alternatives open to us forever.

Anyway, given that I find it difficult to share Searle's optimism that by simply adopting a conceptual strategy that 'consciousness is a higher level feature of the brain' will provide a 'simple solution' to the traditional mind-body problem, let me briefly dwell on Searle's further reflections on this topic beyond what is known from his earlier works.[34] He keeps persistently working on these ideas and has re-stated his position in a very lucid and succinct manner in a paper entitled 'Consciousness'.[35] Here he develops his ideas indicating how consciousness is actually different from 'other phenomena in the natural world'. Searle states that the 'combined feature of qualitative, unified subjectivity is the essence of consciousness and this, more than anything else, is what makes consciousness different from other phenomena studied by the natural sciences'. In other words, what distinguishes consciousness from other natural phenomena is what constitutes the essential feature of consciousness. According to Searle, the essential feature has three aspects—qualitativeness, subjectivity, and unity. This analysis is interesting and illuminating in many ways. Searle himself believes it to be especially helpful for disentangling *some* of the threads of the traditional mind–body problem.

---

33 W. Penfield, 1975, *The Mystery of the Mind* (Princeton University Press).

34 As in Searle, *The Rediscovery of the Mind*.

35 First published in the *Annual Review of Neuro-science*, 2000.

To those who question the possibility of a scientific study of consciousness, Searle's answer to them is that the 'scientific requirement of epistemic objectivity does not preclude ontological subjectivity as a domain of investigation'.[36] In support of his statement, he cites examples of cases of subjective experiences of pain and anxiety that have always been objects of scientific enquiries. Indeed, up to a point this claim cannot be questioned. Nevertheless, from this to proceed to answer the delicate question regarding the extent to which subjectivity can be explored and how far it can be ascertained as accessible to an epistemically objective scientific investigation, let alone as assertable in neurobiological terms, is confronting a domain that is yet pretty much unknown. The 'first person ontology', to which he alludes, seems still to retain deep mystery to keep us bewildered for some time in the future.

It seems to me that in order to make a headway with the kind of theory that Searle proposes, a fuller account of the idea of causation is required in that specific theoretical context. He insists that consciousness is a feature of the brain process and therefore caused by the brain process. However, several questions remain unanswered, precisely due to a lack of sufficient knowledge about what the causal process is bringing about in the case of the occurrence of consciousness—a case that seems to require a radically different elucidation than the standard physiological causal explanations as in the case of digestion. Searle has used this analogy many times in support of his claim, which has nevertheless left me unconvinced as these are not parallel cases.

At this juncture, let me refer back to his comments regarding the religious traditions, mentioned earlier. These sources of ideas need to be considered not for the sake of any justification for any specific reading but in the context of concerns and insights. In his *The Rediscovery of the Mind*, Searle declares 'our problem is not that somehow we have failed to come up with a convincing proof of the existence of God or that the hypothesis of an after-life remains a serious doubt...it is rather that in our deepest reflections

---

36 *Ibid.*

we cannot take such opinions seriously' and this is, he says, due to 'our scientific world-view'.[37]

However, as a contrast to this version of what 'a scientific world-view' is all about, note that not only a Newton belonging to the 17th century but some of the greatest scientists of the 20th century—such as Einstein and Schrödinger who have played a key role in shaping this 'scientific world-view'—saw the matter quite differently. From the statements of such great scientists[38] it certainly seems that one needs to exercise caution against sharing any incorrect assumption about what a scientific world-view must *necessarily* exclude.

I bring up this point simply because this has pertinence for the overall frame within which thinking about consciousness must proceed, without letting any inhibiting preconceived notions for or against the cognitive discourses associated with science or religion.

Interestingly, however, in a paper entitled, 'Consciousness, Free Action and the Brain' Searle comes to argue 'even though somewhat reluctantly', as he puts it, that 'an irreducible non-Humean self' is required, and even that this 'self is not an entity in the field'.[39] As I read this, a host of questions comes before me: In what sense can this 'conscious self' be said to be a part of the natural, physical world, neuro-biologically explicable and what could be its role and status? Moreover, what will be the philosophical account of individuation in the overall picture that he has so far drawn about consciousness? How does an epistemically objective science get access to the inner recesses of subjectivity for further exploration which is indispensable for a deeper comprehension of this absolutely fundamental issue?

37 Searle, *The Rediscovery of the Mind*.

38 cf. Einstien's 1958, 'The World as I see it', a section from his *My View of The World* [Mein Weltbild] and Schroedinger's *Mind and Matter* (Cambridge: Cambridge University Press).

39 First published in 2001, *The Journal of Consciousness Studies*, Vol. 8, No. 8, pp. 59–65, reprinted in his 2001, *Rationality in Action* (Cambridge, MA: MIT Press).

It is possible that naturalistic theories will undergo significant modifications with further advance in the domain of neuro-biology and as neuro-philosophers will dig deeper into this complex and multifaceted question of consciousness. However, in the theory-making endeavour the pictures that have emerged so far, only some of which have been discussed in this chapter, can hardly be said to convincingly demonstrate that naturalism has won over the idea of primacy of consciousness or over substance-dualism. These options seem to still remain open before us.

CHAPTER THREE

Self as Substance

The Basis of I-consciousness

The idea of the 'self as substance' is a cherished philosophical position that has been strongly defended by certain philosophers in India as well as in the West. This is a conceptual paradigm that seeks to provide an answer to the central question regarding what generates and supports the phenomenon of I-consciousness. Many sophisticated philosophical arguments have been forwarded in support of this view and very often common sense also seems to back this reading. The shared perception is that if a substance is that in which qualities inhere, the 'self as substance' is to be conceived as a substratum for certain attributes that are peculiar to it. More importantly, the self is acknowledged as the basis of I-consciousness, it is said to be the referent of the word 'I'. Views that reflect this way of looking at the phenomenon of I-consciousness, in and through their variations, will be considered in this chapter in a cross-cultural philosophical setting with the help of representative examples from Indian and Western philosophical traditions.

Nyaya, Vaisesika, and Mimamsa Schools

In the Indian philosophical scene there have been thinkers who propounded the view of self as a substance quite vigorously. Their reading concerning the idea of the self is particularly interesting as the arguments that they advanced also show why naturalistic explanation is ultimately rejected by them. Thus, while carefully examining the Carvaka contentions that the self is to be identified either with the body (*deha*), or the sense organs (*indriya*) or the mind (*mana*), or to be taken as a conglomeration (sanghata) of all these, philosophers belonging to the Nyaya and Vaisesika schools not only rejected each of these contentions one by one but they also championed the idea of the self as a distinctly separate substance (*dravya*). This view of the self is all the more worth examining since it is defended by philosophers who propounded a pluralistic metaphysics and were hardcore realists. They believed in the independent existence of the external world and were keenly engaged in exploring the nature of space, time, matter, and causality as well as being concerned with cosmology. It is worth noting that it is from among them that arose one of the earliest formulations of the theory of the atom. They came to hold a position of substance--dualism--not unlike the Cartesian view, maintaining that physical properties are to be ascribed to the body and the states of consciousness to the self (*atman*). They firmly held that the self is to be regarded as a substance which is different from the body, the sense organs, as well as the mind, while offering cogent philosophical arguments corroborated by empirical evidence in support of this reading. The position that the self is a distinct reality is supported in their accounts in various ways, such as in their explanation of psychological phenomena as memory and recognition, in their epistemological analyses of the knowledge situation, and also through a scrutiny of everyday language.

Apart from the realists belonging to the Nyaya and Vaisesika schools, the view that I-consciousness (*aham-pratyaya*) is pointing to the existence of a self is also strongly supported by the advocates of the Mimamsa school. Their analysis of experience and the experient led them to hold that the 'I' as the experiencer is indicative of the existence of a self, which is then acclaimed as a substance (*dravya*). In other words, it is the self that generates I-consciousness and is the referent of what is linguistically expressed as 'I'. In the course of their reflection, as documents show, the idea of self stands out as being of capital importance without which, it is claimed, no cogent explanation of experience is possible. Many arguments are advanced in their pluralistic metaphysical system in support of the view that this self is to be held as something distinct from the body, the sense organs and the mind (deha-mana-*indriyatirikta*). Moreover, One finds in the Nyaya-Vaisesika literature a sustained philosophical investigation of the self as the doer (*karta*), the enjoyer (*bhokta*) and the knower (*jnata*), which led them, step by step, to profess the remarkable metaphysical view that in its essential nature the self is eternal (*nitya*), indestructible (*avinasi*), formless (*amurta*), and all-pervasive (*vibhu*). There are of course lengthy records of philosophical argumentations showing the various stages of thinking of these philosophers, how they actually arrived at each of these characterizations, and defended these readings in various polemical situations. Although it is not possible to recapitulate here all the steps of their argumentation in support of such metaphysical claims, a few examples of these exchanges will be alluded to in what follows. What is most relevant for the present study is to take note of how their account of the phenomenon of I-consciousness is distinctly different from the theoretical analysis offered by other schools adhering also to the same Upanisadic tradition, such as Sankhya, Yoga, and Advaita Vedanta.[1] What is noteworthy is that although all the philosophers belonging to the Upanisadic tradition unanimously championed the idea of self and also shared some common philosophical insights, there are some significant differences among them with regard to the notion of self and also about the status of I-consciousness. These irresolvable differences in their philosophical interpretations about the self and the status of I-consciousness expose the difficulties that are integral to the ratiocination process concerning these fundamental questions. However, all the schools of philosophy belonging to the Upanisadic tradition are committed to uncover the self and while pursuing this common philosophical agenda they come up with their distinct readings within their respective metaphysical frameworks.

Anyway, in order to appreciate how I-consciousness and the idea of self are related, it is important to watch various phases of polemical discourse in Indian thought. Granted that according to the realists self is the basis of I-consciousness, let us recall the kind of metaphysical characteristics that they attributed to the self, (documented in the Vaisesika literature), viz. the self as indestructible, etc. These ideas are shared in general by Nyaya and Mimamsa schools as well. This can astound any enquirer, let alone their

1 For more, see Chapter 4.

staunch opponents from the naturalistic camp. Historically, in the Indian context, these naturalists—as discussed in the previous chapter—happened to be predominantly (although not exclusively) the Carvaka philosophers who propounded 'svabhavavada'. However, these naturalists were by no means the only ones to challenge the interpretations I-consciousness and their readings about the self as offered by the realists of the Vaisesika, Nyaya, and Mimamsa schools. Some of the prominent schools belonging to the Upanisadic tradition, despite sharing some of their core insights regarding the self, also questioned some aspects of this specific mode of understanding the issues. The Buddhist thinkers were of course the major challengers of the idea of self as a whole, while offering their own explanation for the phenomenon of I-consciousness. It is of great philosophical interest to follow these controversies that bring to light the intricacies that are unavoidable in any serious inquiry into these issues. Thus, on the one hand, there are the records of arguments and criticism by the advocates of different schools of the Upanisadic tradition, who were themselves *atmavadins* but not necessarily interpreting the idea of the self as these realists do and, on the other hand, there are documents of fierce attacks from the philosophical quarters of the naturalists (*svabhavavadins*) and proponents of the no-self theories (*anatmavadins*) who sought to discard altogether the very idea of an abiding self. These are not only impressive documents but may be considered as pioneering examples in the domain of philosophical investigation in the field of consciousness studies. The varied formulations of the notions of self and no-self theories that come in various versions also entail a range of issues giving rise to centuries of debates and discussions. In fact, reconstruing and recounting these carefully documented controversies can itself make a voluminous study.

In what follows, the focus is on a few of the recorded exchanges in order to exemplify some of the divergent accounts concerning the phenomenon of I-consciousness and to follow up the debates that ensued. The disputes between the Carvaka and Vaisesika philosophers are indeed particularly interesting for examining not only why a naturalistic explanation was found to be unacceptable to the realists of these schools but also to the philosophers of other schools belonging to the mainstream Upanisadic tradition regardless of their own internal differences. In this connection, it is crucially important to keep in mind that even the Buddhist tradition—in spite of its dissimilarities with the Upanisadic tradition and their rejection of the idea of self—had refused to accept the naturalistic accounts of consciousness that the Carvakas offered. This historical perspective enables one to appreciate the rules of debate that were repeated by these ancient philosophers. With reference to the notion of self as advocated by the Vaisesika philosophers, the Carvakas ask sarcastically whether these realists have arrived at this (bizarre) notion of self as being independent of body, sense-organs, and the mind or as being eternal, indestructible, etc., after serious considerations or do they endorse the view simply because the self has been thus described in the revealed scriptures (*sruti*)? This is an ironical remark from the quarters of the atheistic Carvaka thinkers. It is not only suggestive of the fact that they hold these to be absurd but is also a way of ridiculing the authority of revealed scriptures (Vedas, Upanisads) as a source of evidence.

Indeed, there is a long history of deliberation in Indian thought pertaining to the notion of evidence and sources that can be said to be constitutive of knowledge with regard to which the various schools of philosophy held different views. It is easy to surmise that no reference to any utterance in the Upanisads could be cited as 'evidence' in any debate with the naturalists concerning the status or constitution of I-consciousness. Since the rules of debate precluded the use of a source of knowledge as evidence unless all the parties involved in a debate accepted it. It is pertinent to note here that the very idea of a 'revealed' scripture as a valid source of cognition (*pramana*) was not acceptable not only to the Carvakas but also to the Buddhists and the Jainas for that matter. The task before the Vaisesika philosophers was, therefore, to seek to establish the plausibility of the self or atman through other recourses. They attempted to do that precisely by analysing everyday experience (*vyavahara*) as well as by pointing to mutually accepted valid means of cognition by the contending parties such as perception (*pratyaksa*)[2] and/or inference (*anumana*), as the case may be. In this context of dispute with the naturalists, an analysis of perception and of conventional linguistic usage (*sabda vyavahara*) comes to play an important role. Some of these exchanges, as will be seen below, have direct bearing on the philosophical treatment of the phenomenon of I-consciousness.

The Vaisesika philosophers claim that their view about the self (atman) as basis of I-consciousness and as a self-existent substance can be supported by an analysis of the linguistic usage of the word 'I'. In other words, the Vaisesika retort to the Carvakas consists[3] in showing that it is not exclusively the revealed scriptures but an analysis of the very usages of the word 'I' (aham) can demonstrate that the pronoun in the first person, singular number has no other referent than the self, which is an ontological reality. An elaboration on this statement gradually leads the Vaisesika philosophers to spell out what their notion of the atman is, to what specifically the word 'I' refers, and eventually also to provide an answer to the epistemological question about how this self is known.

It has been already indicated that the Vaisesika philosophers, in tune with all other schools belonging to the Upanisadic tradition, cherish the view that the self is not reducible to the body, the sense-organs, or the mind. The ratiocination process discloses why such a stand is to be accepted. One finds them arguing in accordance with this stand, insisting that the primary (*mukhya*) referent of the word 'I' can never be the body, the sense-organ, or the mind. They maintain that wherever there are such conventional usages that seem to identify the pronoun in the first person singular number with either the body (such as in the statement 'I am thin' [aham krsa] or a sense-organ as in 'I am deaf' [aham *badhira*] or a mental state/mind as in 'I am happy' [aham sukhi]), these are to be taken as examples of the secondary (*gauna*) usages of the word.

2 Only perception was accepted by the Carvakas as evidence; the Buddhists accepted inference as well.

3 In Vaisesika Sutra of Kanada, with Muni Sri Jambuvijayi (ed.), *Chandrakanta's Bhasya*, 1961, Gaekwad Oriental Series no. 136, Baroda.

The primary referent is the self which is other than the body, the sense-organs, and the mind.

To this the Carvakas retort by saying that if at all a distinction needs to be made between the primary and the secondary usages of the word 'I', why not let the body, etc., be considered to be the primary referent and treat all other usages as secondary?

In reply, the Vaisesika philosophers point out that if the body were the primary referent of the word 'I' and the body were the self (atman), then the atman, which is the basis of I-consciousness, would be the object of external sense-perception (*vahirindriyagrahya*). However, their claim is that the instrumentality of external sense-organs is not required for apprehending the 'I'. Moreover, in that case, knowledge of 'other selves' could also be obtained using the same means of cognition, i.e., the external sense organs. However, these realists persistently claim that an analysis of experience shows that this is not actually how we cognize either ourselves or others, that in neither case the external sense organs can be said to be the instruments of knowledge. This controversy leads to a detailed exploration of self-cognition and that of the discernment of 'other selves', which is briefly recapitulated below.

The fact of self-cognition, as expressed in the statement 'I know myself' (aham *mam janami*), according to the Vaisesika philosophers, is not a case of external sense-perception but that of internal/mental perception (*manasa* pratyaksa).[4] Following their epistemological analysis, the self is cognized by the mind (manas) which is an internal sense-organ (*antarendriya*). This why it is said that mental perception is to be categorized as a mode of knowing which is neither a case of inference nor a case of external sense-perception. It is precisely an episode where 'cognition of cognition' takes place and that is said to be possible only when it is preceded by an incident of cognition. Thus, it is interesting to note that according to this view the cognition of the 'I'—as in the case of 'I know the jar'[5]—always arises only after the occurrence of a knowl-

---

4 Technically designated as '*anuvyavasaya*', as this is a kind of cognition that always follows a '*vyavasaya-jnana*'.

5 '*ghatamaham janami*', that is, 'I know the jar'.

edge-episode such as expressed in the statement 'this is a jar'.[6] The point that is sought to be emphasized is that the self, which is the basis of I-consciousness, is or can be cognized only when it is preceded by an event that has taken place and has been cognized. This epistemological description also accounts for why in our experience there is never cognition of I as such, which is isolated and abstracted from everything else. The cognition of I is always associated with some other experiences and attributes. As the discussion proceeds further, notice that arguments are given to establish why the self, which is the referent (*artha*) of the word (*pada*) 'I' cannot be the body, the sense-organs, the mind, etc., but has to be a distinct substance called the self.[7] The metaphysical characteristics of the self remain a separate issue to be addressed later on.

In the case of cognition of 'other selves', it is interesting to note that the philosophical account of the process involved in such cognitions is different from that of the cognition of 'I'. The Nyaya-Vaisesika philosophers (not the Mimamsakas) maintain that such cognitions arise *not* by mental perception (*anuvyavasaya*) but by inference (anumana). In other words, it is not only with regard to self-cognition, but equally about how knowledge of 'other selves' is obtained that they disagree with the Carvaka thesis that such cognitions are a matter of external sense-perception. However, as the debate continues, the Carvakas keep on insisting that external sense-perception is the means of our knowing 'other selves', which is exemplified in the case of such a statement as 'I see Devadatta going'. This ascription is considered by the Nyaya-Vaisesika philosophers to be fallacious (*bhrama/upacara*); they claim instead that the knowledge of other selves is established by inference. In this example the inference is made on the basis of the internal sense-perception (manasa pratyaksa) of the effort (*prayatna*) involved in the act of going.

To corroborate further the reading that the self (atman) can never be established by external sense-perception, the realists come up with the following example. Consider the case of a blind man

---

6 '*ayam ghatah*', i.e., 'this is a jar'.

7 cf. Gadadhara Bhattacharya, 1929, *Saktivada*, edited by D. Shastri (Kashi Sanskrit Series).

and a man with sight. They are both entitled to I-consciousness (aham-pratyaya). There is, however, a significant difference with regard to their ability to perceive external objects. In other words, the point is to show that the awareness of the 'I' is not at par with that of external objects, nor is the knowledge of 'I' generated by external sense perception. In short, the conventional usage (*laukika vyavahara*) of the word 'I' (*asmat-sabda*), the fact of internal perception (manasa pratyaksa) and inference (anumana), all in more than one way strengthen the conviction that the self is the basis of I-consciousness. Thus the Nyaya-Vaisesika philosophers demonstrate that the contention of the reality of the self, as apart from the body, the sense-organs, and the mind, is derived not exclusively from revealed scriptures—as the Carvakas had originally accused them of —but also on the basis of evidences that are acceptable to the Carvakas themselves, viz. an analysis of perception as well as of conventional linguistic usages.

At this point, let us go still deeper into the mode of thinking that shapes the conceptual world of the Indian realists and make note of how and why they are convinced of the existence of the self as a distinct entity. For this, they scrutinize the experience of objects and the self/selves as enduring entities. A critical examination of the phenomenon of recognition (*pratyabhijna*) is discerned to be vital. The example as expressed in the statement 'I touch what I saw' shows, they say, that this experience can be accounted for only on the premise that the self as well as the objects persist in time and retain their individual identity by virtue of which they are re-identifiable. Had the self who cognized (as in 'I saw') not been recognized to be the same (as in 'I touch'), there would be no way of ascertaining that the object known in the past through visual sense-organs is the same object which is now known by tactual sensation. Note that this analysis is also at the same time a repudiation of the idea that the sense-organ is the seat of selfhood (*indriyatmavada*). If sense organs were the seats of I-consciousness, there will be a plurality of subjects (*nana-kartrk*) since sense-organs are many. Had that been the case, it would leave the phenomenon of recognition unaccounted for. One cannot say 'I touch what I saw' since vision cannot recognize what was cognized by the touch-sensation. Thus, the notion of personal identity becomes crucial. The notion of individual or singular agency (*eka-kartrkatava*) is needed as the presupposition for understanding how diverse sense-experiences are unified with reference to the same individual as knower. This point is further elaborated below.

What is of crucial significance for the present study is to read the metaphysical implication of this analysis which consists in viewing the self not only as the basis of I-consciousness but also as being distinct, as something apart from being an aggregate of body, sense organs, etc., (*dehadi-samghatamatra*). In other words, just as a substance is conceived to be over and above its parts and qualities, the self must be regarded as something over and above the body etc., (dehadi-*atirikta*) and qualities that inhere in it. Here it is also intriguing to take note of all the steps involved in the conceptualization process that prompt the realists to abandon the idealists' view of an object. The epistemological scenario for the realists is one in which the object is understood as being given and the knower apprehends it with the help of sense-organs, the mind, etc. Notice that the argument for an independent, persistent object is crucially important for establishing the idea of personal identity as well as for maintaining the specific metaphysical notion of the self as they do. If the self had not persisted in time, the sameness of the object could not be ascertained. The other side of the coin is that had the object not been an identical, enduring entity, the sameness of the subject will be equally difficult to establish. The object which was given in vision has to be the same as that which is now grasped through tactual sensation. Had it not been so, one could not point to the 'I' in both cases as the knower and claim these to be non-different (*abheda*). It is precisely in this context that one begins to observe the significance of the idea of self as a substance (*dravya*). Had the self, as some claim (e.g., the Buddhists) been reducible to the states of mind (like touching, seeing, remembering, etc.) and the object to its various parts (like colour, size, etc.), experience will be incomprehensible, nay, impossible. Besides, according to these philosophers, one cannot account for the knowledge-situation without the notion of substance. The very notion of self or an object entails this idea of substance as an indispensable substratum in which qualities inhere. This is so, the realist philosophers insist, both in the case of a substance which is conscious (*cetana* dravya) like the self,[8] and the substance which is material/non-conscious (*jada* dravya) like any object. All knowledge, they claim, presupposes a contact among such factors as the knower, the instruments of knowledge (the sense-organs), and the known.

In this connection it may l e briefly observed that the idea of substance has been a matter of heated controversy between the Upanisadic and the Buddhist philosophers which spanned through the centuries. The Upanisadic philosophers in general vehemently objected to the Buddhist dynamic worldview that sought to do away with the notion of substance on various grounds.[9] Among others, this has important bearing on the philosophical treatment of the theme of I-consciousness in these traditions. It is striking that despite significant internal differences,[10] all the schools belonging to the Upanisadic tradition seem to take recourse to the view that an in-depth analysis of the phenomenon of I-consciousness ultimately points to an unchanging and unchangeable self. To say this is not to overlook the obvious differences that are also present in their estimation regarding the constitution of the 'I'. As will be seen in the subsequent chapters, some Upanisadic philosophers (such as of the Nyaya, Vaisesika, Mimamsa schools) describe the I as simple and homogenous, while others (Sankhya, Yoga) as based on heterogeneous factors, even comparing it as a 'knot of self and not-self' (Advaita Vedanta). While recapitulating these differences among the philosophers belonging to the Upanisadic tradition, this study not only seeks to highlight these differences in their theory-making endeavours, depicting 'I-sense' as simple or composite in character but also the contrasts in their interpretations of consciousness as being necessarily intentional in character or not. Some indeed ascertain that in the last analysis consciousness

8 Consciousness is not an essential property for some realists since a person is found to be not conscious as in the case of swoon, dreamless sleep, or in the state of liberation or mukti (as in Nyaya-Vaisesika) whereas there are other realists who consider it to be essential (as in Visistadvaita Vedanta).

9 cf. Chapter 6.

10 cf. Chapter 4.

is non-intentional. Note that those atmavadins who maintain the 'I' to be an ultimate, indivisible (*akhanda*) entity actually refuse to accept the idea of an objectless mental state (nirvisaya caitanya), whereas there are others philosophers of the same tradition such as the Advaitins, who assert the latter view.

However, let me dwell a bit longer on their analysis with regard to the issue of recognition as it plays a decisive role in support of the idea of self as substance. According to the realists, a philosophical explanation of the phenomenon of recognition necessarily validates the idea of an enduring and abiding self. It is noteworthy that in the episode of recognition, the object is grasped (i.e. cognized) as being non-different from the object perceived before. By the same token, they argue, the 'I' that is cognized in this experience is given as the same 'I' as in the past. The reputed Naiyayika philosopher Jayanta in his well-known book entitled, *Nyayamanjari*, reflects further on this phenomenon of recognition—a phenomenon which is vital for a study of time and self. He considers it as a form of perception, where the object is apprehended as qualified by its pastness.[11] In the episode of recognition, he observes, there is a sense that time has lapsed, that is, the present object is apprehended as being known in the past. This is analysed as being due to the trace (*samskara*) that was left behind combined with the present perception. Moreover, the phenomenon of recognition in turn establishes that the self and the object have remained constant across a stretch of time. Hence, their identity is re-cognizable.

An analysis of this common episode of recognition shows to the realists, as they maintain, the falsity of the claim of the idea of universal momentariness. The notion of universal momentariness that was advocated by the Buddhists was never accepted by any school belonging to the Upanisadic tradition. Controversies continued for centuries. Recall that the Buddhists in turn do not accept recognition (pratyabhijna) to be a means of valid knowledge (pramana), since—as they argue—recognition entails a composite judgement, being a composition of memory-trace, and perception. Incidentally, note that even the Upanisadic schools

---

11 *Atitavasthavacchinnavastugrahanam.*

like the Prabhakara Mimamsa also did not accept recognition as a pramana for the same reason.[12]

As one probes deeper into what is involved in the experience, viz. 'I touch what I saw', one finds that a few intricate questions with regard to the status of the phenomenon of memory are also dealt with in the literature. It is indeed remarkable to recapitulate how these realist philosophers argue step by step to lay bare that the phenomenon of memory can establish not only the existence of the self but it can even lend support to the contention that the self is distinct from the sense-organs as well as different from the mental states that are caused by the contact of sense-organs with the objects.[13] Their opponents, for example the Buddhists, vehemently oppose this contention. They hold the view that the phenomenon of memory can be explained without postulating any idea of an abiding self. They claim that it is the trace (samskara) left by the object seen before is what is now remembered. They insist that memory cannot be treated as a ground for establishing the existence of the self, since what is instrumental to the phenomenon of memory is the samskara and no self is required for that purpose.

The realists seeking to answer this objection press the point that even if it is granted that the self is neither the cause nor the object of memory, the phenomenon of memory itself cannot be explained unless the trace is treated as a quality (*guna*) which resides in the self and which, therefore, shows that the self must be regarded as a substance. This is further demonstrated by the fact that the 'I' which remembers the object as being 'seen before' also perceives itself as the same 'I' that re-identifies the object that is now given in tactual sensation to be the same object.

---

12 Recall that the Prabhakaras claimed that 'so' ham cannot be said to establish the atman, precisely because it is given in recognition (*pratyabhijnamatra iti siddhantam*).

13 *Nyaya Sutra* 3.1.13—*Na smrteh smartavyavisayatvat*—is documented expressly to gear the discussion to disclose what really is at stake as one undertakes a minute analysis of memory. This is taken up in the next Sutra and commentary thereon. The objection is that the self cannot be said to be either the cause (karana) or the object (*visaya*) of memory.

Again, this argument is also used for repudiating the view of the indriyatmavadins, that is, those who claim the sense-organs to be the basis of I-consciousness—a view held by some of the naturalists that has been referred to before. The realists say that if one or more of the different sense-organs were the seat of self, memory cannot be accounted for, since what is given by one sense-organ cannot be remembered by another. In other words, the self is crucial for explaining such phenomena as recognition and memory. Once again, in the case of 'I touch what I saw', the I who remembers the object which is given by tactual sensation is the I who saw it. The tactual sense-organ cannot obviously remember since the object was previously given by the visual sense-organ—only the self can remember and recognize and must therefore be acknowledged to be distinct from the sense-organs. Moreover, if each sense-organ is treated as a seat of selfhood, the situation will be chaotic as there will then be a plurality of selves (*nanatmavada*).

The above arguments offered by the advocates of the realist school is a summary analysis in support of the contention that the self can indeed be established in this way and shown to be as something distinct from sense-organs and as the only possible substratum for memory. Their answer to all those who raise objections against the realists—by saying that an account of memory does not require the self—is that this is due to a lack of awareness of all the factors that memory experiences really involve. It is worthwhile here to refer to Vatsayana, the commentator of the *Nyaya Sutra*. In support of this above view, he makes a careful attempt to bring out all the components of memory-experience. Consider the case of memory as expressed in the statement 'I knew this thing'. He claims that in the case of the knower who knew the thing, the knower, the knowledge, and the thing as known before—all these three are objects (*visaya*) of memory. In other words, one who thus remembers 'I knew this thing', all the three—'I who knew this thing, this thing was known by me, and I who had the knowledge of this thing' are parts and parcel of the memory-experience. I could not say 'I saw this thing' had the memory-experience not disclosed the thing as 'seen', or that it was 'me' who saw it, or that that which 'I see now', 'I have seen before'. The knower who utters 'I will know', 'I know', or 'I knew' is the self which abides in all three times—past, present, and future—is even the same self who seeks to unravel what memory is.[14]

In fact, one of the persistent charges against the Buddhists in the Nyaya-Vaisesika-Mimamsa literature is that the idea of trace (samskara) is totally incompatible with the Buddhist idea of momentariness (*ksanabhangavada*). Similarly, they find that the phenomenon of recognition remains unexplained on the Buddhist premise. For the Vaisesika and some other realists, on the other hand, recognition is precisely a phenomenon which cannot be explained if the object and the self were discontinuous and changed at every moment. Eager as they were to establish that the self and the objects are continuous, enduring entities, they insisted on this phenomenon of recognition, which is accessible to all. They claim that it is a legitimate experience that unfailingly points to the identity of self and objects despite the passage of time.

The Buddhist philosophers on their part are well aware of the fact that to accept recognition to be a form of valid cognition/ judgement will be disastrous for the key Buddhist contention that 'at no two moments anything can be said to remain identical'. These topics thus remain a matter of philosophical controversy. Again, even though the Buddhists accept the pan-Indian ideas of karma and transmigration, for the Upanisadic philosophers these notions would remain entirely unaccounted for if one accepts the Buddhist premise that all existents are momentary in character (*yat sat tat ksanikam*). This is why the Buddhist idea that the moment and the momentary coalesce ontologically has been a target of criticism by the Upanisadic schools of philosophy for centuries.

It is precisely in order to explain all these phenomena that are important for psychological, ethical, and soteriological considerations, that these realists as spokespersons for the Atmavada tradition expounded with great fervour the notions of the enduring, persistent, and abiding character of the self (selves) and objects. For this, the realists find that a defense of the notion of substance becomes necessary. The self is the substance in which the special qualities (*visesa* guna) such as desire, etc., inhere. Likewise, a physical substance is distinct from the qualities of which it is

14 cf. *Nyaya Sutra* 3.1.14.

the substratum. They argue that not all objects are momentary, some may endure over a long or a short stretch of time until destroyed. This is connected with their view of time as well. This is not all. Following their metaphysical probe, one gradually uncovers the category of the unchanging and unchangeable. One sees how they actually arrive at the ideas that this self which is the object of I-consciousness (*aham-pratyaya vedya*) not only endures, it is ultimately shown to be unoriginate and indestructible. The philosophical challenge consists in demonstrating that (a) transitoriness is not necessarily equivalent to momentariness; and that (b) the category of the eternal must have a place in a conceptual scheme simply for the sake of doing justice to our experience.

Remarkable is the way their analysis discloses within the realists' framework of thinking that the idea of the self is not merely to be treated as a postulate without which no knowledge (perception, memory, recognition, etc.) is possible, but that this self can be demonstrated as a knowable (vedya). In other words, the self is not merely a precondition of knowledge but is also an object of knowledge. Like everything else that exists, the self is also knowable (*jneya*), nameable (*abhideya*), and demonstrable (*prameya*).

One can further follow the arguments by which the realists establish the reality of plurality of selves. It is to be noticed that for them the atman or the self which is referred to by the word 'I' is an individual and not a universal self —a conceptual possibility which is outright denied. According to the realists[15] the existence of a plurality of selves is an undeniable fact. This fact, they urge, is supported by experience which discloses the obviously different conditions and states in which these 'selves' are—some happy, some miserable, etc. These divergences in the case of different persons cannot be accounted for with reference to one universal self. Plurality of selves is not any provisional state of affairs. This idea remains intact in their soteriology as well, which also explains why freedom or mukti attained by one does not imply freedom for all. Lastly, as interpreters of the Upanisadic tradition, they humbly submit that the reality of plurality of selves is also supported by the revealed scriptures as well and cite from the Upanisads in support of this contention.

---

15 *Kanada Sutra* 111,2,20 (*Vyavasthato nana*) clearly indicates this.

Now to summarize, to the epistemological question as to how one becomes aware of oneself, the answer is by mental perception (manasa pratyaksa). When asked by what 'pramana other selves' can be said to be known, it is said that 'other selves' are known by inference. The existence of other selves is inferred from the observation of such marks (*linga*) as activity, inactivity in others which are motivated, similar to what one perceives within oneself, viz. by desire, aversion, etc.[16] In their literature, a list of special attributes (visesa gunas) of the self is carefully enumerated. These are desire, aversion, volition, pleasure, pain, cognition, disposition, merit, and demerit. The self (atman) is the substrate for such special attributes.[17] Apart from the schools of Nyaya and Mimamsa, this line of thinking was also shared by the schools of Dvaita Vedanta.[18] Thus, all these philosophers mentioned above share the insight that although the phenomenon of I-consciousness is possible due to the presence of the self, I-consciousness is always grasped in association with something else. This mode of knowing does not confer mukti, for that is needed a direct encounter with the self as such (atma *saksatkara*). This leaves room for spiritual discipline to be practiced in the quest for obtaining freedom.

Although the idea of Atman has been safeguarded by all the philosophers belonging to the Upanisadic tradition, however, there are important internal differences among them concerning the notion of self and consequently with regard to their analysis of I-consciousness, as can be seen in the following chapters.

WESTERN PHILOSOPHERS AND DUALISM

René Descartes and John Locke

Looking at the history of Western philosophy, one finds a scenario—not unlike the Indian philosophical scene with a clear

---

16 *Kanada Sutra*, Upaskara 111,1,19 (*pravrttinivrtti ca pratyadatmani drste paratra lingam*).

17 *Kanada Sutra* 111,2,21 (*sastrasamarthyacca*)

18 cf. Chapter 4, especially the section on 'Controversies among the Schools of Vedanta'.

tension among those who are either for or against dualism. The traditional philosophical distinction between dualism and naturalism is very much present where the latter is often employed in favour of metaphysical materialism and the former highlights the idea of a non-physical substance as being indispensable. This is in opposition to those identity theories that refuse to accept the distinction between the mental and the physical—a distinction which is not only ingrained in our everyday experience but forms a part of our conventional language. Without this, the dualists firmly hold that no cognitive explanation of ourselves and our experiences is possible.

The investigation with regard to the source of I-consciousness has led some of the dualistic philosophers to the idea of self as a substance. Their metaphysical search has always been about detecting the source of identity and continuity, whereas the epistemological query has been about how to discern the criterion, the mark by which we know it to be so. To say that the self is a substance is to assert that it is something in which qualities inhere and that it is not itself a quality. The special qualities of the self are variously classified by these philosophers. In the Indian context, consciousness is one such special quality according to the Vaisesika philosophers, as has been noted above. However, the fact that the ideas of substance, self, and consciousness are not treated equivocally by philosophers may be observed by reading carefully the views of the Indian dualists as well as Descartes and Locke whose views are discussed below.

The idea of self as a substance in which qualities inhere and which is capable of existing separately is strongly present in Descartes. For him, I-consciousness is certainly indicative of a self which is a distinct substance. The peculiarity of this substance is that it is immaterial, that it knows of no extension. It is entirely different from the body which is an extended substance. Indeed, this form of dualism of the body as the machine and the mind as the immaterial substance as propounded by Descartes has had tremendous impact on subsequent articulations and philosophizations concerning this theme in Western thought. This immaterial substance that I-consciousness is said to be is further described as a thinking substance. This is expressed in his famous statement—'I think, therefore I am'. It is to be noted that thinking for Descartes entails, as he has himself elaborated on it, all such functions as doubting, understanding, conceiving, affirming, and denying. To think also means to will, to refuse, to imagine, and to perceive. Descartes not only asserts categorically this thinking substance to be independent of the body but goes as far as to claim that it 'would exist even should the body cease to exist'. Thought and extension mutually exclude each other.[19]

However, it has been noted by scholars that Descartes' notion of the 'I' as the inner observer is one of his many influences received from Augustine.[20] I do not intend to recapitulate here the all too well-known story of the intense search on the part of Descartes to arrive at a first principle that cannot be called into question and which can be ascertained with unshakable certainty. This task has been attempted by a number of scholars since the seventeenth century. What is of crucial relevance for the present undertaking here is to note that for Descartes, 'cogito ergo sum' is 'the first principle of all philosophy'. Even if all else could be doubted, he argued, the existence of the thinking I is beyond any doubt. This is the crux of the statement 'I think, therefore, I am'. To Descartes this seems to be so certain that he wrote that 'the most extravagant suppositions brought forward by the sceptics were incapable of shaking it'. He then further asks himself, 'but what am I' and replies 'a thing which thinks. What is a thing which thinks? It is a thing which doubts, understands, conceives, affirms, denies, wills, refuses, which also imagines and feels'. This self, Descartes argues, is not a material substance possessing the attribute of extension but a mental substance possessing the attribute of thought. Thus ensues a strict form of metaphysical dualism which entails that thought and extension mutually exclude one another. Descartes was aware, as were the philosophers following him, of the problem

19 René Descartes, 1996, *Meditations on First Philosophy* (ed. by John Cottingham), (Cambridge: Cambridge University Press).

20 Augustine in his *Confessions* (Book 10, Chapter 8) described himself as wandering through the many chambers of his memory. cf. Phillip Cary, 2000, *Augustine's Invention of the Inner Self: The Legacy of a Christian Platonist* (Oxford: Oxford University Press).

of the relation between the mind and the body. He postulated that there was a causal interaction between the two, although he never quite fully demonstrated how such a causal relation between a thinking, unextended substance and an unthinking, extended substance is possible.[21]

Note that in the course of history of Western thought, as documents show, many attempts have been made to sort out the difficulties with regard to the mind–body relation. As philosophers offer solutions, one sees that some try even to this day to retain the dualistic framework by proposing psycho-physical parallelism and occasionalism. Again, there are some, who while refuting the theory of substance-dualism advocate in turn, property-dualism, and then there are those who go for an outright rejection of dualism. Gilbert Ryle, for example, criticized Descartes' dualistic position by remarking that the mind a la Descartes is a 'ghost in the machine'.[22] Moreover, since Descartes maintained that although the material and the mental substances are completely distinct, they interact causally, objections were raised against the possibility of interaction between two utterly different kinds of substance. In order to solve this problem, Descartes had himself proposed the pineal gland as the locus of the interaction. However, not satisfied with this theory of causal interaction, some philosophers such as Leibnitz proposed psycho-physical parallelism as an alternative.

However, questions about how the non-physical can causally affect the physical or the physical can give rise to the mental are topics of debates that have remained alive to this day and contemporary Western philosophers are still struggling with these issues. Many of them who are physicalists try to account for it as a species of physical causation. Debates go on and one comes across several versions of epiphenomenalism, mind–brain identity, etc., as proposed solutions to these problems.

Perhaps the Cartesian mode of discerning the I as a disengaged self, as an immaterial substance is a way of disclosing the feature

---

21 Descartes, *Meditations on First Philosophy*.

22 Gilbert Ryle, 1984 [1949], *The Concept of Mind*, (Chicago: University of Chicago Press).

of inwardness (*pratyaktata*) which is inseparably linked with the sense of I-ness. It may be observed very briefly that there are also normative and even soteriological implications of such a construal, since there is little doubt that Descartes' idea of God is intimately connected with this disclosure of 'I' as an immaterial substance. 'The Cartesian proof', as Charles Taylor puts it, 'is no longer a search for an encounter with God within. It is no longer the way to an experience of everything in God. Rather what I now meet is myself: I achieve a clarity and fullness of self-presence that was lacking before. But from what I find here reason bids me to infer a cause and transcendent guarantee, without which my now well-understood human powers could not be as they are'.[23] Anyway, given the seventeenth century scientific picture of a mechanistic universe that Descartes subscribed to and did much to promote, his enquiry into the nature of the indubitable I is a remarkable project. In his reflections, the methodical disclosure of the cogito as indubitable becomes a crucial step for his subsequent ascertainments about what he regards as clear and distinct perceptions where there is no room for any uncertainty.

Interestingly, the Cartesian idea of self as a substance exerted considerable influence on the empiricist philosophers as well, even on those who otherwise held the view that the mind is a tabula rasa and, hence, that all knowledge stems from sense impressions. A prime example of how the idea of self as substance came to be formulated by the empiricists who did not accept any notion of innate ideas is the view proposed in the work of John Locke. It may be noted here that as an empiricist, Locke does not seem to propound the idea of self as substance without some sense of discomfort. The analysis of the very idea of substance becomes somewhat more complicated, prompting more critical reflections in him. Noting that our ideas regarding horses and stones being nothing but collections of simple ideas, he observes; 'yet because we cannot conceive how they should subsist alone, nor one in another, we suppose them existing in and supported by some common subject; which support we denote by the name of substance, though it be certain that

23 Charles Taylor, 1981, *The Sources of the Self* (Cambridge, MA: Cambridge University Press).

we have no clear or distinct idea of that thing…'.[24] However, given these misgivings he continues to assert that—because of the same reason as has been argued in the case of the corporeal substance— one cannot deny the existence of the self substance despite that one has no clear and distinct idea about this. Note that the impact of Locke's view on subsequent European and American thought (such as on William James) has been considerable.

The idea of self as a substance is a central issue not only to rationalists like Descartes but also to an empiricist like Locke. These reflections have important bearing on the subject-matter of I-consciousness. Despite that the notion of substance in Locke is not quite as clear and uniform as in the case of Descartes, the question of personal identity, the idea of 'vital union' with the same immaterial substance surely plays a significant role in his analysis. As he explores the notion of identity, it becomes clear that Locke is aware of the complexities and peculiarities of the notion of substance in a profound way. There is a lengthy record[25] of such deep reflection on the notion of immaterial substance in Locke's writings which has both provoked objections as well as invited support from philosophers such as Reid and Butler.[26]

It is evident that for Locke the question of personal identity was crucial. 'It is in this', he puts it, 'is founded all the rights and justice of reward and punishment'. Describing 'person' as a 'thinking thing', Locke tried to analyse carefully in what consists this identity, this sameness, so that a person—as he puts it—'can consider itself as itself', as 'the same thinking thing, in different times and places'. At this juncture, two important ideas that come up in his writings are the phenomena of memory and self-consciousness. It is by virtue of these two functions that identity and continuity are accounted for. Memory enables one to perceive 'that with which the consciousness of this present thinking thing can join itself,

---

24 John Locke's *Essay on Human Understanding*, first published in 1690.

25 *Ibid.*

26 T. Reid, *Essays on the Intellectual Powers of Man*, first published in 1785; J. Butler, *The Analogy of Religion*, first published in 1736.

makes the same person, and is oneself with it, and with nothing else; and the attributes to itself and owns all the actions of that thing as its own, as far as that consciousness reaches, and no further; as everyone who reflects will perceive'. As per self-consciousness Locke says: 'when we see, hear, smell, taste, feel, meditate, or will anything, we know that we do so'.

However, later on, Locke's critics noted the ambiguous usages of the ideas of consciousness, sameness, etc.[27] Indeed, equally are there ambiguities regarding the way Locke understood the idea of immaterial substance in contrast to that of Descartes' view of the same. For Descartes, consciousness is an attribute of the immaterial substance that the self is, whereas there are passages in Locke in which the immaterial substance that the self is supposed to be seems distinguishable from consciousness. The main thrust of his analysis of self as immaterial substance sometimes appears to go along with ideas of person and consciousness, sometimes these are distinguished, again at other times these are used as though to emphasize their overlapping contents. Consider, for example, the following passage where he writes that

> the personal identity would equally be determined by the consciousness, whether that consciousness were annexed to some individual immaterial substance or not. For, granting that the thinking substance in man must be necessarily supposed immaterial, it is evident that an immaterial thinking thing may sometimes part with its past consciousness, and be restored to it again, as appears in the forgetfulness men often have of their past actions.[28]

The complexity of the question of personal identity becomes evident as Locke proceeds with the intention of claiming the intimacy of the identity of the self and consciousness and writes: 'self is that conscious thinking thing, whatever substance made up of (whether spiritual or material, simple or compounded, it matters not), which is sensible or conscious of pleasure and pain, capable of happiness or misery, and so is concerned for itself, makes the

---

27 cf. Antony Flew, 1951, 'Locke and the Problem of Personal Identity', *Journal of the Royal Institute of Philosophy*, Vol. xxvi, No. 96, pp. 53–68.

28 Descartes, *Meditations on First Philosophy*.

same person, as far as that consciousness extends'.[29] This is then what lies at the core of the idea of personal identity. Indeed, one finds that his search for in what consists of personal identity has led Locke to conclude that it lies not in the identity of substance but in the identity of consciousness. Here too he goes as far as his analysis allows and he seems to suggest that it is logically possible to conceive that this continuity of consciousness can go along with even that of the change of bodies. It is interesting to note that this interpretation is opposed to the Aristotelian view of inseparability of souls and bodies.

In Locke's dualistic theory, the idea of continuity of conscious-ness based on memory and self-awareness is absolutely crucial since, without these, moral life will be meaningless and the ideas of reward and punishment would be irrelevant. His writings amply bring out the difficulty in discerning a criterion for identity as well as in conceptualizing the difference between the notions of 'unity of consciousness' and 'identity of consciousness'. John Locke tried to account for personal identity by linking the sense of first person identity with conscious memory. In his *Essay Concerning Human Understanding*, he writes: 'As far as this consciousness can be extended backwards to any past action or thought, so far reaches the identity of that person'.[30]

Another interesting issue that was not overlooked by Locke is the problem of deep sleep. The problem has long been felt by philosophers while examining the issue of the relation between self and consciousness. John Locke recognized the problem while pondering over the question whether consciousness is 'the same identical substance' that makes personal identity and while seeking an answer to the question regarding in what consists the essence of selfhood. Unlike Descartes who makes a forthright claim that consciousness is the essence of the immaterial substance that the self is supposed to be, Locke is aware of certain difficulties since consciousness does get 'interrupted' as in 'sound sleep having no thoughts at all' giving rise to doubts with respect to 'whether we are

29 *Essay on Human Understanding*, 1690.
30 *Ibid.*

the same thinking thing i.e. the same substance or no'. However, for Locke the problem does not 'concern personal identity at all: the question being, what makes the same person, and not whether it be the same identical substance, which always thinks in the same person'.[31] In other words, the poignant question raised in this dualistic frame is whether this self as substance can be said to remain identical or is it that the continuity of consciousness and self-awareness that makes one the self-same person despite being interrupted by sleep and can also be so interrupted by death. Recall in this connection that for Descartes the immaterial self is indivisible, hence indestructible.

An overall survey can show how Western philosophers agreed and disagreed with Locke regarding the idea of self as substance and on various other issues. However, it must be acknowledged that Locke exerted an enormous influence on subsequent Western thought.

31 *Ibid.*

CHAPTER FOUR

I-consciousness is Composite in Character
Divergent Views within the Upanisadic Tradition

Sankhya, Yoga, and Advaita Vedanta

A startlingly different kind of philosophical interpretation from what has been discussed in the previous chapter will be considered here. In the literature of such prominent schools of philosophy as Sankhya, Yoga, and Advaita Vedanta, all belonging to the Upanisadic tradition, one notices a radical departure from the reading that projects a notion of 'I' as simple and homogenous. This latter view is a philosophical position, akin to common sense, in support of which various arguments have been offered by the advocates of the Nyaya-Vaisesika-Mimamsa schools, discussed in previous chapters.[1] As a contrast to this reading where I-consciousness is seen to be directly identical with the self, Sankhya, Yoga, and Advaita Vedanta propose a radically different view according to which the sense of I is said to have dual aspects. In other words, I-consciousness is generated not by just a simple, homogenous substance but is regarded as being composite in character.

As will be seen below, there are subtle variations in the analyses offered by Sankhya, Yoga, and Advaita Vedanta. However, despite these variations one notices that they are in agreement in their theoretical renditions in making the very subtle and crucial distinction between the notion of self (*atman/purusa*) and the notion of ego (*ahamkara*). This conceptual strategy introduced as well as elaborated in full-fledged forms by the advocates of these schools has important implications for philosophical thinking with regard

---

1 See Chapter 4.

to the question of I-consciousness. In Sankhya and Yoga, the ontological reality of two principles, technically termed purusa and *prakrti*, is retained throughout. The former is the principle of consciousness and the latter is the principle of nature/dynamic matter. A remarkable analysis is made within this dualistic conceptual frame which entails the claim that there is a vital difference between the notion of self as pure consciousness and that of the ego. The interpretations of the notions of 'purusa', 'ahamkara' and 'asmita' within a frame of thinking that operates with the notion of plurality of selves (*vahu-purusavada*) are unique to these systems. These break away from conventional mode of viewing a range of issues pertaining to the theme of consciousness. The depictions of empirical and soteriological scenarios are of equally great significance for the proponents of the Sankhya and Yoga philosophy pertaining to self and I-consciousness, despite their own distinct ramifications of these ideas.

It is noteworthy that in the philosophy of Advaita Vedanta, one not only encounters an amazingly intricate understanding and elaboration of the distinction between self (atman) and the ego (ahamkara) but also a bold projection of a notion of pure consciousness as non-dual. Their emphasis on the primacy and foundational character of consciousness leads to a rejection of dualism and pluralism. This radical understanding of consciousness in the philosophy of Advaita Vedanta is especially intriguing as it not only rejects the idea of plurality of selves propounded by Sankhya, Yoga as well as Nyaya,Vaisesika, and Mimamsa schools but also because it proposes a specific philosophical construal of its own for disclosure of the phenomenon of I-consciousness. The Advaitic analysis became a subject for debates even among the philosophers within the Vedantic tradition. These controversies among the schools of Vedanta are especially interesting because of their otherwise pronounced agreements concerning the ontological reality of the atman and their common soteriological conviction that knowledge of the self is the highest knowledge, since that alone can lead to freedom (*mukti*).

The internal differences among the schools of Vedanta, touching upon a host of key issues merit a careful study since these have pertinence for the enquiry into I-consciousness. These ideas,

documented in ancient texts seem to me to be still of much
relevance for contemporary investigations into various aspects
of this profound problem. A brief review of these controversies is
made in a separate section of this chapter.

Sankhya, considered to be the oldest school of Indian philosophy, propounds metaphysical dualism. It holds that there are
two basic principles—consciousness (purusa) and nature (prakrti).
According to Sankhya, purusa is what prakrti is not. In other words,
these are two entirely distinct principles. Hence, consciousness is
not considered to be a natural phenomenon. What is primarily
worth noting here is the idea that all change is ascribed to prakrti
which is described as insentient (*jada*), whereas the sentient principle, which is aware of change, is said to be free from all mutations
(purusa). The fundamental insight that is operating here is 'that
which changes cannot take note of itself as changing' (being inert),
and 'that which takes note of change (being conscious) must be
unchanging in character'.[2] This complex network of ideas is shared
by the Yoga school as well. While noting the ideas of ever-changing
nature and immutable consciousness, it is interesting to recall that
both schools reject the notion of absolute time a la Vaisesika where
time is perceived as the ultimate substrate in which all contingent
entities arise, persist, and perish. Indeed, although the Sankhya
and Yoga schools both accept the ontological reality of change,
Sankhya combines space–time–matter in the same dynamic notion
of prakrti or nature, which constantly undergoes mutations. The
Yoga school, on the other hand, advocates a discrete view of time—
the temporal datum being the moment. They argued that 'since
no two moments can be said to exist simultaneously',[3] all notions
entailing a collection of moments or the idea of sequence are nothing but conceptual constructions. Despite their differences regarding the notion of time, they agree that all change and mutations

2   T.R.V. Murti, 1955, *The Central Philosophy of Buddhism: A Study of
the Madhyamika System* (New York: Macmillan).

3   *Yoga Sutra*. For a detailed account, see my work, 2009, *A Study
of Time in Indian Philosophy*, 3rd edn (New Delhi: Motilal Banarsidass
Publishers).

are to be ascribed to the insentient prakrti, whereas the principle of consciousness or purusa is to be viewed as immutable in character. Purusa is the seer (*drsta*) or the witness (*saksi*), and prakrti is that which is seen or witnessed (*drsya*) and an object (*visaya*) of consciousness. Indeed, the profound insights of the philosophers belonging to these schools are especially fruitful for a study of time and consciousness. These have significant implications for the constitution of I-sense born—like everything mundane—from interplay of these two ultimate principles.

Indeed, the Sankhya philosophical interpretation, which is largely shared by the Yoga school as well, provides a strikingly different account of the presence of the phenomenon of I-consciousness from the Nyaya-Vaisesika model. Unlike this latter view, the analysis offered by the Sankhya-Yoga schools discloses I-consciousness as having dual aspects. In other words, philosophical reflection shows I-consciousness to be composite in character. On the one hand, I-consciousness is recognized as the seat of empirical subjectivity, conceived in terms of a principle of egoity (ahamkara), which is anchored to the ever-changing, insentient nature (prakrti), and on the other hand, it is viewed as deriving its support from a principle of consciousness (purusa) as a transcendent subject. The dawning of I-consciousness is no more seen simply as referring to the self a la Nyaya-Vaisesika but recognized as that wherein two principles are involved[4]—purusa and prakrti. The naturalistic trend in Sankhya is so strong that it takes the mind–body complex as an evolute of nature and this 'evolution' is understood in terms of interplay between nature and consciousness. Consequently, the analysis of the question of subjectivity takes on a more complex turn. Along with the idea that I-consciousness is composed of two heterogeneous components, there emerges an important conceptual distinction in their philosophy. This is precisely the difference between the self and the ego (projected in the notions of purusa and ahamkara), mentioned before. It is noteworthy that purusa is independent of prakrti whereas ahamkara is viewed as an evolute of prakrti, bearing witness to a strong naturalistic component in

4 cf. *Sankhya Karika* 20: '*tasmat tatsamyogat*'.

Sankhya thinking. Vacaspati Misra in his commentary[5] says that the presence and function of I-ness or 'ahamkara' is discernible in such expressions as 'I am entitled to this', 'I am able to do this', 'these are all for my use, etc'. Further analysis lays bare that for the discernment that purusa is an independent and not a derived principle whereas ahamkara is a product of prakrti 'discriminatory knowledge' (*viveka-jnana*) is needed. This calls for dedicated practice of Yoga as a spiritual discipline.

The very idea that we mistakenly take the 'I' to be ultimate and identify it as the self deserves attention. It is worth noticing that the principle that induces one to see the self in the not-self is listed in the Sankhya literature as one of the five forms of error (*panca-viparyaya*) and in the Yoga literature as one of the five forms of affliction (*panca-klesa*). It is further highlighted that the principle of egoity is anchored to *avidya*—a pan-Indian concept of a 'beginningless' principle of root primal ignorance. Note that in their literature in both cases, this I-principle is placed next to avidya as it derives support from this transcendental principle that covers the face of reality. In other words, the inability to discriminate between the self and the ego—purusa and ahamkara—is a chief characteristic of our mundane existence. It is precisely in order to emphasize its fundamentally pre-empirical and beginningless character that this principle of egoity is listed in the second place immediately next to avidya in their classification. What the philosophical analysis seeks to bring out in the Sankhya–Yoga context is not that the ego is illusory but that the propensity to take the I as though it is underived and ultimate (*antim*) is entirely false and misleading. This reading deserves careful attention in order to grasp that even though pre-empirical, it is still to be viewed as a case of error (Sankhya) and it points to the presence of an affliction (Yoga) because of which we fail to perceive that the I-sense is not really the same as the principle of consciousness that is an evolute of the insentient nature. Indeed, Yoga literature carefully explains the nature of this affliction by amplifying what 'asmita' stands for.

---

5 Vacaspati Misra in his *Tattvakaumudi* explains *Sankhya Karika* 24 that states '*abhimano hankarah*' as entailing '*ahamadhikrtah, sakta khalvahamatra, madartha evami visayah*', etc.

The text says categorically that this mistake is due to looking upon the two principles—pure awareness (*drk-sakti*) and the principle of cognition (*darsana-sakti*)—as though these were the same.[6] In other words, the I-sense, which appears to be undivided and homogenous, is generated by the non-distinction of the two utterly heterogeneous components, the experiencer and the experienced.

Patanjali's insights into the question of consciousness are profound and call for careful exploration of the brief aphorisms/sutras concerning purusa. These are impregnated with layers of meaning. In Yoga Sutra 2/20,[7] we read the description of purusa as the seer, as the 'absolute knower'. Although pure in itself and granted it is immutable and unchanging (*aparinami*) character, the principle of consciousness witnesses as an onlooker the modifications of '*buddhi*'— an evolute of prakrti. This sutra expresses in very few words deep perceptive readings about the nature of consciousness as well as how it stands vis-à-vis the changing states. The changing (*parinami*) character of the mental faculty (technically buddhi) allows it to grasp its contents (visaya). Moreover, it is noted that buddhi may or may not grasp an object present, as that is dependent on other factors as well; purusa, however, is constantly aware (*sadajnata*) of all the modifications of the mind without undergoing any modification itself.

An indispensable part of the striving for freedom is understanding that there is not one but two principles, each playing a part in the ensuing of I-consciousness. It is to be considered as the first crucial step toward unravelling what the self is. This analysis demonstrates how an inquiry into I-consciousness gradually discloses its composite character and lays bare the various levels of subjectivity. The principle of purusa entails the idea of transcendental subjectivity of which we are not aware in our everyday experience as it is ahamkara that is falsely taken to be the experiencer and not perceived as the experienced. Evidently, the notion of purusa reflects the Upanisadic idea of atman as the immutable self. This is the principle of consciousness that remains ever constant.

6 *Yoga Sutra:* '*drgdarsanasaktaurekatmatevasmita*'.
7 '*drasta drsimatrah suddhe'pi pratyanupasya*', translated by Mukherji as the seer, is the absolute knower.

Note that no distinction is sought between self and consciousness. The perception that the phenomenon of I-consciousness (*aham-pratyaya*) is not only indicative of purusa but also of prakrti as its source adds a new dimension to the analysis. Thus, the contention that I-consciousness has dual aspects entails that this phenomenon is not possible without the non-conscious nature (jada prakrti), of which ahamkara is an evolute. It is fascinating to note that in the Sankhya-Yoga interpretation of I-consciousness there is on the one hand, the ontological principle of consciousness—which is entirely independent of Nature and marks a departure from naturalism as a philosophical stance and on the other hand, the principle of ahamkara as evolving from nature/prakrti which lays bare a strong naturalistic component. Taken together, these readings account for the empirical as well as the soteriological queries regarding the status of the 'I'.

What is truly remarkable is to watch that when the Yoga philosophical analysis is pushed further, it clearly acquires, step by step, a soteriological dimension. The disentanglement of the complex constitution of I-consciousness leads not only to the disclosure of the part that nature plays but ultimately also of purusa—the transcendental subject. Indeed, the entire Yoga pursuit is to obtain that discriminatory knowledge (viveka-jnana) by virtue of which empirical subjectivity is no longer mistakenly perceived to be purusa, the transcendental subject. A full uncovering of the principle of immutable consciousness of course calls for dissolution of the affliction called 'asmita', i.e., 'am-ness', eventually of egoity. It is not attainable simply through conceptual and analytical understanding alone, although this process of intellection is undoubtedly acknowledged as an important aid. It is significant that in the Yoga literature asmita is not only placed just next to avidya in the list of afflictions, one also comes across subtle descriptions of the different states and phases of afflictions. It is said that these afflictions may be in any of these four states: dormant, attenuated, interrupted, or active.[8] Knowledge with regard to these above-mentioned four states is also useful for understanding the working of asmita which

8 *prasupta, tanu, vicchinna, udara.*

is vital for the three afflictions – desire (*raga*), hatred (*dvesa*), and fear—especially of death (*abhinivesa*). The Yoga philosophy holds that knowledge of the purusa is possible only after a complete eradication of all the afflictions including egoity. The process requires not only a surface correction but also a deep purging out of 'avidya', the primal principle which is considered to be the generator of all afflictions and to which no beginning can be ascribed. In other words, the goal is to overcome this state of confusion which is pre-empirical but not invincible.

Some observation may be made here with regard to the provocative question that arises in connection with the Yoga categorization of the five afflictions (panca klesa).[9] It may be asked why in the Yoga literature, 'asmita' without which there will be no sense of 'I am' is catalogued just after 'avidya' or primal ignorance, why such afflictions as desire/attachment (raga), hatred/aversion (dvesa), and fear (abhinivesa)—especially fear of death—are listed after 'asmita'? The reason is that the other three afflictions are subordinate to the presence of I-sense which is unquestionably a prerequisite for the arising of such mental states as desire, hatred, and fear. Further on, a closer examination of asmita is made in order to throw light on its constitution as well as for demonstrating that this specific affliction can be analysed into heterogeneous components, as discussed before. Besides, the Yoga tradition claims that a one-pointed focus on I-sense can lead to a state of concentration (technically called '*sasmita-samadhi*'). In this state, it is said that it is possible to unravel the constitution of the sense of I and gradually become aware of the distinction between consciousness and nature. In other words, this discriminative knowledge (viveka-jnana) enables the aspirant to disentangle purusa from prakrti and is considered to be indispensable for the attainment of liberation/*moksa*. This dimension of the analysis also has profound ethical bearings as it carries with it the deep implications of

9 Thus the idea of *asmita* appears in three different contexts of the Yoga discourse; (a) as a *klesa*, (b) as a *tattva*, being identical with *ahamkara* and (c) in *sasmita-samadhi*. cf. my paper, 1991, 'The Notion of *Klesa* and Its Bearing on the Yoga Analysis of Mind', *Philosophy East and West*, Vol. 41, No. 1, pp. 77–81.

freeing oneself from the pulls of desire, hatred, and fear. Evidently, these latter afflictions are sustained by the presence of asmita. It may be emphasized that this is in essence why asmita/'am-ness' is placed next to avidya or the primal (spiritual) ignorance. Ensuing from avidya this I-sense is in effect what lies at the centre as the world-process/*samsara* unfolds.

Thus, a review of the recorded literature shows that a minute analysis at the level of intellection has a deeper purpose. Indeed, this endeavour to comprehend the constitution of I-consciousness is regarded not merely as a response to an abstract philosophical theory-making challenge but is seen as an essential, integral part of the pursuit for moksa. Seeking a riddance of this primal ignorance because of which the not-self is erroneously taken to be the self, is recognized to be what lies at the very heart of this pursuit. Yoga also assures that this error/confusion can indeed be removed through practice (*abhyasa*)[10] and detachment (*vairagya*). Thus, the need for an adequate program and discipline arises. This is precisely why the eightfold Yoga practices (*astanga* yoga) are prescribed. The text says that an intense one-pointed concentration (samadhi) culminates in the discriminative discernment (viveka-jnana), enabling one to discard the not-self. It is this alone that finally leads to the disclosure of purusa. The soteriological goal (*kaivalya*) is accomplished in the successful attainment of isolating the purusa from the prakrti—a bondage to which no beginning can be ascribed.

The puzzle of subjectivity has indeed long been recognized in Indian thought. In the Sankhya-Yoga tradition, Purusa, modelled after the Upanisadic idea of atman, is viewed as the ultimate subject that never presents itself in experience as an object. This purusa is hard to disclose, precisely because it is not a matter of simple analytical thinking, although the latter also has a significant role to play. According to the tradition, the path that an aspirant needs to follow demands practice and detachment: it is undertaking a journey that leads one away not only from all forms of discursive knowledge but eventually also from worldliness.

According to the teachings of the Upanisads, intellection (*manana*) plays a vital role in this process of seeking knowledge

10 cf. my article, 2009, 'Abhyasa', *Journal of IHC*.

about the self. Elaborate records of queries and responses touching upon various subtleties and intricacies of the question of subjectivity are available in the philosophical literature of the various schools that developed within the fold of the Upanisadic tradition. As is to be expected, the philosophical discourse on consciousness, being integral to the preparation for undertaking the soteriological journey, is of major significance.

At this point, let us turn our attention to the philosophy of Advaita Vedanta.[11] The topic of consciousness has been carefully examined in the vast literature of Advaita Vedanta. The crucial question has been described in the Upanisads as 'by what can that be known by which everything else is known'? Indeed, thousands of pages have been devoted to answer that question which reveals the ethos of the tradition. The Upanisadic tradition repeatedly says that the 'highest knowledge' (parama-vidya) consists in obtaining knowledge of the self (atma-vidya). A vigorous study of I-consciousness forms an indispensable part of that undertaking.

Advaita Vedanta has often been considered to be representative of the culmination of the Upanisadic mode of reflections. Here one encounters not simply the idea of the epistemic primacy of consciousness, an idea that has been considered in the beginning of this monograph, but also a reading that favours the ontological reality of consciousness alone. Note that although Sankhya-Yoga also vehemently supports the idea of the ontological reality of consciousness, the Advaita position is even more radical than that of Sankhya and Yoga since the latter also attribute an equal ontological status to nature—a non-sentient, ever-changing principle. Unlike in Sankhya and Yoga, in Advaita Vedanta the aim is to establish the thesis that consciousness is ultimately non-dual, there being no room for plurality of selves.

In the literature of Advaita Vedanta, one encounters a philosophy of consciousness which is based on a refutation of the intentional as well as egological structures of consciousness. The position has points of agreement with Sankhya, viz. that I-consciousness

11 For more discussions on Advaita philosophy based on the works of Sanhara and other notable Advaitins along with their commentators, see Chapters 5, 7, and Epilogue.

involves an intermingling of heterogeneous elements and that a distinction needs to be made between the notions of self and ego. There are well-known texts belonging to the school of Advaita Vedanta where the I-sense is even interpreted to be masking as the self, so the philosophical endeavour has been to lay bare outright its constitution and finally reduce it to the status of not-self. The enquiry into I-consciousness leads to a radical line of thinking, disclosing the 'I' also as an object of consciousness.

The idea of self as unchanging and unchangeable has been variously worked out by diverse schools of philosophy belonging to the Upanisadic tradition. However, one comes across drastic conceptual configurations of the themes of self, ego, and consciousness in the enormous literature belonging to various schools of Vedanta. Like in Sankhya and Yoga, the philosophy of Advaita Vedanta denies the reality of absolute time but unlike Sankhya and Yoga, it refuses to grant any ontological status to any principle of change whatsoever. It not only vehemently maintains that eventually the self is to be identified as consciousness but also claims that in the ultimate analysis the idea of plurality of selves is to be abandoned. The Advaitins seek to demonstrate philosophically the idea of non-dual self in compliance with the motto of the Upanisads, viz. that 'the self is the self of all'. Advaita Vedanta insists upon the reading that consciousness is simply not objectifiable whereas everything else has only the status of an insentient (jada) object, to be revealed (bhasya) by consciousness. All that has the status of an object is conventional (vyavaharika) in contrast to consciousness which alone is ontologically real (paramarthika) and is 'one without a second'.

Let us recall once again that there is no controversy among the philosophers belonging to the Upanisadic tradition with regard to the soteriological conviction that knowledge of the self leads to freedom or mukti. However, regardless of this core agreement about the indestructible character of the self, the idea of self certainly knows of disparate interpretations. Similarly, it may be noted that the philosophical disclosure with regard to the status and constitution of I-sense also knows of significant variations. They all agree that in our ordinary experience there is never a cognition of a pure I. The I-sense is always associated with the apprehension of something else, be that an object of introspection or that of any of the external sense-perception. Thus, it may take the form, e.g., 'I am happy/sad' or that 'I know the jar', or 'I see you'. However, there are striking differences between Advaita and all those schools that project the I to be the self, holding these to be identical. As an example of this, note that one of the most conspicuous differences between Nyaya and Advaita Vedanta lies in the way they do or do not attribute qualities to the self. Thus, whereas all the characteristics (*dharmas*) that are listed in the Nyaya literature as special characteristics and qualities of the self,[12] are—in the case of Advaita Vedanta—all attributed to the ego (ahamkara) and not to the self (atman). In other words, those which are identified as the characteristics of the self by Nyaya are taken to be those of the mind (*antahkarana*) by Advaita Vedanta. For Advaita Vedanta, it is antahkarana that generates the I-sense (ahamkara). Hence, the mind is seen as the agent, the enjoyer. The so-called I-sense is metaphorically described as a 'knot' of the self and the not-self (*cid-acidgranthi*). For Nyaya, on the contrary, the mind (*manas*) is an instrument (*karana*), an internal sense-organ (*antarendriya*). Unlike in Advaita, the I is always considered to be the self.

Note that this understanding of 'I as the self' is commonly held by all the advocates of all those schools of philosophy who oppose the non-dual philosophy of Advaita Vedanta, whether these schools happen to be within or outside of the Vedantic tradition. The Advaitic idea of an objectless (*nirvisayaka*) and indeterminate (*nirvisesa*) consciousness is unacceptable to all its opponents who propound various forms of metaphysical dualism or pluralism.

Again, it is interesting to note that whereas for the naturalists and materialists as well as the realists belonging to the Nyaya-Vaisesika schools, consciousness is an adventitious property (*aguntaka* dharma), it is not so for Sankhya, Yoga, or Advaita Vedanta, which hold the position that consciousness is not derived but a distinct principle which is sui generis. Moreover, the Advaita philosophy makes the explicit claim that consciousness cannot be designated as knowable, hence no evidence is needed to establish it. This claim is made by forwarding the argument that evidence—be

12 Such as *kama, samkalpa, dvesa, iccha, krti, sukha, duhkha*.

that perceptual, inferential, or any other—is needed for establishing everything that has the status of an object. It has already been discussed that generally the schools agree about the contention that no evidence can at all be established without accepting the epistemic primacy of consciousness. The Advaitins insist that self does not fall within the category of knowable (*vedya*), hence cannot be treated as if it were on a par with other objects that are indeed knowable and thus need to be evidenced by one or another of the standard means of cognition (*pramanas*). The valid means for ascertaining the truth-claims concerning any object of knowledge cannot be employed in the case of consciousness. It is so precisely because consciousness cannot be established by any one of the accepted forms of evidence. It must be, therefore, regarded as self-evident (*svayam-siddha*) and as self-luminous (*sva-prakasa*).

The Advaitins emphasize categorically the foundational character of consciousness, declaring it to be the non-dual ontological reality. Diverse layers of complexity are disentangled in the process of the philosophical investigation of subjectivity entailing a daring exploration of I-consciousness. There is hardly a philosophical appraisal that has come up in the history of the Vedantic movement that can match the radical Advaita reading concerning the phenomenon of I-consciousness. Advaita Vedanta takes a philosophical stand where the 'I' is exposed as composite/divisible (*sakhanda*), as constituted (*adhyastha*), as an object (visaya), finally even as the not-self (*anatman*).[13]

Following the Advaita philosophical analysis, the ego principle superimposed on primordial ignorance or Avidya not only induces I-ness (*ahamakara*) and my-ness (*mamakara*) but also masks itself as the self. This in turn also gives rise to the sense of plurality of selves, which according to Advaita Vedanta, happens due to a lack of discernment between the I—which is the agent, the knower, and the experiencer (*karta, jnata, bhokta*)—and the self (atman) identified as the immutable, non-dual consciousness. It is precisely in order to remove these wrong perceptions of plurality caused by

13 See Madhusudana Sarasvati, 1937, *Advaita-Siddhi*, 2nd ed., edited by Ananta Krishna Shastri, (Bombay: Nirnaya-Sagar Press).

this primordial ignorance (avidya) regarding the self (atman) that the phenomenon of I-consciousness needs to be fully examined step by step. In the Advaita texts, it is clearly stated that the I is not entirely a non-object,[14] the 'I' is apprehended by the witness consciousness. It has been mentioned before that I-consciousness is metaphorically described as a knot (*granthi*), as an entanglement of the self and the not-self. This reading shows that according to the Advaitic view consciousness, taken as non-different from the self, can never itself be known by means of any accepted standard sources of knowledge or established by any one of the standard evidences that are used for validating knowledge-claim with regard to that which can be categorized as an object, as a knowable. In other words, consciousness—being a non-object (avisaya)—cannot be categorized as knowable. However, to say that it is not empirically discernible as knowable does not mean that it is unknown. Indeed, it is 'known as unknowable', since knowing is a feature only of that which is objectifiable.[15]

In order to appreciate the spirit of the Upanisadic tradition, notice that the philosophical adventure is aimed at the recovery of the self. The commitment is so deep that it gradually brings to the notice of an investigator the epistemological, metaphysical, and linguistic dimensions of the project and even recognizes it as an integral part of the search for freedom/mukti. To the follower of this path, it is a journey that helps one to arrive at the limits of discursive knowledge and to attain the readiness to be eligible (*adhikara*) for a non-discursive mode of knowing. This is a point, the text says, where the knower and the known merges.[16] No investigator can be expected to be convinced by a piece of revelatory knowledge unless backed by the process of intellection and philosophical cogitation, therefore polemics also has a rightful place. It is said that without reasoning no conviction can be dawn nor can doubts be removed. However, once convinced, it must be meditated upon until a non-discursive intuition emerges that discloses

---

14 '*Nayamatma ekantena avisaya*' in *Bhamati*.

15 For more on this line of thinking cf. Chapter 6.

16 'The knower of Brahman becomes Brahman' (*Brahmavid brahmaiva bhavati*).

'the self as the self of all'. At this level all plurality is transcended. According to the Advaitins, consciousness per se does not posit itself as its own object, just as fire does not burn itself. It is not knowable, since knowing applies only to that which is objectifiable. Ultimately, non-discursive intuition is also ineffable: language cannot express it.

The texts describe the ontological reality as being-consciousness-bliss (*sat cit ananda*). Thus, the philosophical endeavour to unveil I-consciousness fulfils a demand that goes hand in hand with the soteriological quest as well. A sharp line of demarcation between the direct, non-discursive intuition and the discursive, empirical level of experience becomes transparent in the discourse. The study of Vedanta is geared entirely to this project of unveiling I-consciousness precisely because this phenomenon masks as the self. It is categorically stated that if I-consciousness were truly the self (atman), the study of Vedanta, which seeks knowledge of the self, would be superfluous. Even those Upanisadic thinkers— the Dvaitins, Visistadvaitins, etc.,—who maintain the invincibility of I-sense even in the state of moksa are also fully aware of the fact that 'knowledge of the self' (*atmavidya*) is a pursuit that requires a profound grasp and realization of the pure I, which escapes us in our daily life. The Vedantic quest, therefore, starts by questioning the nature of I-consciousness. Vedantic discourse indeed begins there[17]—as one of the principal texts puts it succinctly.

The Advaita account of empirical subjectivity necessarily entails the notion of superimposition (*adhyasa*). The association of the real self with the not-self is so intimately mediated by avidya or the root cause of primal ignorance that the mind (antahkarana) is confusedly identified as self. In Advaitic thinking, the sense of I-ness along with the attributes of the body (I am fat), of the sense-organs (I am deaf), of the mind (I am happy) are seen as superimposed on consciousness and these are as much objects for a subject just as the physical things are, as all these are illuminated

17 *Sarve vedanta arabhyante*. Sankara's commentary on Brahma Sutra.

by the light of the self.[18] In the next chapter, further discussion on the philosophy of Advaita is taken up focusing on the penetrating analysis made by K.C. Bhattacharya, an outstanding Advaitin of the past century. He carefully demonstrates how the awareness of the body, etc., can be described as object awareness from which the subject awareness is to be dissociated. Indeed, it is in this process that the notion of subjectivity gradually unfolds at its various levels, disclosing the absolute and foundational character of the atman.

It has been already mentioned that in the process of their philosophical analysis the Advaitins make a differentiation between the ego and the self. This distinction is not only extremely difficult to be aware of experientially but also hard to tackle conceptually. However, in Advaita Vedanta this distinction remains of crucial significance. Advaitins insist that if one takes the 'I' to be the self the study of Vedanta will be redundant. However, this last observation becomes a matter of keen philosophical controversy among the philosophers who represent different schools of Vedanta. These documents show that the ancient Indian philosophers through the centuries have remained engaged in exploring the topic of I-consciousness. A review of some of these polemics is important for appreciating the intricacies and challenges that are part of this investigation.

CONTROVERSIES AMONG THE SCHOOLS OF VEDANTA

Vedantic literature is an immensely rich repository of ideas. In this section, some of the controversies among the advocates of the Dvaita, Visistadvaita, and Advaita Vedanta schools are looked at. Although there are many schools of Vedanta, the three mentioned above are among the most influential schools of Vedanta philosophy. What is of particular interest for this study is the fact that for all Vedantins—no matter which stream of the Vedantic movement they come from—the question of I-consciousness

18 A.C. Mukherji, 1943, *The Nature of Self* (Allahabad: The Indian Press).

occupies, absolutely, a central position in their reflections. The main issue under consideration is whether the phenomenon of I-consciousness is to be regarded as being due to a homogeneous and irreducible metaphysical entity, a self, or is it constituted by heterogeneous principles. Despite all other variations and differences in their philosophical interpretation of the phenomenon of I-consciousness, their debates nevertheless show their common adherence to the atman-paradigm. While interpreting the core message of the Upanisads no school has sidetracked the question of I-consciousness, since the philosophical scenario is one where 'no one doubts whether I am or not, nor does anyone maintain the contrary of I am'.[19] This makes the present investigation even more intriguing. The philosophical perceptions of the advocates of different schools of Vedanta of course differ; consequently, their philosophical explanations of this phenomenon of I-consciousness vary significantly.

A perusal of the relevant literature discloses a wide variety of issues that have been raised in the context of the Vedantic enquiry pertaining to the question of 'I'. To list some of them at random: is I-consciousness indicative of an ultimate, indivisible (akhanda) entity or is it composite (sakhanda) and derived? In the latter case, what is it derived from? What does the word 'I' refer to? If it does not refer only to the self, if it is composite in its constitution how does one discern the meaning of the word? Or, while considering the nature of I-consciousness, it is asked: how is the I presented in this consciousness and to whom? This involves the so-called problem of 'ego-split', the subject-ego (jnata-aham) and the object-ego (jneya-aham). How is I-consciousness related to time-consciousness? How is it related to the consciousness of the body as well as consciousness of others?

One of the most important differences that lead to sharp controversies between the Advaita and other schools of Vedanta centred around the contending issue whether or not the I—an universally acknowledged phenomenon—signifies the presence of

19 'Na hi jatu kascidatra sandigdhe aham va naham veti', as Vacaspati Misra remarks while commenting on the Sankara-Bhasya.

an irreducible, indivisible metaphysical entity. Documents show that the Advaita reading is quite contrary to that of the Dvaita or Visistadvaita schools of Vedanta. For Advaita, the I-sense is explicable as being due to adhyasa or superimposition, a notion that is severely challenged by the opponents. The Dvaita (dualist) and the Visistadvaita (qualified non-dualism) schools of Vedanta raised several objections and strong criticisms against the Advaita stand in this regard, which is discussed in what follows.

One of the most impressive examples of such criticisms from the standpoint of Dvaita Vedanta can be found in the famous work by Vyasatirtha entitled *Nyayamrta*. He insists that I-consciousness is not due to any superimposition and that the apprehended 'I' cannot be reduced by any means to the status of not-self. The position that Vyasatirtha takes is that the 'I' is ever-abiding and never absent either in mundane life or in the state of liberation (moksa) for that matter. He even maintains that I-sense is there also in the state of deep sleep. Vyasatirtha and later his followers made repeated attempts to expose what they perceived to be the fallacies of the Advaita claim regarding the composite character of the constitution of the I and even more radically the Advaitic ascription of the status of not-self to the I. With great logical skill a case is made in order to indicate the indissolubility of the 'I' in the Dvaita literature. The Dvaitins insisted that the notion of pure consciousness without a self as a substrate is as unacceptable as the idea of non-intentional consciousness.

However, in his famous work, entitled, *Advaitasiddhi*, Madhusudana Sarasvati makes an all-out effort to answer all the objections raised by Vyasatirtha and other opponents of Advaita Vedanta. Adopting a staunch Advaitic standpoint, he attempts to demonstrate that in the long run the I cannot but be accorded the status of not-self. Among other arguments, he insists that the I is absent in the state of deep sleep whereas the self is unsublatable. Again, the I-sense is, as it were, a 'knot' of self and not-self, it is not entirely a non-object since it is knowable whereas the self is never objectifiable, hence can never be categorized as a knowable. These debates are truly illuminating as they push their cogitations to the absolute limits of intellectual endeavour in order to grapple with the theme of I-consciousness.

Ramanuja, the principal proponent of the School of Visistadvaita Vedanta equally launched an attack on the Advaita interpretation of I. Holding the view that consciousness is always intentional and a quality of the self, he analyses the knowledge-situation with the help of simple examples such as 'I know the jar', precisely in order to demonstrate that consciousness is always directed to an object, e.g., the 'jar', and is an attribute of the agent (karta), here referred to as 'I'. He opposes the Advaita contention that the I is reducible to the rank of not-self or that it is external to consciousness. He maintains, on the contrary, that the I is never experienced as an external entity (bahya-padartha). He argues that the quality of inwardness (pratyakta) is inseparably associated with I-consciousness alone, claiming further that the very distinction between external and internal rests upon this fact. He repeatedly declares that the I is the self (pratyagatma).[20] He decries the Advaita effort to grant to the I the status of the not-self (which in his interpretation is equivalent to saying 'not-I') and ridicules the reading by saying that such an idea is as absurd as the statement 'my mother is barren'.

Ramanuja sought a conceptual space for an understanding of consciousness that could, on the one hand, steer clear of the view advocated by the Indian realists (naiyayikas) belonging to the Nyaya-Vaisesika schools—that consciousness is an adventitious property of the self—and avoid, on the other hand, the position held by those who championed the cause of Advaita Vedanta— that self is consciousness or that this self is non-dual. In other words, Ramanuja wanted to preserve a notion of consciousness where its eternality could be preserved alongside its attributiveness that would account for its temporality. Thus, he advocated a notion of self whose essence is to be conscious. Again, this self is also conceived as the substratum where consciousness of an object has its origin and end. In the latter case, consciousness is no more than an attribute (guna) of the self and thus a non-eternal property.

In this way Ramanuja could disavow the realists' position where consciousness is seen exclusively as an adventitious quality, hence,

---

20 See especially the section on *Ahamartha Anatmattvaupapatti* in *Advaitasiddhi* of Madhusudana Sarasvati with *Gauda Brahmanandi*.

by very definition is non-eternal. Note that this latter reading is not without consequence in the context of speculations concerning the state of liberation (moksa). The idea that consciousness is adventitious and not an essence of the self led the realists to hold that, in the state of moksa, the self is non-conscious—an idea which has been profusely criticized in the Indian philosophical circles. The followers of the Visistadvaita school stay away from this absurd situation by highlighting the view that consciousness is not merely an attribute (dharma) having a temporal character, as the proponents of Nyaya school hold. However, unlike the latter, Ramanuja clearly regards consciousness as the essence of the self (*svarupa*) and thus to be eternal. In other words, according to him and his followers, the atman is never deprived of consciousness, it is never non-conscious (*acit*). This is a position which not only differs from that of the realists but also seeks to shun the Advaitic idea of pure consciousness as indeterminate (nirvisesa) and objectless (nirvisayaka). Ramanuja insists on holding the position that consciousness is intentional and that the self is fully conscious and is a subject.

However, the emphasis on the idea of consciousness both as a substrate and as a quality (guna)[21]—a view that Ramanuja and his followers were advocating—has its own difficulties. Objections have been raised against this position and the charge of inconsistency has been brought by their opponents. When he says that consciousness is a guna, it entails a temporal character, but when he says that the self is of the nature of consciousness (cidrupa), eternality is implied. Recall that indestructibility of the self is accepted by all schools of Vedanta. However, when Ramanuja says that the self is of the nature of consciousness, his reading—unlike in Advaita Vedanta—still focuses on the notion of the self as the cognizer (jnata), and not only as cognition (jnana).[22]

To summarize what is especially of relevance for the present study is to note that Ramanuja was striving to provide support for his philosophical view about the self as expressed in I-consciousness.

---

21 '*Evamatma cidrupa eva caitanyagunakah*': *Sribhasya* 1.1.1.

22 '*Atma jnata eva na prakasam matram*': *Ramanuja Bhasya (RB)* 1.1.1.

One significant move was to proclaim a philosophy of language, stating unambiguously that the referent of the word 'I' is invariably the self.[23] Moreover, the idea of the self here, unlike in Advaita Vedanta, does not imply any notion of undifferentiated consciousness. Ramanuja actually launched a series of arguments against the view that consciousness can be bereft of I-sense (ahampratyaya). He argued that such a reading not only goes against our empirical experience, it fails as well to lend meaning to any ethical or soteriological pursuit. The distinction between the knower and the known, the subject and the object, according to Ramanuja, cannot ever be obliterated. The self, in his view, is always the subject and consciousness is always object-directed. Finally, no distinction is made between the ego principle and the self (ahamkara and atman).

Besides firmly rejecting Sankara's ideas of an indeterminate consciousness and of I-consciousness as being composite in nature, Ramanuja also insists that the idea of self cannot be equated with that of consciousness. Self and consciousness are not equivocal. Against Sankara's readings, Ramanuja objects by saying that had it been true that the self and consciousness were identical, we would have an experience equivalent to 'I am consciousness'. However, our actual experience, he argues, always assumes the form 'I am conscious'.[24] Hence, Ramanuja alleges that the idea of self is one which is never void of its I-ness.[25] For him, it is incongruous to say that the self is there but not I-consciousness. It is also for the same reason that he kept on insisting that even in the state of deep sleep that the sense of I is preserved.[26] Since I-consciousness as a theme has pertinence not only with reference to the waking— or dream—state, the analysis of the phenomenon of deep sleep has been a topic that has received much attention in the Vedantic discourse, as will be more clearly seen in what follows.

☞ For Ramanuja the episode of self-consciousness is important. He holds that for consciousness to appear to itself necessarily involves that it does so in the form of an 'I'. Thus what constitutes

---

23 '*Svarupam eva ahamartha atmanah*': RB 1.1.1.
24 '*Anubhutiraham iti pratyeta, na anubhavami aham iti pratitih*'.
25 '*Ahampratyaya siddho hi asmadarthah*': RB 1.1.1.
26 '*Sususptavapi naham bhava vigamah*': RB 1.1.1.

the inward self is not an impersonal consciousness but the 'I'[27] and this, he insists, can in no way be explained as an illusory phenomenon or as a result of any superimposition (adhyasa).

The above readings are obviously targeted against the Advaita interpretation. In this connection, it is worth noting that in the discourse of Advaita Vedanta attempt is made to give a cogent account of consciousness both at the level of empirical experience (vyavaharika) as well as at the transcendental level (paramarthika). This is a multiple-layered discourse where the approach is to maintain the distinction between the ontological/transcendental and the empirical/conventional levels. The distinction between the knower-known-knowledge was certainly not denied any empirical validity by the Advaitins. However, the point that Advaitins have insisted upon is that this distinction cannot be taken as final, as ultimate.[28] Why so? The Advaitic answer is that ultimately all these three—the known, the knowledge, and the 'I' as knower—are all knowable and are to be seen as superimposed on a distinctionless consciousness (nirvisesa *caitanya*). These are apprehended by the witness-consciousness (*saksi*). Hence, consciousness is neither necessarily intentional, i.e., object-directed nor owned by a subject—as Ramanuja would have it.

Moreover, the Advaitins have also confronted Ramanuja's objection, viz. that if consciousness did not have a substrate in the form of self or had consciousness been identical with the self, there would have been cognition such as 'I am consciousness' (*anubhutiraham*), which none of us have. This objection is seen to be pointless since in the Advaita context the 'I' is itself a knowable hence is not the self which is never a knowable.

An in-depth analysis of these controversies among the philosophers belonging to the schools of Visistadvaita, Dvaita, and Advaita Vedanta is crucial for comprehending why the *distinction between selfhood and the ego-principle* is deemed indispensable for the latter whereas it is untenable to the former. In this connection, it is relevant to take note that the 'internal' instrument/mind (antahkarana) that generates I-ness or Ahamkara is perceived to

27 '*Ahamartha eva pratyagatma na jnaptimatram*': RB 1.1.1.
28 '*Avidyakalpitam vedya-veditr-vedana bhedam*': SB 1.1.4.

be non-conscious (jada) by the Advaitins, since it is a knowable (vedya). Hence, it has the status of an object. However, consciousness in its transcendental aspect is not a knowable, as it is not objectifiable. Thus Advaita philosophy highlights and explores subjectivity to its ultimate limit.[29] The identification of consciousness (cit) with self (atman) precisely implies that no duality can be attributed to it. Consequently, there is no room for a notion of a plurality of selves in Advaita Vedanta. This is how Advaita Vedanta brings out the profound significance of the Upanisadic utterance that the 'self is the self of all'.

Note that much technical ingenuity has been employed by the Advaitins in support of such a reading. They, for example, undertook a sharp analysis of the notion of difference (*bheda*) in order to highlight the idea of a distinction-less, immutable, and non-dual consciousness. Difference is categorized under three headings: '*svagata*', '*sajatiya*', and '*vijatiya*'. If we take the example of a tree, the first of the three kinds of differences points to such internal differences as the trunk, the branches, the leaves, and flowers, etc., that are there in the tree itself, the second one implies the kind of difference that is noted between one tree and another and the third is exemplified in the difference that is there between a tree and a stone. The idea of consciousness as an immutable and non-dual ontological reality implies that ultimately the foundational consciousness knows none of these three forms of differentiations, there are no parts within it, there is no 'other' that is similar or dissimilar to it.

The question whether I-consciousness is ultimate or not raises another interesting point of debate among the philosophers belonging to the schools of Dvaita, Visistadvaita, and Advaita Vedanta. This has bearing on how the epistemological situation is described. The Advaitins say that in order to be an agent (karta) of the knowing activity, the knower (jnata) has to undergo variation or modification. This is why the I-function (ahamkara) is not ascribed to the immutable principle of consciousness, it is a function of antahkarana or mind. This is precisely why the Advaitins attribute agency to the I or ego (ahamkara) principle, which being

29 For more, see Chapter 6.

an 'other' to consciousness is a knowable and not-conscious (acit/
jada). Hence, it can and does undergo variation and alterations,
whereas consciousness in the ultimate transcendental sense is
free from all modifications, it is unchanging and unchangeable
(*kutastha*). This is one crucial reason that brings us back to why
the I-sense (ahamkara) cannot be said to be identical with the self
(atman). As mentioned earlier, the Advaitins have described I-sense
as having dual aspect; it represents as it were a 'knot' (granthi) of
the conscious and the non-conscious principles (cit-acit granthi).
Viewed ontologically, this so-called knot is itself indicative of an
illusion; it is precisely that which covers the face of the real (sat),
projecting the unreal to be the real under the influence of the primal ignorance (avidya). Hence the I-sense is mistakenly identified
with the self since the self according to Advaita Vedanta is identical with consciousness, it is non-intentional (*nirvisaya*), indeterminate (*nirvisesa*), without any substrate (*nirasraya*). Ultimately,
no duality can be ascribed to the self.

However, the debate continues through the centuries. Ramanuja
and his followers belonging to the school of Visistadvaita Vedanta
vehemently deny the characterization of I-sense (ahamkara) as an
inert (jada) principle. This they find to be an absurd statement.
Had it been so, they argue, it could never be an agent (*kartr*) or a
knower (*jnatr*). Moreover, they claim that the notion of a knower
does not entail any concept of a changing consciousness in the way
the Advaitins describe the epistemological scenario. The 'I' as the
knower is the self and is the unchanging substrate of consciousness. It is noteworthy that the idea of a changing self is unacceptable to all the contenders, since all accept the Upanisadic idea of
self as eternal and immutable. The debate is really about whether
consciousness is necessarily intentional in character and whether
it needs a substrate. For the Advaitins, ultimately consciousness is
non-intentional and does not require any substrate. The Advaitins
are not simply interested in providing an account of the empirical scenario; their aim is to uncover the self in its transcendental
nature without which no cogent and coherent explanation of
empirical experience is deemed possible.

It is precisely this search for discerning whether or not the 'I'
is ultimately indissoluble that has led the Vedantins to examine

not only the states of waking (*jagrata*) and dream (*svapna*) but also that of the dreamless sleep. The analysis of I-consciousness in the different schools of Vedanta becomes intense and interesting when the state of deep sleep (*susupti*) becomes the focus of philosophical scrutiny. The issue of the identification of I with the self (aham with atman) is once again examined in the context of the state of susupti. Serious controversies arise concerning the question whether I-consciousness that prevails in the states of waking and dreaming can also be said to do so in the state of deep sleep i.e. dreamless sleep. The Dvaitins and the Visistadvaitins maintain that the I is invariably present in all the three states—waking, dream, and dreamless sleep. It pervades through all our experience as the permanent substratum, giving it unity. The 'I' is not an 'other' to consciousness. In other words, the I-sense is not interruptible. They insist that I, the knower, is the self[30] hence it does not need anything outside of itself for being self-luminous.

What is noteworthy in philosophical documents cross-culturally is that most epistemological analyses of I-consciousness generally concentrate on the waking state, when the psycho-physical organism is, so to speak, on full alert and the agency of the 'I' is easily traceable. To the extent that dream-analysis has been attempted, it is usually focused on the significance of the contents of dreams, often in relation to the dreamer's waking-state. Although the external world is not grasped and the sense-faculties are at rest, the sense of I is not, subjectively speaking, remarkably different from the waking state. However, among the Indian philosophers the phenomenon of deep sleep has been an issue of crucial importance.

The Advaitic analysis of *deep sleep* has profound bearing on their theorizing concerning the idea of the non-dual Atman as the ultimate ontological reality as well as for the general account with regard to the empirical understanding of how to interconnect the three states through which we alternate, viz. the waking state, dream state, and the state of dreamless sleep. The vulnerability of I-consciousness in the state of deep sleep becomes the focus of philosophical attention.

---

30 '*Jnata-ahamartha-evatama*'.

The Advaitins maintain that in the state of deep sleep, i.e., in the state of dreamless sleep, not only all mental activities cease, I-consciousness is also totally absent. Indeed, this specific characteristic of the state of deep sleep is conspicuous. The Advaitins emphasize that the state of deep sleep clearly discloses that I-consciousness is not ever-present, that is, it is eliminable. In other words, I-consciousness as a phenomenon is not constant since it is apprehended in the state of wakefulness and that of dream but cannot be traced in the state of deep sleep. Hence, I-consciousness cannot be held to be identical with the Atman which is regarded as unsublatable in all three times: past, present, or future (*trikala-badhya*). Most importantly, for Advaita, the state of deep sleep is indicative of the fact that the self transcends I-consciousness, laying bare the latter phenomenon to be 'other' than the self (*atmanyah*).

Thus, the philosophical explanation of such experiences as are reported by persons upon waking from the state of deep sleep, expressed in such statements like 'I have slept during this period blissfully'[31] and 'I knew nothing all this time'[32] vary in the Advaita, the Dvaita, and Visistadvaita discourses and are explained in harmony with their respective view of I-consciousness.

The questions that are raised are, how does one account for that cognition of bliss, what is the status of the I which knows it to be a blissful state? Is this cognition to be described as a case of perception, recollection, or inference? Moreover, can this state of dreamless sleep be assessed as one where there is a total lapse of the sense of 'I' because the 'I' itself is markedly absent?

Note that a logical response to these questions was attempted by the advocates of Nyaya school. They said that since consciousness is a property (guna)—which arises in the self when appropriate factors conjoin, such as in the case of perception (*pratyaksa*), inference (*anumana*), comparison/analogy (*upamana*), and verbal testimony (*sabda*)—cognition knows of both origination and destruction. No cognition is possible during the state of dreamless sleep since no sensory organ or the mind functions during that state. There is not only no external object to be cognized; there

---

31 '*Etavantam kalam sukham aham asvapsyam*'.
32 '*Naham kincit avedisam*'.

is no dream-object to be grasped. There can be no awareness in the absence of the functioning of the sensory organs and the mind (*indriya* and antahkarana). Thus, they account for that experience of bliss as follows: there can be no experience of bliss during the state of dreamless sleep, since there is no possibility of experience or of self-awareness when sensory-organs and the mind are not functioning. Recall that '*anuvyavasay*' presupposes '*vyavasaya jnana*'. Therefore, the sense of bliss under discussion is an event that takes place only on the waking, as absence of suffering, similar to the experience that 'I did not know anything so long' (i.e. during the state of sleep),

In the Advaita scheme, the notion of *jiva* is interesting. It is wider than I-sense. It is said that empirically (*vyayavaharika*) jiva always presents itself as I-sense. However, the I-sense is there in waking (jagrata) and dream (svapna) states. In the state of dreamless sleep (sususpti) the jiva persists of course but there is no I (aham). All Advaitins agree on this—the *bhamati, vivarana,* and *prasthana*. They explain that in deep sleep, there is no awareness of I which is there in the waking and the dream states, since antahkarana is then in a dormant state. Note, for them the I is no more than mind or antahkarana superimposed on consciousness.

However, Ramanuja does not agree. His point of departure is totally different. He holds the world to be real and does not admit of any such principle of Avidya. He asks, if the I is absent in the state of deep or dreamless sleep, how does it return to the waking state with all its propensities and traces (*vasanas, samskaras*)? How to account for the sense of I as persistently the same as it was fifty years ago?

For the Advaitins, this sense (*pratiti*) of identity is simply due to the persistence of mind (antahkarana), whether it is in gross or subtle form. Until there is total destruction (*vinasa*) of this mind, the sense of identity will continue in the regular rotation (*avartana*) of the three states, i.e., the waking, dream, and deep sleep.

The question is asked to those who argue that the I persists in the state of dreamless sleep but it is not experienced (*anavabhasat*). Why not? It is said since the I has no object/content (visaya), therefore it is not grasped. This argument, note, is as such acceptable to all the Upanisadic philosophers as they all agree that there is no sense of a pure I to be encountered in our experience without association with something else as content of that awareness. But then how is this lack of awareness of object (*visayanubhava*) to be accounted for? Is it because there is no awareness at all or is it because that although there is awareness still there is no awareness of object/content? Note that the seer-function (*drastrtva*) is absolved in the state of deep sleep in the same way as in the waking state. The most vital condition for perception is contact of sense-organs (indriya *sannikarsa*) with the object. Without that even if there are objects present, perception does not occur, In the state of deep sleep, this contact is absent, sense-organs do not function and the mind is said to enter the gland called '*puritat nadi*'.[33]

To those who say that there is I (aham) in deep sleep (sususpti), but there is no awareness (pratiti) due to other reasons, the important question that arises is on what basis can such a claim be made? In other words, if there is no awareness, how does one establish that the I is there? It is not enough just to make a stray claim that something exists, for that there has to be an awareness which is backed by evidence. Incidentally, the Vedantins while arguing against Sankhya remarked that without evidence nothing can be established.[34] Had that been not the case, they argued, it should be enough to establish the existence of thousand lamps inside a wall simply by claiming that it exists.

At this point, it is pertinent to recall that there are technical discussions in the Advaita scheme indicating that not everything can be established by any of the accepted forms of evidence (*pramanasiddha*) such as perception, inference, etc.; despite that many are indeed established that way. The presence of I or states of sadness, happiness, etc., for example, cannot be established by any of these evidences; these are said to be established by the witness consciousness (*saksisiddha*) whereas the existence of the absolute, non-dual consciousness is simply self-evident (svayam-siddha). Thus the existence of I/Aham does not need any evidence (pramanas) nor can it be said to be self-evident (*svayamsiddha*). In their

---

33 Descartes referred to pineal gland.

34 As the Naiyaikas would say that claim of any existent has to be backed by a *pramana*: '*manadhinameyasiddhi*'.

analysis, the I being a knot[35] of the two principles—conscious and non-conscious (antahkarana) is established by the witness-consciousness (*saksisiddha*).[36] Recall the observation recorded in Sankara's commentary on the *Brahma Sutra*[37] that the I is not entirely a non-object (*avisya*). This is clearly exemplified in the statement 'I know an object' which shows that all the three components of the statement—'I', 'knowing', and 'object' —are knowable.

Ramanuja, however, has an altogether different view. He emphasizes that the I is there continuously in all the three states; it is there even in the state of freedom or mukti. There is no principle of 'avidya' in this conceptual structure. He as well as his followers—similar to the case of the Dvaita Vedanta school—are all upholders of the 'reality of the world' (*jagat-satyatavadi*, not *maya-vadi*).

A significant step in the Advaita analysis regarding the I is that although the I-sense is said to be totally absent in the state of deep sleep, it does not imply that on waking the I that is confronted is a different I. This is explained by saying that the mind or antahkarana is not destroyed but remains in a latent state in deep sleep. The individual continues whereas no I sense is there. Thus, although there is no static I (*sthira* aham), the I remains the same I by virtue of the fact that it is the same mind that is superimposed on consciousness tinged with the beginningless principle of avidya.

It is not possible here to go into many of the details of these debates here. However, what needs to be emphasized is that both expository and polemical literature pertaining to this topic shows unfailingly that I-consciousness is indeed a key question for all Vedanta. Unhesitatingly, it may be said that as each of these major schools of the Vedantic tradition seeks to interpret the teachings of the Upanisads a distinct and clear formulation with regard to the status and nature of 'I-consciousness' emerges. This in turn becomes an integral part of that specific line of philosophical

35 '*Cidacidgranthi*'.

36 For a full discussion, see Srimohan Bhattacharya and Dinesh Chandra Bhattacharya Sastri (eds), 1979, *Bharatiya Darsana Kosa* (Calcutta: Sanskrit College).

37 '*Nayamatma ekantena avisaya, asmadpratyayavisayatvat*'.

interpretation declared as a fundamental tenet (*mukhya-siddhanta*) of that particular tradition.

The above is a brief survey of the diverse positions that are held by various schools of Vedanta. Now a few general observations about these readings can be made. Firstly, the disputes concerning I-consciousness need to be appraised in the Vedantic context by keeping in mind that all the contending parties have a common background as a starting point and that the primary focus of their quest is to understand the self. They all accept the ontological reality of self (atman) and share unanimously the conviction that 'knowledge of the self' (atma-vidya) alone can confer mukti. Thus a philosophical probe into I-consciousness is indispensable in order to fulfil the soteriological demand, since no phenomenon can be closer to that search for self than I-consciousness. The Vedantic tradition, therefore, spares no effort towards a rigorous exploration of this experience which is witnessed/testified by all (*sarvanubhavasiddha*). It is also equally recognized by them that I-consciousness despite being accessible to all yet is an open problem.

What is essential to observe in the course of this discussion is how the school of Advaita Vedanta, as opposed to other schools of Vedanta philosophy, puts forward a set of ideas which not only goes against the commonsense view but also shocks its sophisticated opponents. An amazing shift of perspective is seen in the Advaita treatment of this crucial issue. Radically different from other Vedantic theories, I-consciousness is here explained not by holding the 'I' or aham as a metaphysical entity, nor is the apprehended I identified with the self or atman. With the key concept of adhyasa or superimposition, Advaita Vedanta develops a complex theory which carefully unravels the constitution of I-consciousness and in the process demonstrates that no ontological reality is to be ascribed to the 'I' as it is composite in character.

Given that any Vedantic philosophical scheme requires a definitive account about the nature of I-consciousness, a phenomenon that no one doubts or denies, the following question has been of special interest : Is the 'I' a simple, homogenous entity or is it composite? Is it identical with the 'true' self (atman) or to be granted a merely conventional but no ontological status? Lastly, is it to be considered as being external (*bahya*) to consciousness, to be treated in the final analysis as the not-self?

Reference has been made to the vigorous controversies that ensued with regard to each of these aspects. These are all documented in the literature. It has been noted in this study that while all Vedantins agree that knowledge of the self is indispensable for emancipation from bondage, the quest for self has yielded a stunning result in the case of Advaita Vedanta. It needs to be highlighted that the Advaitins, unlike the Dvaitins or Visistadvaitins thoroughly reject the idea of plurality of selves. Moreover, the self is distinguished not only from the 'body', the 'sense-organs', the 'mind' but also from the 'I'[38]—all are labelled as the not-self (anatman) and carefully disclosed as various cases of superimposition.

The Advaita Vedanta school, as anyone familiar with the literature knows, makes much use of the notion of superimposition (adhyasa) which entails the idea of the ground (*adhisthana*) as well as of that which is superimposed (*aropya*) on it—as in the classical example of the 'illusory' snake superimposed on the 'real' rope. This idea of superimposition is applied not only in the case of illusion in the domain of the objective but also in case of the subjective as well. Many notable Advaita texts, using technical vocabulary, describes the presence of 'I-consciousness' as being due to superimposition on pure-consciousness which is 'beginninglessly' tinged with ignorance (*ajnana*).[39] Special mention may be made of such important works as *Advaitasiddhi* and *Siddhantabindu* by Madhusudana Sarasvati, where the author displays remarkable philosophical ingenuity as he defends the Advaita claim by answering the objections raised by its opponents.

To the Dvaita and the Visistadvaita schools, on the contrary, the idea that the I is ultimate and irreducible is not only crucial in order to account for empirical experience, it is also very much a soteriological demand. They argue that a loss of I in the salvaging scheme is an absurdity. These philosophers emphasize that the cancellation of the I is equivalent to the annihilation of the self. The I is never interpreted by these opponents of Advaita

38 cf. section on '*ahamkara-anatmattvaupapatti*' in *Advaitasiddhi*.
39 '*ajnanavisita-caitanye ahamkaradhyasa*', *ibid*.

Vedanta as something 'constituted', be that as it may result from superimposition or otherwise. They discard vehemently the idea that I-consciousness can even be interrupted, eliminated or dissolved, so to speak, be that in the state of deep sleep or liberation.

At this stage, it is worth recapitulating some of the salient points in the different readings showing how the discernments about the nature and the status of the 'I' are intimately connected with the general conceptual formulations regarding what consciousness is in the final analysis. Many of these distinctions that have been recorded in various expository and polemical documents also bring to light a network of issues that no investigation of the large theme of consciousness can really evade. One such central question in their discussions and debates is: can the presence of consciousness be proved or disproved?

The Advaita reply to this question is the following: As a contrast to everything else, designable as object (visaya), as 'this' (idam) that duly require evidence (pramana) for their establishment, consciousness does not need any evidence as it cannot be treated as a 'knowable'. The Advaitins claim that consciousness is to be described as a non-object (avisaya), not-this (anidam) and independent of all evidences (pramana-nirapeksa). In the final analysis, consciousness is self-evident (svayamasiddha). All attempts to prove or disprove anything fall back on this last idea. Recall that Vacaspati Misra, while examining the Buddhist Sunyavadins' reading on this matter, commented that even if one denies the whole world as being void (sunya), it presupposes the witnessing consciousness.[40] That which reveals the entire world of things (objects), the Advaitins argue, cannot itself be apprehended as a knowable, as this or that.[41] In other words, the characteristic features of the 'known' cannot be attributed to the 'knower'. Moreover, noteworthy is the fact that to say that consciousness cannot be presented to itself as an object (visaya) does by no means render its reality questionable. Again, the very fact that the I is 'known' shows that it is not the self. This clarifies why consciousness cannot be treated as

40 'sunyasyapi svaksitvat'.
41 cf. Chapter 6. Note K.C. Bhattacharya's remark that consciousness is 'known as unknowable'.

being on a par with any object that can be discerned as a knowable by means of any of the accepted sources of cognition such as perception, inference, etc. However, what is especially noteworthy is that the philosophy of Advaita Vedanta goes one step further in the way it develops the notion of consciousness as foundational. Consciousness is not only granted epistemic priority but is claimed to have ontological reality, expressed even more radically as being non-dual. This latter idea is intended to claim that there is no room for plurality or difference.

In other words, consciousness is sui generis, it is not caused, and it is not a derived principle. The self-evident (svayam-siddha) character of consciousness goes hand in hand with the Advaita contention that consciousness is self-revealing (*svayam-prakasa*). No distinction needs to be made between self and consciousness but a distinction must be made between self and the ego (atman and ahamkara). In the ultimate analysis, consciousness is non-intentional (nirvisayaka) and indeterminate (nirvisesa).

The issue whether consciousness is intentional or not has been a topic for endless debate in Indian philosophy. The Dvaitins and the Visistadvaitins have vehemently rejected the Advaitic notion of non-intentional consciousness. In fact the ideas that consciousness is non-intentional (nirvisaya) and does not belong to an ego (nirasraya) are unacceptable to them. Ramanuja, for example, while considering the idea that consciousness is self-evident, defines this latter feature thus: consciousness is self-evident only when it reveals its object to its owner.[42] These readings clearly show that the 'I as self' plays a distinctively crucial role in their epistemology as well as in their ontology. Ramanuja categorically asserts that anything that is real must necessarily be determinate and definable or else it will be simply nothing.[43]

As has been said before, Ramanuja and his followers maintained a view according to which consciousness is both of the essence of self (*cidrupa*) and a quality (*cidgunaka*). The importance of this position is to be understood in the following way. Ramanuja wants

---

42 'svasrayamprati visayaprakasana-velayameva'.
43 'sadharmata syat, no cet tucchata': RB 1.1.1.

to work out a position where, on the one hand, the self is viewed always as conscious and, on the other hand, also as the subject of all cognitions.[44] This position seeks to avoid any reading where the self can be described as non-conscious (acit) at any stage.[45] Consequently, consciousness must be the essence of the self, yet it is never without a subject and equally never without an object. It is clear from the accounts of the debates why and how these predominant schools of Vedanta philosophy come to hold different views when considering such issues as whether consciousness and self are identical or not or a distinction needs to be maintained between the self and the ego, etc. The Advaita position is a radical one in which no distinction is made between self and consciousness. Consciousness is an unchanging principle. It is not a product or a quality (dharma) but the very essence (*svarupa*) of the self and by self is meant 'the self of all'. These ideas leave no room for any notion of plurality of selves.

For Ramanuja,[46] as it is for all the realistic schools of Indian philosophy, knowing or cognizing is defined in terms of revelation of an object.[47] However, the process of knowing entails, according to Ramanuja, a self as the knower to whom the knowledge of the object is revealed. In other words, while revealing the object also implies being revealed to its locus—the self—without the intervention of any other knowledge. This position thus differs from that of the Naiyayikas and others who explain it otherwise. For the Naiyayikas an episode of 'cognition of cognition' (*anuvyavasaya*) requires: (a) knowing the object and subsequently; (b) 'I the knower' becomes aware of the knowledge of the object. Among the dualists, there are indeed many shared convictions yet in their theories, for example in explaining the epistemological procedures with regard to 'cognition of cognition' or how the atman is known, there are

44 '*evamatma cidrupa eva na prakasa matram*'.

45 Recall that the Naiyayikas described the self as devoid of consciousness in the state of liberation (*mukti*).

46 For primary sources concerning Ramanuja's rendition, cf. *Sribhasya* by Ramanujacarya (Nirnayasagar edition) and *Yatindramatadipika* by Srinivasa (Anandaasrama edition).

47 '*Arthaprakasah jnanam*'.

many interesting variations[48]. It is not possible to get into these details within the compass of this monograph. One fascinating question asked in the soteriological context is how does one distinguish one individual from another when the external stripping weans away? A Dvaitin like Madhva's[49] answer is that there is an intrinsic difference between one individual and another. In other words, individuality is irreducible, it is ultimate.

It is evident that all schools of Vedanta—be that Dvaita, Visistadvaita, or Advaita—regard knowledge of the self to be the highest knowledge. They all share this Upanisadic insight. The thinkers of this movement identify the unmasking of the I-sense as of capital importance for this purpose since nothing is closer to the project of unravelling the self than understanding I-consciousness. The profound involvement of the Vedantic movement with the issue of I-consciousness can be seen on metaphysical, epistemological, and linguistic levels. While seeking to lay bare the nature of I-consciousness, the major philosophers of the different schools of the Vedantic movement express openly their philosophical differences. They have fearlessly faced the sceptics, the agnostics, and the naturalists. They have polemized against the proponents of the no self theories. However, despite important conceptual overlaps in their thinking, the Vedantins have put forward their specific analysis of I-consciousness that displays significant variations.

---

48 Such as the 'Prabhakara Mimamsa' theory of 'Triputi', etc.
49 Madhva elaborates this idea in his theory of 'svarupabheda'.

CHAPTER FIVE

On the Meaning of the Word 'I' and the Layers of Subjectivity

Profuse discussions on semantic and indexical analysis concerning the pronoun 'I' are available in the literature. Indeed many analytical and linguistic studies relevant to these queries have been carried out in recent time in the West. Documents also show that in the ancient Indian philosophical circles,[1] many of these concerns have actually been anticipated and discussed. The theoreticians, Indian as well as Western, who have engaged in the intellectual struggle have all contributed insightful ideas, producing skilful methodical work in the area of philosophy of language. A survey of such works alone can be the subject of a comprehensive study in a cross-cultural context.

Given the immensity of the material that has accumulated in course of time regarding the theme of consciousness and which in turn has considerably augmented a critical appreciation for the difficulties associated with various interpretations of the word and the notion of 'I', a review of the current discussions in the West shows the treatment of these issues in a more poignant and

---

1 cf. T.R.V. Murti's comment in his presidential address, Indian Philosophical Congress, 37th session:

> It is no exaggeration to state that Indian philosophy is repeated twice over—once in the accredited metaphysical systems as we know them and once again in their standpoint with regard to language. Almost all types of metaphysics-Absolutism and Pluralism, Empiricism and Transcendentalism, Realism and Nominalism and their shades and sub-shades are found here. Every system of philosophy had to consider language at some stage or other; and each one had to ponder over ultimate questions concerning the relation of the word to Reality, of the modes of meaning and the validity of verbal knowledge.

pronounced manner. However, when one takes into account the deliberations and controversies that have gone on from ancient days in India, it enables one not only to recognize the overlaps in philosophical enquiries but also the originality in the mode of reflections that are there and which deserve to be more widely known.

REPRESENTATIVE EXAMPLES FROM INDIAN PHILOSOPHY

A search for the meaning of the word 'I' is important not only for a purely linguistic evaluation but also has bearing on epistemological and metaphysical concerns pertaining to the questions of subjectivity and of self-awareness. When the analysis is pushed further and further, going beyond epistemological and linguistic concerns, the need for a deeper comprehension of the phenomenon of I-consciousness surfaces that has ontological as well as soteriological dimensions. Thus, in the philosophical context of the Upanisadic tradition, it seems to me, that a profound and a critical understanding regarding consciousness emerges when the theoreticians belonging to the schools of the Nyaya, Vaisesika, and Mimamsa as well as Advaita Vedanta[2] directly begin to look at the phenomenon from multiple perspectives.

However, in this chapter focus will be especially made on the school of Advaita Vedanta as here one encounters, as it were, a map of an intricate journey that is extraordinarily rich, gradually leading even to soteriological insights. Philosophical deliberations documented in the literature on statements, beginning with 'all living beings have I-sense', to the culminating moment of the liberating experience as expressed in one of the great sayings (*mahavakya*) of the Upanisads 'I am Brahman' (aham *Brahmasmi*), bear witness to a remarkable conceptual journey. A colossal amount of material is available within the context of the Advaita Vedantic discourse, let alone the commentaries thereon by a band of Advaitin scholars over the centuries. An over-all appreciation of how these various perspectives are interlinked, considerably

---

2 The works of these stalwarts are numerous. Many original and good secondary sources are available.

enriches reflections on this topic. This is a vast area that can be treated only selectively within the compass of this monograph.

As I have said earlier, the disagreements among philosophers have never been with regard to the whether or not one could deny or doubt the presence of I-consciousness, the issues have rather been focused on such questions as to what the word 'I' refers to, what forms the basis of I-consciousness, whether it is homogeneous or heterogeneous in composition, etc. I would like to briefly draw attention to a few representative examples of philosophical discussions from both Indian and Western sources that help us to comprehend the nature of the philosophical struggle. For this purpose, let me narrow the scope of this extensive linguistic enquiry and focus on a few specific analyses of the word 'I' from relevant literature.

The Upanisadic philosophers, while reflecting on the word 'I' (*asmad-pada*) and its meaning (*artha*), were keenly aware of the fact that the manner in which the meaning of the word I is discerned is bound to have an important impact on the philosophical establishment of the atman or the self. The Nyaya-Vaisesika literature has plenty of technical discussions on this issue that are stimulating reading for those interested in philosophy of grammar or semantics as well. The concern here, however, is to grasp how an account of a specific linguistic usage of the common word I can be used as an evidence in the making of a philosophical theory explaining the structure of I-consciousness. Note that the advocates of *atmavada* did seek to establish their views as autonomous philosophical arguments; they did not try to propagate the central philosophical core of the tradition simply by referring to *sruti* or the revealed scripture, which for many of the opponents—such as the Carvakas, the Buddhists and the Jainas—was in any case not acceptable as a valid source of cognition or as an evidence. This is precisely why the Vaisesika philosophers said in their exchanges with the Carvaka materialists, that apart from sruti, their view with regard to the self or atman is also supported by the linguistic usage of the word 'I'.[3] Already in this ancient Vaisesika

---

3 *Ahamiti-sabdasya vyatirekannagamikam.*

text one comes across discussions about what may be considered to be the primary (*mukhya*) and the secondary (*gauna*) meaning of that word. The linguistic evidence is sought both for establishing the claim that the self (atman) is the very basis of I-consciousness, that it is the referent of the word I as well as for demonstrating what this word discloses about the self. It is with regard to this last question that the differences between the Vedantins and the Nyaya-Vaisesika philosophers become transparent. In fact, it is highly interesting to watch closely some of the dissimilarities among the Upanisadic philosophers themselves in determining the referent of the word 'I'. This is particularly so since these diverse interpretations need to be appreciated in a context where all these philosophers otherwise unanimously agree about the absolute and foundational character of the atman or the self—the fact that has earned the Upanisadic tradition the designation of atmavada. This latter observation, however, is not intended to obliterate the fact that there are indeed subtle differences among them with regard to their views about the self. On the contrary, the analysis of the word 'I' by different schools precisely puts these divergences en relief.

Thus, the linguistic problem concerning the word 'I', which is the most universally used pronoun (*sarvanama*) in first person singular number and accepted as an essential component of our conventional language, brings to the forefront the following questions: What does the word 'I' exactly refer to? How does one discern its meaning? The enormity of the literature available in the Indian context is somewhat startling as it at the same time lays bare to the critical gaze unsuspected complexities of this theme, indicating how delicately the metaphysical, the phenomenological, and the linguistic concerns are knitted together.

In the case of the Nyaya-Vaisesika philosophers, their philosophy of language supports the view that the referent of the pronoun in the first person, singular number directly points to the self, interpreted metaphysically as an entity that stands apart from the body-sense-organs-mind—each taken separately or as a collection. This self is the basis of I-consciousness and there is a plurality of selves. All these ideas are part and parcel of their pluralistic metaphysics, which has been discussed before. The Mimamsakas have also made important contributions demonstrating a keen preoccupation with some of these issues. Their original works as well as the secondary sources based on ancient texts are available.[4]

In this chapter, however, the main focus is to further explore the thesis of Advaita Vedanta which is distinctly different from other readings—viewed phenomenologically, metaphysically, and linguistically. Unlike the advocates of Nyaya-Vaisesika-Mimamsa schools, for the Advaitins, the 'I' is not is discerned as a simple, homogenous entity nor is it supportive of the view of the onto-logical reality of a plurality of selves. There are several stalwarts of the Advaita tradition such as Sankara, Vidyaranyamuni, Nrsim-hasrama, Madhusudana Saraswati, and others who have master-fully dealt with various issues that are intertwined with the analysis of the word 'I' in consistency with the philosophy of non-dualism. This endeavour was seen as integral to the pursuit of exploring the Atman.

My task here is not to give an outline or a summary of the enormous literature of Advaita Vedanta but rather to focus on exponents of this school who sought to lay bare the intricacies of subjectivity by analysing I-consciousness linguistically and phe-nomenologically. For this, I would like to focus on some aspects of the profound reflections of K.C. Bhattacharya. The writings of this twentieth-century Advaitin provide a fine case in point, disclosing how linguistic analysis of the pronoun (sarvanama) in first per-son singular number and exploration of subjectivity are delicately intertwined.

The remarkable analysis made by K.C. Bhattacharya[5] in his essays entitled, 'The Subject as Freedom', 'The Concept of Philos-ophy', 'The False and the Subjective'[6], among others, reflect his

4 B.K. Matilal, 1985, *Language, Truth, and Reality* (Delhi: Motilal Banarsidass).

5 Professor K.C. Bhattacharya (1875–1949) was a convinced Advaitin of the twentieth century. Well-versed in the subtle technicalities of the expository and polemical moves that are elaborated in the Indian philosophical literature both for and against Advaitic thinking, he embarked on the arduous project of exploring subjectivity.

6 K.C. Bhattacharya, 1953, 'The False and the Subjective', *Studies in Philosophy,vol.2*, edited by Gopinath Bhattacharya (Calcutta: Progressive Publishers).

profound interest in laying bare the structure of I-consciousness and his skill in analysing the peculiarities of the word 'I'. Keenly aware of the objections that the adversaries of Advaita thought had raised, Bhattacharya attempted a novel analysis of the word 'I' that gradually discloses some atypical features of the phenomenon of I-consciousness and in the process brings out the deep significance of the Advaitic idea of the self as non-dual.

Given that the Advaitins unanimously hold the idea of the ontological reality of the non-dual atman as central, they are keenly sensitive to the various issues associated with the theme of subjectivity. An important consequence of their position is that they perceive the notion of plurality of selves along with the commonsense appraisal of the I-sense as being identical with the atman to be eventually 'false' (*mithya*) and as illusory (*mayic*)—technical notions that play a crucial role in the philosophy of Advaita Vedanta. The analysis of the experience of falsity is especially pertinent for understanding subjectivity in various ways. Bhattacharya in his essay 'The False and the Subjective' takes this question up and shows how intimately the consciousness of the false and that of the subjective are interrelated, by showing what the experience of falsity actually entails. To be conscious of falsity, he maintains, implies that the content is speakable as a belief which is disbelieved. The consciousness of the false is a consciousness of the past belief which at present stands refuted. Even if a belief is reaffirmed, to be conscious of a belief does involve a distinction between content and its intentional reference (fact). While elaborating on Bhattacharya's insights into the question of falsity and illusion, T.R.V. Murti in a paper entitled 'Illusion as Confusion of Subjective Functions' further argues against the realists who hold the view that illusion could be explained in objective terms (without reference to the subjective). Murti maintains that 'the transition from illusion to cancellation is not an objective change, a becoming in nature: it is something subjective'.[7] Moreover, he goes on to show that the implication of the essentially 'reflective' nature of the cancelling

7 T.R.V. Murti, 1963[1935], 'Illusion as Confusion of Subjective Functions', *Recent Indian Philosophy, Vol. I,* edited by Kalidas Bhattacharya (Calcutta: Progressive Publishers).

consciousness is not that it is just another 'unitary subjective state' as the illusion is. The cancelling consciousness does not derive its 'corrective force' from the fact of its being merely temporally posterior to the illusion, since cancellation 'is disbelief or withdrawal of belief and not a new belief'.[8] Indeed Murti's comments constitute an interesting attempt to elaborate on Bhattacharya's interpretations regarding the implications of illusion as opposed to that of the realists' explanations.

In brief, what is argued is that the awareness of subjectivity is implied in the awareness of falsity, since the content of consciousness can be discerned in this context to be a belief as opposed to fact. The awareness of 'subjectivity', he says, is 'other than the meaning-awareness', it is different from consciousness of an object since 'the object is what is meant'.[9] These ideas are discussed in what follows.

Bhattacharya's account of the word 'I' is very closely connected with the question how a speaker communicates to the hearer her own subjectivity by expressing herself as 'I'. This term, he says, has a uniquely singular reference; but as understood, it is general in the sense the term unique is general'.[10] A quick look at the over-all analysis offered by Bhattacharya shows that to the question whether the word I has a 'meaning' (artha), his reply is in the negative, although he says that it is 'speakable'. Note carefully the technical significance of the ideas of 'speakability' and that of 'meaning' in this discourse. Speakability, according to him, is a large concept, and the speakable may or may not have a meaning (artha). Granted that the speaker refers to themselves as 'I' and to the object as 'this', both the subject and the object are to be regarded as speakable. However, the question of meaning is a different philosophical issue according to Bhattacharya, as explained below.

'Meaning' (translated from the Sanskrit word 'artha') evidently has a technical significance and is of crucial importance for his analysis of the word I. By 'meaning' what is meant is an episode

8 *Ibid.*
9 *Ibid.*
10 Bhattacharya, 'The False and the Subjective'.

in which the auditor and the speaker can utter the same word and thereby intend the same meaning, i.e., refer to the same object. When, however, this is not the case the speakable cannot be said to have a meaning, although it may still be significantly speakable. Note that this picture of how the theoretic consciousness actually functions is vital for Bhattacharya's analysis of the word 'I' and eventually for his readings with regard to the phenomenon of I-consciousness.

In his deservingly famous essay entitled, 'The Subject as Freedom', he analyses in detail the peculiar features of the word 'I' by distinguishing it from the word 'this' and points out, in the process, its implications for making a careful distinction between the subject and the object. He writes: 'the object is what is meant'.[11] In accordance with what has been observed earlier, the object is to be understood as that which can be designated/referred to by a word, which can also be employed by the hearer to convey exactly the same as intended by the speaker who utters it. (For example, both the speaker and the hearer can utter the word 'table' and refer to the same table).

For Bhattacharya the word 'this' stands 'as the symbol of the object or what is meant'; since the word 'this' can be used by the hearer to mean the same object as it is intended by the speaker, even though it can be used to mean something else as well. The point to note here is that the word 'this' represents all those words where one can discern an identity of the general meaning, an applicability to the same thing. Bhattacharya develops the notion of subjectivity step by step by dissociating the awareness of the subject from that of the object as meant. He claims that there is no such similar 'meaning-awareness' in the case of the subject as expressed in the word 'I' as opposed to the word 'this'. To use his own words: 'The word I as used by a speaker is not understood by the hearer to convey what he would himself convey by the use of it'. If he uses the word, he would intend himself and not the speaker. In other words, the hearer understands the word I in a

11 K.C. Bhattacharya, 1953, 'The Subject as Freedom', *Studies in Philosophy, vol.2*, edited by Gopinath Bhattacharya (Calcutta: Progressive Publishers).

manner which is not the same as he would in the case of the word 'this', which is through the meaning of the word. The word I, then, cannot be said to have a meaning since it is evident that the word 'I' can never be used by the speaker and the hearer to intend the same which in the case of 'this' is possible. He brings out succinctly the peculiarity of the word I by observing: 'The I is not unmeanable nor is it meant—meant even as unmeanable. It is not unmeanable in the sense that it presents no problem in meaning at all....'[12]

Bhattacharya further points out that the word 'I' cannot be said to have a singular or a general reference. He elaborates the point as follows: 'the term is, in fact, not singular in the sense that different people use it of the same thing and not general in the sense that it is understood by any of the different things at a time'.[13] Indeed, it is equally interesting to note that the word 'I' is understood by the hearer even though no two persons use the word to refer to the same thing. The speaker is using the word to refer to herself, the hearer understands what is intended not because the word has a meaning but because it has, to use Bhattacharya's own vocabulary, 'a meaning-function', which in tune with the Advaitic trend he calls the 'I-function' (ahamkāra). This 'meaning-function' of the word 'I' is a specific use of language which expresses the speaker in her 'actual introspection but the understanding of the word by the hearer is indicative of a form of consciousness subtler than introspection'. In other words, the hearer understands the word 'I' uttered by the speaker not because the word has a singular reference. The hearer would use the same word if he were to refer it to himself. The point to note is that the function of the word is not the same for the speaker as it is for the hearer. This is what Bhattacharya seeks to express by saying that as if it were the self-consciousness of the speaker that 'incarnates' in that word. The word, he insists, cannot be taken as merely having a symbolizing function. He states emphatically that 'the word I is at once the symbol and the symbolized', although as symbol it is 'better known than what is symbolized by it'.[14]

12 *Ibid.*
13 *Ibid.*
14 *Ibid.*

This brings us to an important perception that speaking is essentially a social matter; even introspection can also be said to be 'implicitly social'. Bhattacharya insists that it is not through the meaning of the word that the speaker understands her self-consciousness, 'the word only reveals it to another', that is, it is a case of self-evidencing in a social context. In other words, the possibility of being intuited by the other self is open for the self-evidencing self who uses the word 'I'. Again, while expressing herself through the word I and communicating to another self, the speaker is also aware of herself as a distinct self.

This remarkable analysis of the words 'I' and 'this' brings out other interesting features that distinguish the object-awareness from the subject-awareness. What is communicated in the case of 'this' is the object and not the communicating itself, whereas in the case of 'I' it is not the meaning that is communicated but it is the speaker as speaking and communicating. The self-consciousness of the speaker, as it were, to put it in Bhattacharya's words, is not merely 'expressed but incarnated in the word "I"'.[15]

The major thrust of this exceedingly interesting study is on demonstrating how grades of subjectivity imply grades of objectivity, finally leading up to the threshold of what the Advaitins have described as the absolute and foundational consciousness. It is indeed with great ingenuity that Bhattacharya discloses before the reader how subjectivity at every step is 'felt to be free or dissociated from the object'. In another context of this phenomenological analysis he, in consonance with the Advaitic insight, points out that the object can indeed be conceived to be

illusory as the denial of reality is intelligible about what is meant, the negation of the meant being also actually or problematically meant. The unreality of the subject, however, as intended but not meant by the word I is meaningless. It is not only inconceivable like the opposite of an axiom; it is not even tried to be conceived... The word I expresses an unique and unanalyzable content....[16]

15 *Ibid.*
16 *Ibid.*

These perceptions of the word 'I' as contrasted with the word 'this' and of grades of subjectivity as opposed to those of objectivity led Bhattacharya to observe that that the so-called debates in metaphysics concerning the subject are all indicative of a notion of subject 'viewed in some sense as object'. He even goes on to make the bold assertion 'there is properly no metaphysic of the subject, if by metaphysics is understood an enquiry into the reality conceivable as meanable'.[17]

A question may be raised here is that if the knowable is meant and if the subject, as Bhattacharya insists, must be treated as unmeanable, in what sense then is a philosophical enquiry into the subject possible? To find an answer, the idea of speakability needs to be looked into more closely, since as he says 'the subject is communicable by speech' boldly claiming that the awareness of the subject prior to its expression in speech through the word 'I' is 'somewhere midway between a mystic intuition and the consciousness of a meaning, being the believing content of a speakable content...' The peculiarity of the spoken word is such that its negation cannot be said to be a meaning. To the extent, however, 'that the subject is communicable by speech' it is to be considered as a legitimate theme for a philosophical discourse.[18]

The charge that his language is terse, sometimes difficult to penetrate perhaps is not untrue. However, once one enters into his conceptual world, the clarity and depth of his thinking becomes evident. To put it in his own words, it is by 'conceiving in general after Vedanta as conscious freedom or felt detachment from the object' that he goes for a phenomenological disclosure of the absolute and foundational base of the Atman. Bhattacharya succeeds in disclosing before the reader with remarkable skill, how subjectivity at every step is 'felt to be free or dissociated from the object'. The point has been to highlight how the awareness of the subject always remains as that which cannot be meant, that is, as that which is eventually not objectifiable, trying to carefully demonstrate how the awareness of the body, awareness of others can all be described

17 *Ibid.*
18 *Ibid.*

as object-awareness from which the subject-awareness is to be dissociated, disentangled. An important point to note is that this investigation lays bare the notion of subjectivity at various levels. He writes: 'the grades of subjectivity implies grades of objectivity, the terms being conceived in a relative sense. To spiritual subjectivity, the psychic is objective and so to psychic subjectivity, the bodily and to bodily subjectivity the extra-organic is objective'.[19]

While reviewing Bhattacharya's treatment of I-consciousness, one appreciates particularly his analysis of the word I and the phenomenological description of the different grades of subjectivity that he offers, gradually disclosing how it frees itself from any objectification. He is conscious of his project as being modelled after Vedanta, seen 'as a substitute of metaphysics'.[20] Indeed, his study does bear a stamp of authenticity, rigour, and depth which is hard to match.

I had suggested earlier[21] that Advaita Vedanta cannot be classified as a specimen of descriptive psychology, nor can it be treated as what is called 'metaphysics of the natural standpoint' by the phenomenologists. The Advaitic insistence on the idea of consciousness as the absolute ground and that of the world—thereby included the I-ness (ahamkara) as superimposed (adhyastha) is to be appreciated in the context of a discourse that exemplifies a definite departure from all traditional ontologies. Mithyatva or falsity in the context of Advaita is a notion that needs to be radically distinguished from the idea of falsity from the natural standpoint. In the Advaita literature the I-principle is considered to be the very first of the superimposition of nescience on absolute consciousness—all that is classified as 'karyadhyasa'. Moksa or freedom involves an annulment, so to speak, of all forms of superimposition (Adhyasa), including as well that of the I-sense (ahamkaradhyasa). The intricacy of this venture is remarkably

19 Ibid.

20 Ibid.

21 cf. my essay,1992, 'Analysis of I-Consciousness in the Transcendental Phenomenology and Indian Philosophy', in D.P. Chattopadhyaya, et al (ed.), Phenomenology and Indian Philosophy (Delhi, India: Motilal Banarsidass), pp. 133–40.

expressed when Bhattacharya says that one is never introspectively aware of one's individuality in the similar vein as one is in the process of successively freeing oneself 'as body from perceived object, as presentation from the body, as feeling from presentation and as introspective function from feeling...'.[22] He concludes his essay, 'The Subject as Freedom', with the following observation:

> I am not introspectively aware of my actual introspective individuality but I am aware in my introspection into feeling that the self from which the feeling is distinguished may not actually introspect and may not even possibly introspect, that individual as it is as introspecting... it may be free even from this distinctness, may be freedom itself that is de-individualized but not therefore indefinite—absolute freedom that is to be evident...[23]

Let me conclude this section here by recapitulating that knowledge of the self is hailed in the Upanisadic tradition to be the highest knowledge (*atma-vidya hi parama-vidya*). A philosophical exploration of I-consciousness has been deemed to be indispensable for comprehending what is entailed in the very notion of self. Thus, an analysis of the word I has been recognized as an important cognitive tool and that eventually this kind of a phenomenological investigation discloses a strong soteriological dimension that is implicit in it. The significance of the postulation that the awareness of the subject is 'other than the meaning awareness', has been ably demonstrated by Bhattacharya while re-affirming the readings of the Advaitins. Note that the Advaita understanding and analysis of consciousness as foundational is a radical departure from other traditional systems. In the long run, what is striking is that the investigation into the question of subjectivity, even though closely tied to the first person perspective, gradually points to an experiential reality which, to repeat Bhattacharya's words, gets 'de-individualized'. This implies a negation of plurality of selves and makes room for an idea of impersonal consciousness which is devoid of duality. Cognitively, it is not possible to further uncover the Upanisadic claim that the 'self is the self of all'. The function of discursive knowledge is at best to lay bare the

22 Bhattacharya, 'The Subject as Freedom'.
23 *Ibid.*

structure of consciousness within the domain of duality where language is operative; the phenomenological investigation pushes the boundary and unravels the experiential reality. Here, 'all words come to a stand-still'.[24]

REPRESENTATIVE EXAMPLES FROM WESTERN PHILOSOPHY

At this point, let me turn to Western philosophy and focus on a few interesting examples of analyses of the word I in connection with specific notions of self or no-self, as the case may be. Here the purpose of focusing on certain accounts of the word 'I' is much less born of any curiosity for purely grammatical, semantic, or indexical exercises documented in the literature but has much more to do with the motive of observing the concerns which are part and parcel of the investigation into the large theme of consciousness. It is also in this process that one comes to see how both philosophy of language and metaphysics actually can serve the common project of unravelling the consciousness. The enigmatic features of the phenomenon of I-consciousness inevitably begin to surface, and one understands why no unanimity can be expected among the investigators.

Recall that Descartes' famous statement 'cogito ergo sum' has been open to many critical probes, not only with regard to the question of appropriateness of his metaphysical dualism but also how far he was led to that position by way of analysing the meaning of the word 'I'. Descartes had said that 'I could suppose I had no body but not that I was not'.[25] Further on he came to the conclusion that 'this I is not a body'. In other words, while attempting to discern the meaning of the word 'I' and analysing the cognition of I, he was led to the ascertainment of a notion of self as an immaterial, non-physical substance.

It is noteworthy that the usage of the reflexive pronoun 'I' has been analysed by such philosophers as Kripke and Anscombe

24 yato vaco nivartaute, Mundaka Upanisad.
25 René Descartes, 1993 [1641], *Meditations on First Philosophy*, 3rd ed., trans. Donald A. Cress Indianapolis: Hackett.

among others, who indicate what they see as Descartes' pitfalls. The analysis in Anscombe's work[26] certainly discloses how the word 'I'—a personal pronoun—can function syntactically like a name and yet it can never be confounded with a proper noun, although, as she points out, that whenever a speaker uses that word I, he means that which can as well be referred to by his proper name. Indeed, the question of reference of the word 'I' poses considerable problems since it cannot be treated as any other ordinary demonstratives since the latter is subject to reference-failure unlike the word 'I'. Moreover, if thinking is the essence of selfhood, as Descartes holds, the difficulty lies in concluding that the referent of different I-thoughts to be the same. Anscombe asks: 'how do I know that 'I' is not ten thinkers thinking in unison'?[27] In other words, the challenge is how to account for that 'I' has a singular reference.

Anscombe tends to think that it is wrong to take 'I' as a referring expression. She finally reaches the conclusion that 'I is neither a name nor another kind of expression whose logical role is to make a reference, at all'. For her then, unlike an array of thinkers, 'the (deeply rooted) grammatical illusion of a subject is what generates all the errors'.[28] Is this a move toward a no-ownership theory?

Indeed, the difference in the linguistic function of the first person pronoun from that of proper names, common names, even from some demonstrative pronouns has been noticed and scrutinized by philosophers in India and the West. Consequently, there is a general consensus regarding the ontological and referential priority of the word 'I' and an awareness concerning how this reference differs from a third person perspective of a speaker who utters the word 'I'. The ambiguities and the possibilities of mistakes, for example, that can be discerned in the usages of a proper name and of other descriptions in order to identify the speaker are virtually impossible in the case of reference of the word 'I'. Some have carefully scrutinized the usages of such demonstrative pronouns as 'this', 'that' only to uncover that none of these have

26 G.E.M. Anscombe, 1975, 'The First Person', *Mind and Language*, ed. S. Guttenplan (Oxford: Clarendon Press) pp. 45–65.

27 *Ibid.*

28 *Ibid.*

the character of 'pure indexicality' as the word 'I' has. In order to unerringly identify the referent of the demonstrative pronouns, one may need to know which among the many possible referents is actually intended by the speaker or even whether a referent at all exists or not. Given this situation, one cannot help but notice that the status of 'I' is different. This is why some philosophers are inclined to think that when a speaker utters the word 'I' at a given moment, it guarantees, as it were, the presence or existence of the referent of that word. This reading tends to confirm the Cartesian intuitions and provides the reason for the general assertion that statements like 'I am not' or 'I don't exist now' are inconsistent and that these even sound absurd.

Gilbert Ryle[29] in his well-known work *The Concept of Mind* makes elaborate analyses of the word 'I' in the hope of solving what he calls the 'systematic elusiveness' of the concept of 'I'. He observes that pronouns such as 'You', 'she' and 'we' feel unmystifying, while 'I' feels mystifying'. He ends his chapter on self-knowledge by noting that 'one influential difference' among these indexicals is that 'I' in my use of it, always indicates me and only indicates me. 'You', 'she' and 'they' indicate different people at different times 'I' is like my own shadow; I can never get away from it'. Ryle goes on to provide the reader many examples of how index words are 'used in different senses in different sorts of context' and shows, quite interestingly, the 'elasticities in the uses of "I" and "me"', accounting for why 'so many people have felt driven to describe a person as an association between a body and a non-body'. Ryle is mentioned here not as much for the purpose of making a critical review of his own understanding of the mind, but as one of the earlier examples that demonstrates how this sort of analysis of indexicals led to more endeavours in this direction, provoking further reflections on I-consciousness. While exemplifying not only how theorists and thinkers but also unsophisticated people including children are perplexed by this puzzle, Ryle notes that even children ask such questions as 'where was I before I began'?, let alone that theologians wonder about 'what is it in an individual

---

29 Gilbert Ryle, 1949, *The Concept of Mind* (Chicago: University of Chicago Press).

which is saved or damned'?, and that philosophers speculate about 'whether 'I' denotes a peculiar and separate substance and in what consists my indivisible and continuing identity'.[30]

Indeed, there are many puzzles that have bewildered thinkers while seeking to account for how one is presented to oneself and why this phenomenon cannot be described in the same mode as one's awareness of anything else 'as an object'? Attempts to analyse these sorts of questions, showing the difference between the two cognitions, can be seen in the writings of several Western philosophers. As a pertinent example of such an analysis, consider the following contributed by Shoemaker:

> The reason one is not presented to oneself 'as an object' in self-awareness is that self-awareness is not perceptual awareness, i.e. is not a sort of awareness in which objects are presented. It is awareness of facts unmediated by awareness of objects. But it is worth noting that if one were aware of oneself as an object in such cases (as one is in fact aware of oneself as an object when one sees oneself in a mirror), this would not help to explain one's self-knowledge. For awareness that the presented object was ø, would not tell one that one was oneself, unless one had identified the object as oneself; and one could not do this unless one already had some self-knowledge, namely the knowledge that one is the unique possessor of whatever set of properties of the presented object one took to show it to be oneself. Perceptual self-knowledge presupposes non-perceptual self-knowledge, so not all self-knowledge can be perceptual.[31]

Recall that precisely for this reason that the category of 'mental perception' (*manasa pratyaksa*) was admitted by many Indian philosophers in contrast to sense-perception, as discussed earlier in connection with the Naiyayika theory of self-cognition.

There has been considerable amount of discussion regarding the differences between the linguistic usage of 'I' (*asmad-sabda*) and the ordinary demonstrative such as 'this' (*idam*) both in Indian and Western philosophy. The obvious noticeable differences

30 *Ibid.*

31 S. Shoemaker, 1984, 'Personal Identity: A Materialist's Account', in S. Shoemaker and R. Swinburne (eds), *In Personal Identity* (Oxford: Blackwell).

between these is that when the speaker utters the word 'I', the referent of that word cannot be intended by other speakers when they utter that same pronoun, which is not the case with the indexical 'this' since the same referent can be intended by all of them. Again, there can be a certain possible ambiguity about the referent of 'this' which goes against any claim of absolute unerring reference. The hearer has to be sure of the object which is intended by the speaker among various possible objects by the demonstrative 'this'. Finally, what has puzzled philosophers most is how to account for the referent of the word 'I', leading to the question whether the word 'I' has a reference at all. If it has, the question will be whether this can be used in the same manner as to enable one to point out one object among other possible objects, which would mean that a third-person perspective can well capture the meaning of the word. Alternatively one should abandon that possibility and go for a theory that claims that the referent of that pronoun is always a subject.

While reflecting on such issues, Anscombe comes up with the thoughtful comments:

> Whether 'I' is a name or a demonstrative, there is the same need of a 'conception' through which it attaches to its object. Now what conception can be suggested, other than that of thinking, the thinking of the 'I'-thought, which secures this guarantee against this reference-failure? It may very well to describe what selves are; but if I do not know that I am a self, then cannot mean a self by 'I'.[32]

Thus, one comes to note the subtle nuances of the meaning of the pronoun in first person and singular number and the way these tend to lend or withdraw support for self or no-self theories as the case happens to be.

Interestingly, the Indian conceptual world provides us with various theories that can be categorized under the self and no-self general headings. It has been seen that the affirmation of the self has given rise to an entire tradition of thinking that knows of inner variations, discussed in previous chapters. Philosophy of language

---

32 G.E.M. Anscombe, 1975, 'The First Person', *Mind and Language*, edited by S. Guttenplan, pp. 45–65 (Oxford: Clarendon Press).

came to play a decisive role both in support as well as against the idea of self. Those who denied the ontological reality of self generated a vehement debate, bringing forth in the process a strong tradition of thinking, which also knows of inner divergences. The no-self view will be the focus of discussion in the following chapter of this monograph, essentially with the view of noting its relevance for the theme of I-consciousness.

Indeed, in a cross-cultural framework many contending and conflicting observations can be noticed pertaining to the theme of self. At the very beginning of his essay, entitled, 'The Self', G. Strawson remarks that 'The substantival phrase 'the self' is very unnatural in most speech contexts in most languages, and some conclude from this that it's an illusion to think that there is such a thing as the self, an illusion that arises from nothing more than an improper use of language'.[33] He, then tries to make a case for the existence of self in the face of such counter-attacks, as by Kenny, who maintains that 'the self is a piece of philosopher's nonsense consisting in a misunderstanding of the reflexive pronoun'.[34]

However, the idea of self seems to have many variants. The metaphysical assumptions that lie behind the theories can be wide apart, in a few cases even to the point that it becomes questionable how far that same word 'self' can be said to bear conceptual overlaps for meriting the same designation. This may well be a point in favour of those who put forward rebuttals to the idea of self and propound instead one of the many possible versions of the no-self theory. Let us dwell on this issue for a little while, as this is interesting not only for understanding how standard nomenclatures camouflage significant differences but also for appreciating philosophical endeavours for exploring the question of self in the cross-cultural context.

It has been earlier noted that the idea of self that Descartes projected was in his view an immaterial substance. When Descartes—after asserting 'I know that I exist'—asked the question but 'what is

33 Galen Strawson, 1997, 'The Self', *Journal of Consciousness Studies*, Vol. 4, Nos 5/6, pp. 405–28.
34 Anthony Kenny, 1988, *The Self*, (Milwaukee: Marquette University Press).

this 'I' that I know'?, he gave the answer within a clearly conceived dualistic metaphysical framework of thinking. But when Strawson, not unlike several other contemporary philosophers, upholds the idea of the self, it is unmistakably a denial of dualism. Although he describes the idea of self as entailing the notions of a 'mental thing', a 'subject of experience', an 'agent', etc., this is not the same as holding a 'belief in an immaterial soul, or in life after bodily death'. Proclaiming himself to be a philosophical materialist, he declares that 'we are wholly physical beings'. However, he claims that all philosophical materialists have a 'sense of self' despite their belief 'that animal consciousness of the sort with which we are familiar evolved by purely physical natural processes on a planet where no such consciousness previously existed'.[35]

This brings us to an interesting point of discussion, viz. the meaning of 'mental' in a discourse that vigorously lends support to metaphysical materialism. In this connection, recall the internal divergences among the ancient Indian materialists. They not only advocated *dehatmavada* but also *indriyatmavada* as well as *manatmavada*. In all three cases, as has been mentioned earlier, the body, the sense-organs or the mind were all understood in terms of physicalism. All theorizations are conceived within a naturalistic framework. Consciousness was never perceived by any of them to be a distinct principle but an epiphenomenon. This is precisely why when the Buddhists rejected the idea of self that was championed by the Upanisadic tradition, the Carvakas thought that the Buddhists could just as well join them. However, the Buddhist understanding of consciousness had nothing in common with the materialists' interpretation. Detailed and pointed debates took place among them where the Buddhists carefully show exactly how their no-self theory as a philosophical position differs, on the one hand, from the self theories advocated by the Upanisadic philosophers and on the other hand, from the physicalist theory of consciousness as proposed by the Carvakas.[36]

35 Strawson, 'The Self'.
36 cf. Santaraksita, *Tattavasamgraha*, 1968, with commentary 'Panjika' by Kamalasila (edited by Dwarakanath Shastri [Varanasi]).

In the case of contemporary Western discourse by naturalists and materialists, the distinction between physical and mental are not always unambiguously explained. In some cases of course, it has led to a propounding of attribute-dualism, while avoiding substance-dualism. These issues deserve further attention.

David Hume's reflections on the question of self and his analysis that the so-called self as no more than a bundle of experiences has had profound influence on subsequent Western philosophical thinking on this topic. Certainly, many of the contemporary naturalists exhibit the same trend. However, some in the course of their reflections have also come to abandon Hume's reading, such as John Searle. However, prior to referring to Searle's view on this matter, let us recall that Immanuel Kant already saw Hume's account of the self as problematic. Kant indicated that the self is a category of understanding that stands for the transcendental unity of apperception without which one cannot account for the unity of conscious life.

If Searle who after a long search finds Hume's position to be not satisfactory, it is because he thinks that an explanation is needed in order to account for how different experiences can be seen 'as part of a single unified conscious field'. He argues that without the idea of the self 'we could not distinguish between one consciousness having ten different experiences....and ten different consciousnesses each with one experience'. On his view that 'self is not an experience, nor is it an object that is experienced'. How, even, could one justify the assumption, if it is an assumption, that there is just one thinking which is this thinking of this thought that I am thinking, just one thinker? How do I know that 'I is not ten thinkers thinking in unison'? This is why, Searle argues that Hume's reading 'of each perception as separate and distinct' leads us astray.

A most interesting development in Searle's thinking showing the passage from Neo-Humean to a non-Humean conception of the self is delineated in his work, entitled *Rationality in Action*. He has come to adopt that point of view 'since an analysis of rationality, volition, freedom of will and action' has shown him that the 'Humean bundle, even if unified and embodied, is not enough.... An agent is more than a bundle....Agency requires an entity that can consciously try to do something'. The idea that the agent must be a self and that this latter notion cannot be eliminated, is also prompted by the perception that the entity to which volition is to be ascribed has also conation and cognition. Moreover, Searle points out that 'rational behavior and its explanation' needs to be understood 'from the first person point of view, because they have a first-person ontology. They only exist from the first-person point of view. It explains both why I did what I did, and why I did that rather than an alternative that was causally open to me'. Thus, for Searle, 'neither a Human bundle nor a Strawsonian 'person' is sufficient for a satisfactory account of agency. He comes to the conclusion that the self cannot be eliminated. It is not that 'action creates a self, but that action presupposes a self'.[37]

For an Advaitin of course, Hume's effort to find a self through introspection was a totally misguided venture. They insisted that the self is not a knowable as an object, its transcendental subjectivity cannot be questioned.

---

37 John Searle, 2003, *Rationality in Action* (Cambridge, MA: MIT Press).

CHAPTER SIX

I and the No-self Theories
Differences within the Buddhist Tradition

The pivotal role that I-consciousness plays in our mental life is accepted by philosophers, in conformity with the commonsense view. This indubitable experiential base, therefore, serves as a common starting point for all subsequent inquiries and interpretations about ultimately who and what we are. Given this is the case in a cross-cultural context, it is no wonder that there is a perplexing variety of theories vying to account for this phenomenon of fundamental importance. In the beginning, one is baffled by the divergences present in the theory-making front since there is really no controversy about the discernment with regard to the presence of I-sense, but as soon as the investigation begins, one comes to note that disagreements arise with regard to such questions as what forms the basis for this awareness, how to account for self-awareness or what actually is the referent of the word 'I', and so on and so forth.

Indeed, the philosophical significance of these diverse cognitive undertakings seeking to unveil I-consciousness can be captured only by staying vigilant to the genre of queries that highlight the bewildering facets of this seemingly simple phenomenon. It is in this process of reviewing the cross-cultural history of ideas that the many inherent philosophical difficulties become explicit on the theory-making front.

Reference has been made in previous chapters to a number of views where the notion of an abiding self plays a central role in various accounts explaining and analysing I-consciousness. However, historically, the philosophical scene is much more complex than that. What is particularly perplexing is to take note of theories that exhibit sharply divergent, even contradictory, metaphysical trends. These, contrary to those self-theories discussed earlier, are often results of attempts that have been made to explain the flow of mental life and the presence of I-sense without the postulation of any notion of an identical, enduring self. It is this latter a position that we intend to discuss in this chapter.

INTERPRETATIONS BY DIFFERENT BUDDHIST SCHOOLS

A survey of Indian thought hardly leaves any doubt in the mind of an investigator that the ancient Indian thinkers were keenly aware of the conceptual subtleties and complexities of the various alternative strategies while affirming or denying the notion of self. Interestingly, whereas the schools of philosophy belonging to the Upanisadic and the Jaina traditions developed diverse conceptual models regarding the idea of self; this very idea of an abiding self received a severe blow with the advent of Buddhism. These distinctly different traditions of thinking thus become the carrier of a contrasting range of theory-making endeavours, exploring the theme of I-consciousness along distinctly different lines. This inevitably resulted in an intense battle of ideas giving rise to a considerably large amount of polemical literature. These are of great philosophical significance and an invaluable resource for anyone who is involved with consciousness-studies.

Buddhist thought, which has exerted profound influence over the centuries in many parts of the globe, is a source of ideas that challenged the Upanisadic notion of self in all its variations. It is perhaps the earliest document in the recorded Indo-European history of ideas where one encounters the emergence of a full-fledged theory of 'no-self'. '*Anatmavada*' is the other name for the Buddhist tradition. This reading has contributed to the making of a complex and a distinct conceptual tradition. It is worth mentioning here that it is precisely in the process of explaining the no-self stand that significant internal differences arose also among the Buddhist thinkers themselves.[1]

1 My essay, 1988, 'An Appraisal of I-consciousness in the Context of the Controversies Centering around the No-self Doctrine of Buddhism', *Journal of Indian Philosophy*, Vol. 16.

Buddhism as a tradition forthright decries the notion of self as an unwarranted assumption. The idea was seen from the outset as logically absurd and psychologically redundant. This reading is closely tied up with the idea of 'universal flux', which is central to Buddhist thought. The notion of universal impermanence (*sarvam anityam*) is said to have been preached by the Buddha himself. Putting forward the notion of causal efficiency as the criterion of reality,[2] the Buddhist logicians claimed to have shown that nothing can be exempt from change. Thus the idea of a permanent entity entailing the notion of an unchanging and unchangeable self is held to be fictitious or at best a linguistic construct having no reference to reality. They equally attempted to demonstrate that the idea of an abiding self is unnecessary as an explanatory tool to account for such psychological phenomena as memory, recognition, etc. Indeed, the Buddhist thinkers went further and insisted that even ethically as well as soteriological the notion of an unchanging, abiding self is nothing but a hindrance. Thus, the no-self view becomes the distinguishing mark of Buddhist thought. This nomenclature itself exhibits a metaphysical contrast to the philosophical claim of the ontological reality of self that has been highlighted in the Upanisadic tradition, which for that reason is designated as *atmavada*.

In the Buddhist conceptual world, there is no room for any immutable core that can even remotely be considered to be the vestige of the 'permanence' in the midst of change. Consequently, the initial theory-making endeavours by the sophisticated Buddhist philosophers led to a thorough refutation of the ideas of the universal, the permanent, and the substance. In the Indian philosophical scene, this was a novel theoretical strategy accounting for all existence in dynamic terms and even claiming to explain the constitution of human personality without any reference to the idea of self. As we will see shortly, the idea of universal impermanence, which the Buddha is said to have preached already in his first sermon, became a major conceptual tool in the hand of Buddhist thinkers belonging to the different phases of Indian Buddhism.

2 The idea of *arthakriyakaritva*.

They retaliated against the Upanisadic tradition in many ways in order to render the idea of substance, mental or material, to be no more than a conceptual construct. This network of ideas, as can be expected, provoked centuries of debates and discussions that shaped the Indian philosophical discourse.

In this connection, it needs to be evoked as well that a critical deliberation of the philosophical analysis of I-consciousness stirred internal divergences within the fold of the Buddhist tradition itself, although these theoretical differences hardly failed to underscore Anatmavada—the main characteristic that distinguishes the Buddhist position from the Atmavada of the Upanisadic tradition. An in-depth look at all these various interpretations clearly bring out the essential features of Buddhism as championing the cause of 'no-self' from its very inception. It is perhaps the first time in recorded history that the 'idea of the self as fictitious' emerged and gradually assumed the form of sophisticated theories. Here note that following David Hume, to be discussed later on in this chapter, several versions of the no-self view appeared in full-fledged form in contemporary Western philosophy questioning various non-Humean renderings of the theme.

As it stands, the development of this idea made its first appearance in the Indian conceptual scene sometime around fifth century BC. It is a story of a vigorous intellectual adventure that not only went against the prevalent popular belief but also the well-established philosophical view of an abiding self or atman that was preponderant at the time of the birth of the movement. This also makes the task of assessing the various Buddhist readings of the ideas of karma, rebirth, and nirvana all the more intriguing, since these obviously reflect the shared convictions of the Upanisadic as well as the Jaina projects of thinking. These are pan-Indian ideas.

The Buddhists indeed ushered in a new way of thinking by arguing in favour of a viewpoint where the idea of an unchanging self—whether standing apart from or underlying various mental states—was seen as having no basis in reality. In the discourses of different Buddhist schools, it is worth noting that the major metaphors used for describing human personality are expressed in terms of an aggregate (*sanghata*), a series (*vithi*) or a stream/a flow (*santana*). The point of the sanghata metaphor is to emphasize the fact that it is futile to conceive of a 'whole' that stands apart from its constituent parts. Again, while explaining how the illusory view of a permanent self arises, they adopted the view that the so-called sense of identity is due to nothing more than the recurrence of similar conscious moments,[3] thereby emphasizing the fact that continuity or resemblance cannot be passed as 'identity'. What is significant from the point of view of philosophy of language is the gradual emergence of the idea that the term 'self'/'soul' is a mere word that has no referent in reality. Note that there are not only significant metaphysical and psychological implications of such a reading; there are also important epistemological, ethical, and even soteriological overtones of the idea of no-self (*anatman*).

Prior to referring to a range of other philosophical texts, it must be mentioned that an amazingly vivid and lucid description of how exactly the metaphor of aggregate (*samghata*) applies in the context of the no-self view can be read in the well-known text entitled, *Milinda-Panha*. This is admirably exemplified in the conversation between King Milinda (Greek Menander) and the monk Nagasena.[4] This powerful and insightful conversation is designed to show the mistaken outlook that leads one to think of an immutable self as something over and above the mental states or to construe it as the underlying core that remains constant in the midst of changing states. The conversation lays bare that the notion of substance[5] in general (be physical or mental) as something more than its constituent parts is one that cannot be demonstrated as having any basis in reality (*vastu-sat*).

The salient features of Buddhist thought become evident as the monk Nagasena asks the king, whether he has come on foot or on a chariot. The king, who was dissatisfied with the idea of no-self, was obviously unaware of the philosophical trap. He replies promptly that he has come in a chariot. The monk immediately launches a thorough scrutiny with regard to the referent of the word 'chariot', insisting on an answer to the question

3 *ati-sadrsa tadatmya bhrama.*
4 cf. Milinda-Panha, 1923, *Les questions de Milinda*, trans. by Louis Finot (Paris-Bossard).
5 *satkaya-drsti.*

whether that word refers to the wheels, the poles, or any other component parts or whether it designates anything over and above these constituents. In this process it is made explicit that the word 'chariot' is merely an appellation and the chariot is no more than an assemblage of all these component parts. Similar, the monk argues, is the case with regard to the 'self', claiming that the so-called selves are not self-contained entities but are mere names for complexes, aggregates, etc. The analysis of the human personality into five aggregates (*panca-skandha*) deserves mention as it is scattered throughout early Buddhist texts. Of these five, the '*rupa-skandha*' stands for the physical whereas the other four, viz. cognition (*vijnana*), feeling (*vedana*), designation (*samjna*), and mental disposition (*samskara*) make for the psychical. Despite the internal differences within the Buddhist tradition, what is vitally important to note is their persistent denial of the notion of an identical self, assumed by laymen as well as by many philosophers either to be the basis or a decisive factor that gives rise to I-consciousness. This notion of self is simply held by the Buddhists to be an erroneous belief, a transcendental construct that is ultimately due to nescience (*avidya*). Propounding a view of universal flux that demolishes any vestige of a permanent entity anywhere, the Buddhist philosophers have repeatedly argued why it is logically untenable and psychologically superfluous to postulate a permanent self as a substratum or as a unifying principle in order to account for mental life.

The purpose here is not to highlight details that are of interest for Indological research, or delving into textual analysis or showing how the origination of specific schools and the syncretic character of some of the texts are related but to discern the major philosophical implications of such renditions that make the Buddhist network of ideas stand out as a distinctly original tradition, bringing in new insights for understanding the phenomenon of I-consciousness. The focus of the meticulous analysis that was undertaken by these thinkers was to lay bare the fact that there is absolutely nothing perdurable in the psychophysical complex (*nama-rupa*) that the individual can be said to be identical with. Indeed, the source of this line of thinking and analysis is attributed to the 'Master' himself. This key idea that there is no self, the tradition holds, can be traced back to the second sermon of Gautama Buddha, the founder of Buddhism, the originator of anatmavada.[6]

Note that, it is not to any revealed text but to the sermons of Gautama Buddha that anatmavada owes its origin. A vivid description of the impermanent and transitory character of all existence, where nothing whatsoever can be said to endure was already present in the first sermon. However, it is especially the literature documenting the second sermon, entitled 'Anattalakkhana Sutta', that contains the key statements which provides the explicit source for this revolutionary idea. Gradually, a minute analysis of human personality was undertaken. Without going into the details of the significant phases of the historical contexts of development for this philosophical analysis,[7] it may be noted that the idea that 'all is without self' (*sarvedharmah anatmanah*), is said to be one of the three fundamental characteristics (*trilaksana*) of all existence. This idea is intimately related to the other two characteristics, viz. all is impermanent (sarvam anityam) and all is suffering (sarvam *duhkham*).

The analysis, documented in several ancient texts, aims at demonstrating that there is nothing unchanging in the psychophysical complex (nama-rupa) that the individual is identical with. An introspective search is recommended with the intent of seeing for oneself the vain and illusory character of the idea of a permanent self, as having no basis in reality.[8] Thus gradually the idea of no-self emerges with all its philosophical sophistications, lying bare that the so-called self is fictitious, a mere name (*sanjamatra*), only a designation that serves the purpose of conventional life.

However, in spite of the steady focus on this principal tenet, viz. the abandonment of an unchanging and abiding self, the development of the actual train of ideas that came to the forefront in the different phases of Indian Buddhism show that each of

6 This sermon is termed in Pali as 'Anattalakkhana Sutta'.

7 cf. G.C. Pande, 1974, *The Origins of Buddhism*, 2nd edition (Delhi: Motilal Banarsidas).

8 There is repeated use of the phrase in the sermon 'O monks, look into yourself', etc. This view has been often compared with that of David Hume.

these phases has its own predominant philosophical orientation that distinguishes it from the other phases. Moreover, although a chronological reading is often attempted in scholarly renderings of the 'three phases'[9] of Indian Buddhism, it is interesting to keep in mind that the advocates of the major schools of each phase have all claimed that their specific interpretation is supported by the Master's own sermons. This is significant as these claims rightly bear witness to the fact that the 'words of the Buddha' (preserved in the tradition as Buddha—*vacanam*) allow for these different philosophical interpretive possibilities. Moreover, it is not only the Master's words but also the 'silence of the Buddha' has equally been seen as impregnated with his awareness of the antinomian character of reason—an awareness, as will be seen shortly, led to the Madhyamika interpretation of Buddhist thought.

Let me observe in this connection that the Buddhist intellectual tradition, like the Upanisadic, represents not merely a single and a simple scheme of philosophical ideas but a matrix of systems. Just as there is no uniform view of self (atman) or of I (aham) in the Upanisadic tradition and yet there is adherence to a common conceptual pattern discussed earlier; similarly the no-self theory along with the theme of I-consciousness knows of diverse interpretations in the different phases of the Buddhist tradition which saw the rise of diverse schools of Buddhist philosophy. It must be emphasized that in the case of Buddhism, the adherence to a central paradigm implies primarily the denial of a substance-view of reality (i.e., *sat-kaya drsti*). However, despite the common commitment to represent the 'middle path' that the Founder was said to have preached, the precise understanding regarding in what consists 'the middle path' varies from school to school.

While rejecting the atmavada of the Upanisadic tradition, the Vaibhasika and the Sautrantika schools belonging to the first phase of Indian Buddhism show a remarkably strong realistic trend where both consciousness and object are said to have ontological reality. An interesting development can be seen during the middle phase with the rise of the Madhyamika school when a

9 cf. Ancient Buddhist historian Buston speaks of 'the three swingings of the Law'.

dialectical mode of thinking emerged. What is remarkable about this middle phase of Indian Buddhism, as shown in the works of Nagarjuna and Chandrakirti, is not just a full re-assertion of what was thought from the beginning of the movement to be the shortcomings of the atmavada of the Upanisads. There was also a keen awareness of the limitations of the interpretations of anatma-vada during the first phase of Buddhism as well. The philosophi-cal reading of the middle phase is that consciousness and object are totally dependent on each other and consequently cannot be said to have any separate reality or essential nature of their own (*nihsvabhavaba*). The central doctrine of dependent origination is interpreted radically in order to emphasize that mutual depen-dence does not signify temporal sequence but the lack of essence or thinghood (*sunyata*). This philosophy highlights the implica-tion of the 'silence of the Buddha' as indicative of the importance of the rejection of all thought-categories. The philosophers of this school made use of the reduction ad absurdum arguments in support of this reading laying bare the falsities of all theorizations. The self-understanding of this conceptual move is that a dialecti-cal rejection of all theories is not itself a theory but an expression of freedom from entanglements of all theory-making devices, an autonomy from all standpoints (is, is not, is and is not, neither is nor is not).[10] Thus, the Madhyamika dialectical analysis was geared to show the limitations not only of atmavada but also of the *abhidharmika* interpretations as well, which led to deeper reflec-tion on the question of consciousness.

However, the dominant school of Yogacara Vijnanavada that appeared in the third, i.e., the last phase of Indian Buddhism reclaimed the ontological reality of consciousness. The philoso-phers of this school characterized the realistic trend of thinking in the first phase as an inevitable form of dogmatism (that goes with realism) and the *sunyavada* philosophy of the middle phase as scepticism. In the literature of this third phase of Indian Buddhism, one comes across an elaborate theory of consciousness. Indeed, the ideas propounded by the advocates of the Yogacara Vijnanavada

10 cf. the *Ratnakuta Sutra* clearly expresses the critical standpoint of Madhyama-Pratipad.

school have played a predominant role ever since and are present wherever Buddhism has spread. While holding on to the central idea of the sole reality of consciousness, they shaped Buddhist philosophy along idealistic lines. In the process, these philosophers radically modified the early realistic theory of elements (dharma theory) by ascribing to it only a phenomenal reality. No detailed study of the complex network of ideas entailed in the metaphysical orientation of the school can be undertaken here.[11] However, it may be briefly mentioned that seen within the pale of Buddhist thought, the philosophers of this idealist school supported the Madhyamika rejection of the category of the object that the realist Sautrantika philosophers had proposed. On the other hand, they vehemently opposed the Madhyamika position by defending the idea of the ontological reality of consciousness. This Vijnanavadin standpoint led to elaborate debates and discussions. A detailed theoretical account was worked out for explaining the status and constitution of empirical experience in consistency with the principal thesis of the school which is the view of a foundational consciousness (*parinispanna-vijnana*) that, in the ultimate sense, is said to be free from all dualities. The vast philosophical literature shows how meticulously the great Vijnanavadins like Vasubandhu and others sought to capture and formulate the significance of this idea to its fullest possible extent as it was crucial for their understanding of the pursuit of nirvana as well.

It may be mentioned in this connection that three important notions come to the forefront while the Vijnanavadins elaborate on the theme of consciousness (vijnana), accounting for experience. These are the notions of '*alaya-vijnana*', '*pravrtti-vijnana*' and '*mano-vijnana*'. These deserve special mention as in the light of these ideas the question of I-consciousness obtains a new significance. The *alaya* or the store-house consciousness is conceived as a basic substratum where the individuality has not yet arisen.[12] Noteworthy is the internal difference with regard

11 cf. Chapter 8, section on Vijnanavada Buddhism and Sartrean Existentialism.

12 It is said that Jung was inspired by this idea in framing the notion of the collective unconscious.

to this notion. Some conceive it in the singular, as a universal receptor, as a collective repository of seeds of all impressions; whereas others maintain that it is peculiar to each ego, hence, needs to be conceived in the plural. In all cases, it is perceived as that dynamic layer of consciousness where the presence of the ego is not yet fully manifest. It is because of the presence of 'alaya', that there is an incessant flow that supplies content to the sense of ego as well as to that of the external world. There is nothing outside of consciousness.

The idea of mano-vijnana is crucial for understanding the emergence of I-consciousness, hence is of great relevance to the present study. Note that according to this philosophy the projection of the 'I' is due to the operation of 'manas' which represents the stage of categorization of the objective and without it there is no awareness of the objective. It is said that 'I know' is invariably connected with any knowledge imparting unity to it. Nevertheless, the I is only an imposition even though it is an indispensable presupposition for all empirical experience. The 'I' dissociates itself from the content as a subject; this itself provokes a substance-view, a false sense of selfhood. It is said that the absence of knowledge with regard to the dynamic operations of the alaya-vijnana gives rise to this sense of ego, which in turn is always accompanied by a false notion of the ego (*atma-drsti*), ignorance about ego (*atma-moha*), a sense of conceit and of egoity (*atma-mana*) and even a sense of attachment to it (*atma-prema*).

The analysis of I-consciousness has two significant aspects—it is a presupposition for all knowledge, it is as well as a reflex. The contention is that all episodes of knowledge are accompanied by the sense of 'I know', even if it may not be present in an explicit form (e.g., there is a pot and I know the pot). It is insisted that this is an invariable condition of all knowing. The knowledge of the object is appropriated by the 'I', to which a full-fledged reference takes place in the reflexive act in which the subject can be dissociated from the object/content. The awareness of the object/content is intimately related to I-consciousness. These two aspects are woven together in their conception of 'Svasam-vedana'. Thus, the Yogacara Vijnanavadins, in tune with the general ethos of the Buddhist conceptual tradition that highlights the momentary character of all existence, perceives the ego as masking the fleeting character of alaya-vijnana by imposing on it an air of permanence and stability, which ultimately is no more than a construction.

The awareness of the category of the object is possible only with the arising of what is technically termed as 'pravrtti-vijnana'. It is not possible to go into the elaborate details of the theory here. Let it be noted that the idea of pravrtti-vijnana is developed with the view of showing that the category of the 'object' is self-contradictory. There are long discussions focusing not only on the problem of whole and parts but also why even the notion of whole and that of parts are both to be seen as subjective constructions. For the advocates of this school of absolute idealism, all these are projections of consciousness—due to the seeds present in alaya-vijnana—that make them appear as though these are outside of consciousness.

Anyway, as one takes an overall view of these diverse conceptual configurations of ideas that the Buddhist cognitive enterprise has brought about, one becomes aware of the subtle intricacies of the problem of I-consciousness in the context of the no-self view. One finds that although the abhidharmika tradition openly rejected atmavada, the issue in question was not seen as resolved either by the advocates of the Upanisadic or Jaina traditions. Consequently, debates continued. Moreover, what is particularly interesting is that philosophical disagreements ensued among the Buddhist thinkers themselves. A review of some of these disputes, to be discussed in what follows, shows how the interpretations of the various versions of the self as well as the no-self theories exerted a tremendous impact on the construal of epistemology, metaphysics, etc.

It is not difficult to imagine the challenge that the Buddhist ideas posed to the Upanisadic philosophical tradition, a tradition that championed the cause of the ontological reality of self. The various theoretical moves from rival camps provoked attacks and counter-attacks that resulted in centuries of lively debates. If there are criticisms that aim at demonstrating the inadequacies of the Buddhist theory of no-self in providing a coherent account of human experience, there are also records showing how the

Buddhist thinkers in turn defended their position, critically demonstrating the limitations inherent in the notion of an unchanging self. These exchanges constitute important chapters of Indian philosophical reflections on a range of issues, including the topic of I-consciousness.[13]

In order to appreciate these readings found in the literature of the different phases of the Buddhist conceptual history, it is indeed useful to be acquainted with the basic philosophical views proposed by the advocates of various schools that emerged within the Upanisadic tradition. The latter set a contrasting pattern and thereby put in relief the distinctness of the Buddhist conceptual models that appeared in course of time. Since the principal views on I-consciousness advocated by the Upanisadic thinkers have already been discussed in previous chapters, only a few brief observations may be made here. With the advent of Buddhism the idea of an unchanging and abiding self—in all its various versions—was severely criticized. The Upanisadic philosophers in turn counteracted these criticisms and launched attacks against the Buddhist notion of universal impermanence which is crucial for the propagation of the no-self view. While struggling to meet the objections that their opponents came up with, the Buddhist philosophers developed alternative explanatory models of the no-self view. In this connection, it is important to note that certain difficulties were felt by some Buddhist thinkers themselves in totally abandoning this notion of an unchanging, abiding self, to be discussed shortly. However, mainstream Buddhism regarded the idea of an immutable self to be logically incongruous, psychologically unessential, ethically and soteriologically as an impediment, and decried the idea of self as an unjustifiable postulation. It may be observed in this connection that if there are different versions of the no-self theories available within the Buddhist tradition, some pronounced differences can also be found among the advocates of different schools within the Upanisadic tradition regarding the interpretation of the notion of atman, although the core idea

13 See, Udayanacarya, 1940, *Atmatattvaviveka* (Varanasi: Chowkhamba Sanskrit Series Office).

of atman as abiding, unchanging, and ultimately free from the influence of time (*kalaprabhavamukta*) has always been defended.

Before concluding this chapter, it may be noted that the treatment of the question of I-consciousness acquires a novel dimension in the hands of the Buddhist philosophers. Since there is no atman in Buddhist philosophy that could be pointed to as the basis of the awareness of 'I', the conceptual move, unlike the Nyaya-Vaisesika accounts, leads up to a different explanatory model. It has been already noted that the idea of the individual as nothing else but an aggregate of momentary elements gradually becomes commonplace in the Buddhist philosophical context. The doctrine of *panca skandha* (the five aggregates) comes to exert a profound influence on subsequent Buddhist thought. Records are available that show how the Buddhist philosophers take the bold step to interpret mental life purely in terms of a process, where the chain of conscious moments are said to adhere to the law of dependent origination[14] which is the Buddhist version of the notion of causality. The well-known formula in which this law is expressed is: 'that being this is'.[15] In other words, no event is a haphazard, arbitrary occurrence but is necessarily dependent on some other factor. The Buddhist philosophers have repeatedly kept on arguing that it is needless—logically or psychologically—to postulate a permanent self as a substratum or as a unifying principle. The commonly held notion of the identical self as an ontological reality is elucidated as an erroneous belief. The sense of identity that is part and parcel of the experience of I-consciousness is accounted for as being due to the recurrence of similar conscious moments; the argument emphasizes that 'similarity' is mistakenly interpreted as 'identity'.

Again, one of the pertinent accounts is the way analysis of language has been undertaken. What is significant from the point of view of philosophy of language is the gradual emergence of the idea that the term 'self'/'soul' is a mere word that has no referent in reality. Further analysis lays bare that the 'I' is a conceptual construction (*vikalpa-pratyaya*). In reality, it is either one or a combination of the skandhas that is referred to as 'I'. Reference has

14 *Pratityasamutpada.*
15 *Asmin sati idam bhavati.*

been made above to the well-known dialogue between the monk Nagasena and king Milinda regarding how this philosophical insight is worked out with power and skill in support of the Buddhist denial of an abiding self. As a matter of fact, this kind of analysis is scattered throughout many texts, such as in *Samyutta Nikaya*, *Dhammapada*, etc. Indeed, there are many interesting details that various schools of Buddhism have worked out in their renditions while confirming this same reading. Mention must be made of the Sautrantika school, which rendered an invaluable service to the cause of the no-self theory. The Sautrantika philosophers provided a logical device for rejecting any claim to the ontological reality of any entity as permanent. Employing the idea of causal efficiency as the criterion of reality, the so-called permanent entity is shown to be fictitious. It has been demonstrated that whatever can be said to exist (i.e., which is not fictitious) is governed by the law of causation and is necessarily momentary in character. The idea of the permanent self meets with the same fate. According to these philosophers, time as instant and being as instantaneous are made to coincide ontologically, their so-called separation is attributed only to an arbitrary linguistic convention. This view at one stroke annuls any conceptual move that seeks to affirm a substance-view of reality.

In other words, the rejection of the idea of a non-temporal self as standing apart from the conscious states induces the setting up of alternative theories concerning I-consciousness. The impact of this paradigm on such areas as epistemology and psychology alone makes it an important subject for a careful and a critical study. Especially interesting are the later philosophical works dealing precisely with such issues as how phenomena like 'consciousness of consciousness', memory, as well as recognition can be accounted for on the Buddhist premise that repudiates the idea of a permanent self. There are many documents that directly deal with the objections raised by the opponents who doubted the possibility of ethical and soteriological ventures on the basis of the no-self theory. These issues reappear and are discussed throughout the different phases of the development of Buddhism.

The Buddhist philosophers were keenly aware of the *ethical* implications of the idea of 'anatman'. This question has been highlighted both in the early as well as in the later texts. Detachment from all sense of selfhood is seen as a very effective moral tool and as indispensable for cultivating an attitude that is favourable for achieving nirvana. The sense of I-ness, falsely assumed to be the core of selfhood, is perceived as the source of egoity (ahamkara) and as supportive of the sense of my-ness (*mamakara*), which creates serious obstacles for the pursuit of nirvana.

The story of centuries of exchanges is simply fascinating. On the one hand, the Upanisadic philosophers were fully aware that no conception of atman, in any of its accepted versions, was compatible with the Buddhist theory of momentariness (*ksanab-hangavada*). The vigorous attempts to repudiate the idea are well-known. There are fascinating documents related to these controversies that span over centuries.

On the other hand, the Buddhist philosophers, being convinced of their own logical acumen, were no less conscious of the challenges that the theory of ksanabhangavada offered to its opponents. Recall the sharp comment made by the respected Buddhist philosopher Kamalasila. In his well-known work *Tattva-samgraha Panjika*, one comes across a pointed remark that the Buddhists did not need to reject one by one the notions of such metaphysical entities (as substance, self, etc.) that are posited by their opponents; the idea that all entities disappear immediately after their appearance without leaving any trace[16] can alone demolish those views.

However, the centuries of debates and discussions have made one thing vividly clear, viz. that the rejection of the idea of an abiding self is no easy and simple intellectual enterprise. What is remarkable to note is that despite the stringencies of early formulations, the subsequent Buddhist philosophers themselves did not find it easy in the process of reflections to completely abandon the idea of self that serves as a unifying principle. It is fascinating to observe how the no-self theory in its radical Sautrantika version was actually challenged by some significant Buddhist philosophers. Indeed, for a deeper appreciation of the complexities of I-consciousness, it is essential to comprehend why philosophical differences arose

16 ahetuka-niranvaya-vinasa.

among the Buddhist philosophers with regard to the evaluation of the status of consciousness as well as of that of I-sense in both empirical and ontological contexts. The subtle problems ingrained in the wholesale abandonment of the idea of self were keenly felt not only outside of but also within the Buddhist philosophical circles and these are amply documented. Two important examples are discussed below in order to demonstrate how the adequacy of the skandha (aggregate) theory was questioned not only by the non-Buddhists but even by some notable philosophers within the Buddhist tradition itself. Discomfort was felt with regard to the skandha theory regarding the extent to which this theory could be said to legitimately replace the atman paradigm and yet account for a range of phenomena that were perceived to be unaccountable without the notion of an identical, abiding self. The Vatsiputriyas and the Madhyamika philosophers were aware of the weakness of the claim that an aggregate or a series of states (skandhas) could substitute the atman—a view that was widely propagated during the first phase of Buddhism.

In the *Abhidharmakosa* and *Kathavastu* we find reference to the Vatsiputriyas. Their theory called *pudgalavada* merits attention. *Pudgala* is the term used by the Vatsiputriyas for the principle of individuality. These thinkers were, on the one hand, keenly aware of the limitations of the skandha/aggregate theory and on the other hand, were reluctant to accept atmavada/self theory. In other words, they were seeking a compromising stand. They thought that simply to insist on the rejection of selfhood without the postulation of 'pudgala' is the same as falling into nihilism (*ucchedavada*) but then, they were equally convinced that if pudgala is taken as distinctly different from the aggregates, the theory could barely be distinguished from the atmavada of the opponents' view that was branded by the mainstream Buddhist thinkers as a form of eternalism (*sasvatavada*). In other words, the Vatsiputriyas were looking for a principle that could give a synthetic unity. They, therefore, conjured the idea of 'pudgal' as a quasi-permanent entity. It was conceived neither to be completely identical with the flow of mental states, nor to be entirely different from the latter. However, the mainstream interpreters of Buddhist thought vehemently criticized the idea since they held that such an entity as pudgala cannot be regarded as momentary. It was seen as a sort of a compromise with the atman theory which was considered to be untenable.

The critical observations offered by the Vatsiputriyas, nevertheless, deserve consideration. The idea of panca skandha or the five aggregates, into which the human personality was analysed during the first phase of Buddhist philosophy, was seen as questionable by the Vatsiputriyas. Their objection was that in the absence of any unifying principle the multiple states and psychical factors would be a chaotic situation. Thus, *pudgalavada* was an attempt to construe a theory that could do without the postulation of a permanent subject outside the aggregates and could be expected to do away with the difficulties that are inherent in a position that accepts the reality of the skandhas alone.

This notion of pudgala was invented not merely as a response to questions regarding the referent of the word 'I' or what forms the basis of I-consciousness but to explain phenomena that are integral to empirical experiences. Leaving out all other difficulties that are of concern while accounting for such everyday experiences as remembrance, recognition, etc., they also sensed that without the postulation of a quasi-permanent principle, which is neither different from nor identical with the mental states, there will remain acute problems even with regard to the possibility of a moral life or achievability of nirvana, as preached by the Master. It is noteworthy that the Vatsiputriyas refer even to the words of the Buddha himself in support of their theory and ask directly: If the aggregates were to be taken as the person, why then did the Buddha say that 'I shall teach, O monk, about the burden, acquisition of the burden, throwing away of the burden and what throws that burden away'? [17]

Vasubandhu, in support of the mainstream understanding of anatmavada, takes this issue up in the *Abhidharmakosa*. He clarifies the meaning of the 'burden' as that which causes suffering and the 'thrower of the burden' as the set of the aggregates that destroys the previous set. He further comments that by the 'thrower of the

17 cf. Bharahara sutra in *Abhidharmakosa and Bhasya of Vasubandhu with Sphutartha commentary by Acarya Yasomitra*, vols. 1–11, edited by Dwarikadas Shastri, Bauddha Bharati, Varanasi, 1971.

burden' is not implied anything 'eternal' as some say (referring to the eternalists), nor anything 'indefinable' (as the Vatsiputriyas hold). While insisting on the idea that a person is nominally/conceptually existent, as a class (meaning a collection of many elements or dharmas) or a flow (meaning a stream of physical and psychological aggregates which are constantly in flux), he claims that no postulation of a self is required nor is the notion of pudgala necessary. In other words, although 'pudgalavada' postulates no immutable substance underlying the changing states that could by any means be identified with any version of atmavada, the idea found no favour within the mainstream Buddhist fold. Various objections were raised by different Buddhist schools against this specific interpretation of the teachings of the Buddha. Some even outright labelled the Vatsiputriyas as pseudo-Buddhists. The extent to which the idea of pudgala can be considered as distinct from the aggregates, the notion was seen as un-Buddhist. The mainstream Buddhist philosophers opposed it mainly because the pudgala could not be categorically taken to be momentary in character—a position that was found to be entirely untenable.

Again, in the literature belonging to the middle phase of Indian Buddhism, one comes across a powerful critical analysis by the Madhyamika dialecticians, led by the famous philosopher Nagarjuna (AD 150). These dialecticians were even much more radical than the Vatsiputriyas in their review of the prevalent radical formulation of the no-self theory of the first phase. Their revolutionary interpretation reflects not only an acute awareness of what they saw to be the limitations of the atmavada tradition but also of the insuperable difficulties that beset the abhidharmika interpretation of the teaching of the Buddha. These dialecticians questioned and criticized the above-mentioned views as well as 'pudgalavada', the theory advocated by the Vatsiputriyas as a compromising stand. Thus, one comes across in the literature a thorough scrutiny of several self and no-self theories as well as of various views of time[18] that support such theories only in order to lay bare

0018 cf. *atma-pariksa* and *kala-pariksa* in P.L. Vaidya, ed., 1960, *The Madhyamakasastra of Nagarjuna*, with the Commentary Prasannapada by Candrakirti (Darbhanga: Mithila Institute of Postgraduate Studies).

their eventual untenability. The Madhyamika intention is to focus on the idea that ultimately the real is 'sunya', that is, free from all conceptual constructions.

It is interesting to notice that in the theory-making front, whereas the Vatsiputriyas insisted that the skandha could not be taken as a substitute for the atman, the Madhyamika philosophers hold that 'there are no states without the self, nor is there the self·without the states and therefore both are unreal, being relative'.[19] Both the views are seen as unhelpful and misleading since one takes the unchanging and the other the changing to be the real. The entire thrust of the Madhyamika philosophy is to seek disentanglement from all views. It is through a dialectical method that critically exposes the intrinsic limitations of all theories and highlights the idea of things as they are free from all standpoints (*bhuta-pratyaveksa*). Thus, the Madhyamika undertaking was not to attempt to weave one more theory but rather to show the ultimate real as emptiness (sunya) that cannot be captured by thought-categories. This they did with the help of reductio ad absurdum arguments (*prasangapadanam*), by bringing out the inner contradictions inherent in all views. In brief, these dialecticians were keenly aware of the fact that no matter whether the phenomenon of I-consciousness is theoretically accounted for in terms of either self- or no-self theories, these are all equally beset with difficulties and contradictions.

HUME, PARFIT, AND NOZICK

Given that early Buddhism is a forerunner of no-self theory, it marks a novel initiative and forms a prominent chapter in the documented history of global ideas dealing with the enquiry into the fundamental questions about consciousness and human personality. This is a theoretical stand that rejects thoroughly the

19 For a pointed summary of the elaborate analysis of the middle position as documented in the *Ratnakuta Sutra* (Kashyapaparivarta), cf. T.R.V. Murti, 1960, *The Central Philosophy of Buddhism* (London: George Allen and Unwin).

idea of an enduring, unchangeable, indivisible self underlying or standing apart from the stream of consciousness, which is widely assumed by many notable traditional thinkers across cultures. It is important to take note of the fact that since the advent of Buddhism this radical no-self idea has come to play a significant role in the sphere of consciousness-studies. This is a paradigm of which there are several interpretations in cross-cultural philosophical discourses. What is especially interesting while making such a review is the kind of arguments that are forwarded by the proponents of this no-self view and to observe their overlaps as well as the divergences. Indeed, diverse formulations that can be found within the Buddhist tradition itself of this no-self view have been already discussed earlier.

In the history of ideas in the West, this no-self theory—as a contrast to the theories of self advocated by many distinguished thinkers in the West as in India—has also come to assume several distinct renditions. In these diverse interpretations of the no-self view in Western thought one sees a determined attempt to reject the Cartesian view of an abiding, indivisible self. In fact, one comes across various elucidations in support of this reading especially in the writings of David Hume and his followers. Contemporary discussions that have drawn considerable attention in the area of consciousness studies in the West also exemplify in many ways a refutation of Descartes' view. In what follows, a few representative philosophical views will be alluded to that propagates this no-self stand. However, before attempting a brief review of some of the principal arguments offered in the philosophy of David Hume who has pioneered and championed this view in a full-fledged form in the history of Western philosophy, let us note that the two disparate ways of looking at reality—expressed in dynamic and static fashions—have been known both in ancient India and ancient Greece. Some have labelled these points of views as substance or modal views. The well-known Heraclitean reading that everything is in a state of flux opposed the Parmenidean static picture of reality in a similar fashion in which the Buddhist view contrasted with the Upanisadic notion of an unchanging and unchangeable reality. 'One cannot dip into the same river twice' (Heraclitus) or that 'what does not change does not exist' (Buddhist) are readings that know of significant metaphysical consequences. Indeed this dynamic view of reality when applied to consciousness studies can provide support in the direction of a denial of any identical self underlying the changing stream of consciousness, as has been previously noted in detail in the case of Buddhist thought.

Indeed, the anti-Cartesian stand takes on a radical form in the philosophy of Hume who was a devout empiricist. Hume critically questions the idea of self (or substance) that many philosophers find to be indubitable. In his well-known work entitled *A Treatise of Human Nature*, he observes directly that this idea of self like all ideas—in order to be 'clear and intelligible'—must be shown to be derived from some impression. Moreover he says as he continues to argue, that 'if any impression gives rise to the idea of self, that impression must continue invariably the same, through the whole course of our lives; since self is supposed to exist after that manner. But there is no impression which is 'constant and invariable'. He is therefore sceptical of this idea of self that some other philosophers seem to be so certain that it is considered to be 'beyond the evidence of a demonstration, both of its perfect identity and simplicity'. He asks 'from what impression can this idea be derived'? Hume does not find in introspection any such constant and invariable impression and consequently concludes that no such self can be said to exist.[20]

Indeed, it is not surprising that of all the 'no-ownership' theories that we are familiar with in the Western philosophical tradition, the one which has drawn most attention as a parallel to the Buddhist philosophical analysis is that of Hume. It is not without good reason that in several comparative works that draw on Buddhist thought, Hume's memorable rendering on the question of 'personal identity' in Book 1 of *A Treatise of Human Nature* has been cited over and over again. He writes: 'for my part, when I enter most intimately into what I call myself, I always stumble on some particular perception or other, of heat or cold, light or shade, love or hatred, pain or pleasure. I never can catch myself at any

---

20 David Hume, 2000, *A Treatise of Human Nature*, edited by D.F. Norton and Mary Norton (Oxford: Oxford University Press).

time without a perception, and never can observe anything but the perception'.[21]

Thus, unlike Locke who was also an empiricist, Hume leaves no room in his theory for an identical self which endures in and through change as Locke's concept of a person suggests. For Hume any ascription of identity—a self that remains unchangingly—is an idea which is due to the 'operation of imagination' and must therefore be held as fictitious. He goes on to 'affirm of the rest of mankind that they are nothing but a bundle or collection of different perceptions, which succeed each other with an inconceivable rapidity, and are in a perpetual flux and movement'.[22]

Hume's rejection of the substance-view is clearly expressed in his *An Enquiry Concerning Human Understanding*, in these words: 'as our idea of any body, a peach, for instance, is only that of a particular taste, color, figure, size, consistency etc., so our idea of any mind is only that of particular perceptions without the notion of anything we call substance, either simple or compound'.[23]

In a cross cultural philosophical study with regard to how identity of self is established, the analysis of the phenomenon of memory plays a crucial role in various discourses. Earlier it has been noted how the phenomena of memory and recognition have been scrutinized by the Vaisesika philosophers in order to demonstrate how the identity of self and object are discerned and how these mutually confirm the sameness that persists in each case. For Locke also, as has been discussed before,[24] the phenomena of memory and self-awareness mutually reinforce the discernment of identity. Hume, however, questions the account of memory that Locke forwarded in order to establish the identity of a person and says categorically that 'memory does not so much produce as discover personal identity by showing us the relation of cause and effect among our different perceptions'.[25] He emphasizes, however,

21 *Ibid.*

22 *Ibid.*

23 cf. Charles W. Hendel, ed., 1955, *Hume: An Enquiry Concerning Human Understanding* (New York: Pearson).

24 See Chapter 4.

25 Locke.

that 'memory alone acquaints us with the continuance and extent of this succession of perceptions, it is to be considered, upon that account chiefly, as the source of personal identity'.[26] He argues that without memory we will not have any notion of causation, nor consequently that chain of causes and effects, which constitute our self or person. It is by virtue of this that it is possible for us to extend our sense of identity even to a period about which there is no memory. So memory does not produce but discover personal identity. Thus, the ideas of resemblance and causation become explanatory tools accounting for what is passed as identity, be that of the self or of an object. It is an ascription of continued existence which is a fiction. A. J. Ayer explains that by 'fictitious' is meant that it is not a 'true' identity, that is 'the identity of a single unchanging object, but one that can be resolved into a relation between perceptions'.[27]

Being fearless of the implications of the religious doctrines of his time, Hume raised sharp questions regarding the enquiry into in what consists identity. Failing to find any impression that corresponds to the idea of identity, Hume explores how identity is attributed to impressions in empirical experience, indicating that although there is no invariableness, there may be close resemblance in a series of perceptions. Again, it is interesting to note that in the records of cross cultural philosophical analysis of personal identity, the questions of sleep and death invariably come in. Hume is aware of these issues and says:

> When my perceptions are removed for any time, as by sound sleep; so long am I insensible of myself, and may truly be said not to exist. And were all my perceptions remov'd by death, and cou'd I neither think, nor feel, nor see, nor love, nor hate after the dissolution of my body, I shou'd be entirely annihilated, nor do I conceive what is farther requisite to make me a perfect non-entity.[28]

Finally, one cannot avoid noticing the sceptical dimension of his reflections when he comes to the 'conclusion, which is of

---

26 *Ibid.*

27 A.J. Ayer, 2000, *Hume: A Very Short Introduction* (USA: Oxford University Press).

28 *Ibid.*

great importance in the present affair, viz. that all the nice and subtle questions concerning personal identity can never possibly be decided, and are to be regarded rather as grammatical than as philosophical difficulties'.[29] However, the impact of Hume's distrust in the substance-view—whether with regard to his analysis of an external thing or the mind—has been important for all subsequent Western philosophy, both in terms of obtaining further support or by way of challenging and rejecting his views. This can be seen in both phenomenological as well as analytical tradition, first in the writings of those who followed his insights and then by those who went against his analysis.

Hume is by no means a singular example among philosophers in the West who found the idea of an identical self untenable while struggling with the issue of identity across time or has found the question of self-awareness puzzling. Indeed, the idea of a permanent self has been questioned by several philosophers in recent times who, however, attempted to tread different paths which are not entirely in line with that of Hume. Some of them are aware of the difficulties that the 'bundle-theory' of the mind gives rise to.

Roderick M. Chisholm, for example, has carefully examined Hume's view and criticizes his bundle theory. He insists that our idea of a physical object or the mind is not an idea only of 'particular perceptions' as Hume suggested while negating the notion of substance. In his essay entitled, 'On the Observability of the Self', he summarizes his objections against Hume's view that a person is 'nothing but a bundle or collection of different perceptions'. He writes, 'one may ask, with respect to any bundle of things, what is the nature of the bundle and what is the nature of the bundled. What is it that holds the particular items together, and what are the particular items that are thus held together'? He concludes that 'the items within the bundle are nothing but the states of the person' and 'what ties these items together is the fact that that same self or person apprehends them all'.[30]

29 *Ibid.*

30 Roderick M. Chisholm, 1969, 'On the Observability of the Self', *Philosophy and Phenomenological Research*, Vol. 30, pp. 7–21.

There are also interesting criticisms by Indian philosophers of various forms of no-self theory. S. Bhattacharya, for example, writes:

> Hume himself admits that there are gaps between any two successive ideas. As there is nothing in the gaps, there cannot b any personal identity. Hume seems to be aware of this difficulty and tries to cover, not solve it, by his theory that 'the different perceptions...succeed each other with an inconceivable rapidity', for there will be nothing during the gaps to experience then.[31]

Among the philosophers who find the idea of an enduring, identical self to be unquestionably inadequate and thus approach the debate over the issue of personal identity quite differently from those who cherish the notion of self, notable is the view of Robert Nozick. It can be seen that thought experiments and a specific form of linguistic approach to the question of I are of crucial importance for thinkers who offer philosophical views as a rebuttal to the notion of an identical self. As such some of these philosophers do not question the usefulness or legitimacy of the pronoun in the first person singular number, notwithstanding the kind of metaphysical predicament the notion of an enduring self meets with at their hands. The distinctive features of their thought become evident when they are pressed for philosophical explanations with regard to specific issues. Nozick says that the Cartesian statement 'I think' is not satisfactory, at best Descartes can state that 'thinking is going on'. However, Nozick's view is different from Hume's theory of self as a 'bundle of perceptions'. Given that the idea of self enduring in time is not acceptable to him, he raises the question: 'if the self synthesizes itself at a time isn't it only a momentarily existing self? How then can we have identity over time'?[32] Nozick does not opt for a Humean solution but proposes 'the closest continuer theory of identity over time to specify how a whole may differ from the sum of its parts'.[33] However, this 'closest

31 Sibajiban Bhattacharya, 2001, 'The Emergence of the Person: Some Indian Themes and Theories', *Sandhana*, Vol. 1, No. 1.

32 Robert Nozick, 1981, *Philosophical Explanations* (Oxford: Clarendon).

33 *Ibid.*

continuer' theory entailing synthesis of acts has been criticized on various grounds. According to his critics this theory does not render a meaningful explanation of the self.

In his well-known book *Philosophical Explanations*, Nozick has presented his 'closest continuer' theory precisely in order to account for personal identity. He analyzes certain philosophical difficulties centring the question of I, which can be seen as part of the fabric of a linguistic approach to explore the idea of self. He seems to hold that the ability to say 'I' is a defining feature of the self. He also points out that the 'reflexively self referring' character of the indexical I entails features which are specifically different from other indexicals such as 'this', 'here', 'now', etc. This observation plays a significant part in Nozick's explanation of self creation. He takes the term 'I' as a linguistic device which, as he says, 'necessarily self-refers in virtue of a feature bestowed in the token act of referring'. However, he elaborates on the idea by further observing that

> from the fact that I have this property of being a self, it does not follow that the property is essential to my nature. Moreover, even though the capacity for reflexive self-reference is essential to being a self, and even though reflexive self-referring provides access of a self to itself, it does not follow that it is of my essence (though I am actually a self) to be a self.[34]

While holding the view that to lose the capacity for reflective self reference must imply a loss of self, Nozick makes room for an explanation of such cases as the state of sleep when this capacity is interrupted or in the case of a foetus, when such a capacity is yet to emerge. The fragility of personhood is evident with the loss of this capacity of reflective self reference which happens not only in death but also in the case of senility.

Again, a brief reference can be made to Derek Parfit (sometimes described as the Oxford Buddhist).[35] He has argued against the importance of personal identity, the idea of an identical self.

34 *Ibid.*
35 D. Parfit,1984, *Reasons and Persons* (Oxford: Oxford University Press).

He pursues the idea of no-self in his characteristic manner, although his mode of argumentations and the manner of persuasion is quite unlike the Buddhist philosophers. However, it is interesting to take note of why he thinks that the belief in personal identity is more harmful than helpful. This is a belief, he argues, in something that 'makes people assume that the principle of self-interest is more rationally compelling than any moral principle. And it makes them more depressed by the thought of aging and of death'. He thinks that if people can be 'freed of this presupposition...the question about identity has no importance'.[36]

In his book entitled *Reasons and Persons* he works out a distinction between qualitative and numerical identity with the view of demonstrating the pitfalls of 'what we believe ourselves to be'. This he does with the help of an imaginary case of what he calls 'teletransportation' where a scanner reproduces an exact replica of a person (Parfit). Parfit uses his science fiction like imaginary scenario where his replica is shown to be confusing Parfit's thoughts[37] to be his own and is really not aware of the 'continued existence of a separately existing subject of experiences'. From this, Parfit concludes that just as the replica is not aware of the psychological continuity between his life and Parfit's, similarly we are not aware that we are in the most part states of mind and not separately existing entities. He does this in order to persuade his readers to perceive that 'most of us have a false view about ourselves, and about our actual lives'. Despite the artificiality of such a conceptual scenario, the ingenuity of his analysis is expressed in the way in which he lays bare the standard construals of both the physical as well as the psychological criteria of personal identity with the help of such ideas as physical 'continuity over time' and the psychological experience of 'memory'. However, Parfit has by no means solved but has elaborated with considerable philosophical acuity the vexed question of personal identity. His is again another example of a philosophical attempt to adopt a strategy for showing why the notion of an abiding self needs to be abandoned. The questions of identity and continuity appear once again in his

36 *Ibid.*
37 For details, see his description ('snow is falling, so it must be cold', etc.)

writings as fundamental to this enquiry. He denies the Cartesian ego as an irreducible, indivisible, and enduring entity especially because there is no evidence that one self is not replaced by another since neither introspection nor a publicly detectable criterion of observability are applicable. Hence, he argues that there is no guarantee in support of the identity of a person through change. He tends to think that it is due to a false belief with regard to this identical self that 'most of us have a false belief about our actual lives' and he observes in a moral tone that 'if we come to see that this view is false, this may make a difference to our lives'. This stance has overlaps with the over-all reading of the Buddhist theory of no-self that has strong moral implications. As has been discussed earlier, the Buddhists argue that our attachment to the false belief of an identical self leads to various delusions by provoking self-interest, egoity, pride, etc. As often is the case with certain advocates of no-self theories, the practical moral tone is vibrant in the case of Parfit too. In his endeavour to deny the commonsense notion and the well-established philosophical view of a stable self, Parfit claims to show that identity is not what matters.

In any case, irrespective of the theoretical preference for the self- or the no-self view—a matter that is bound to remain controversial—the quest for a philosophical explanation for the phenomenon of I-consciousness can be expected to continue with the same zeal.

CHAPTER SEVEN

Some Conceptual Scenarios in Cross-cultural Context

It is evident from the preceding discussions that both in India and the West, the philosophical enterprise concerning the exploration of the theme of I-consciousness knows of a long history. This study makes it apparent that the explanatory models and analyses that have emerged in a given cultural setting may indeed be profitably scrutinized as well as evaluated in the light of another, thereby creating a larger and more comprehensive framework. It seems especially fruitful to engage in such a venture when notwithstanding the many distinctive differences in the various views, one also encounters concerns, queries, and approaches that sometimes bear striking resemblances at different levels of investigation with regard to this intricate phenomenon.

With the view of noting some of the overlaps in cross cultural philosophical thinking, the purpose of this chapter is two-fold:

(a) To highlight some aspects of the analyses offered by Edmund Husserl in the context of his elaboration of transcendental phenomenology and those by Madhusudana Sarasvati in support of the philosophy of Advaita Vedanta, especially with regard to the methodological devices that are employed and the structures of consciousness that are thereby disclosed, laying bare in the process the various levels of the constitution of I-consciousness.

(b) To focus on some striking parallels in the philosophical treatment of the question of self-awareness in Vijnanavada Buddhism and Sartrean existentialism. In other words, the conceptual scenarios that are delineated below with reference to actual texts from cross-cultural philosophical sources are interesting for reflecting on two major issues. One of these is pertinent for the question of construing various layers of subjectivity that are entailed in the constitution of I-consciousness, while the other is relevant for the topic of self-awareness or 'consciousness of consciousness'.

TRANSCENDENTAL PHENOMENOLOGY AND ADVAITA VEDANTA

It may be noted at the outset, that the Advaita philosophy of consciousness, despite whatever dissimilarity it may have with the transcendental constitutive phenomenology a la Husserl, has some important elements in common. These ideas, it seems to me, are to be grasped in a philosophical terrain dealing with transcendental problems. Unlike other systems, we find in the philosophy of Advaita Vedanta, metaphysics of consciousness which has abandoned, so to speak, 'the natural attitude'. Advaita philosophy of consciousness can hardly be categorized as a species of descriptive psychology.[1] Indeed, it is noteworthy that the philosophy of Advaita Vedanta, not unlike transcendental phenomenology, projects a conception of consciousness which is conspicuously different from those presupposed by traditional ontologies. This mode of philosophizations leads to the recovery of being-consciousness-bliss (*sat-cit-ananda*). This is a reading which has crucial bearing on Advaita philosophy as well as soteriology.

Within this philosophical frame, it is worth emphasizing that ultimately the idea of consciousness as foundational is disclosed not in *relation* to mundane realities of which the empirical ego is an example, it stands in that sense in contrast to all natural attitudes displayed in traditional ontologies. It is important to appreciate

1 Given that consciousness is a common subject-matter for both psychology and phenomenology, Gurwitsch observed that in psychology, consciousness 'is accepted as one reality among others and is studied in its dependence on extra-conscious data' in Aron Gurwitsch, 1974, in L. Embree (ed.), *Phenomenology and Theory of Science* (Evanston: Northwestern University Press).

that the Advaita understanding of the absolute and foundational character of consciousness, not unlike that of transcendental phenomenology, is a radical departure from the conceptions of consciousness that one encounters in the history of philosophy. Also, that none of these are examples of metaphysics of consciousness that are in consonance with the 'natural attitude' nor are these specimens of descriptive psychology. Note that Advaita philosophy is not committed to such traditional alternatives of either naïve realism as advocated by Nyaya or Mimamsa or subjective idealism as proposed by Vijnanavada Buddhism. Advaita does not side with Indian realism in maintaining that objects are entirely independent of consciousness and that consciousness only reveals what is given to it. It also does not side with the Indian idealists in propagating the view that consciousness projects its own forms, the so-called object being reducible to the latter. What needs to be perceived here is that the notion of '*vyavaharika*' or the empirical/ the conventional acquires a technical significance in the Advaita context. The Advaitic understanding of the I or ego-principle as being due to superimposition (*adhyasa*) is precisely both a subtle and a complex rendition that needs to be carefully looked at and it is in this specific context that I suggest that Husserlian analysis can throw light. However, prior to discussing this important issue, let me briefly outline a few significant steps of Husserl's phenomenological investigations.

The intricacy of the Husserlian phenomenological investigation concerning the 'I' or the ego becomes obvious as one notices the development of the theory discussed in his *Logical Investigations* (1900, 1901), *Ideas* (1913) and *Cartesian Meditations* (1931). In order to retrace the different stages of the complex egology, one has to notice that in his works there are levels of description which point to a gradual delimiting of the study of ego achieved by an employment of the methodological device technically called 'reduction'. As the theory of ego unfolds, there emerge such notions as the 'empirical ego', the 'phenomenological ego', the 'pure or polar ego', and the 'monad or transcendental ego'. The idea of 'empirical ego', as described in his *Logical Investigations*, is not very different from what is understood in ordinary discourse by a 'person' with his/her mind and body, having conscious agency.

Agency here is not understood as something in consciousness but simply as the person undergoing experiences. This ego, as he puts it, is a 'thing-like object and can be perceived' just as we perceive an external thing'.[2]

It is important to notice that, starting from this, the three successive steps of reduction that Husserl successfully employs are obtained by gradually bracketing the thesis of natural attitude concerning the question of ego.

The notion of 'phenomenological ego' in his *Logical Investigations* is arrived at by means of a reduction that entails a process of abstraction by turning away from various external objects with which consciousness is ordinarily occupied. However, this is still in the natural–psychological domain and not yet the 'transcendental reduction' of *Ideas*. The ego that is encountered at this level, even if its focus is on inner experience, is nothing unfamiliar; it is the psychologically functioning ego. At this point phenomenological psychology is not that much remote from the empirical psychology operating with naturalistic assumptions about the ego. 'The phenomenologically reduced ego', Husserl observes, 'is nothing peculiar, floating above many experiences; it is simply identical with their interconnected unity'.[3] Many have noticed that this reading is not dissimilar to that of David Hume. Husserl explicitly states that he was unable to find any pure ego enduring as a 'center of relations' or as a transcendental subject. It is probable that in his understanding of the 'interconnectedness' which accounts for the unity of consciousness Husserl was influenced by Brentano's idea of 'primordial association'. He found it unnecessary to postulate a transcendental ego above or behind the conscious processes since the contents of consciousness have 'the law-bound ways of coming together, losing themselves in comprehensive unities'.[4] This itself constitutes the phenomenological ego or unity of consciousness without the need of any additional ego. In any case, what needs

---

2 E. Husserl, 1970, *Logical Investigations*, trans. J.N. Findlay (New York: Humanities Press).

3 *Ibid.*

4 *Ibid.*

to be noted is that Husserl at this stage rejected the notion of an ego-principle 'which supports all contents and unities'.

This position, however, underwent serious revision in his *Ideas*. It is here that the second step of the reduction is employed. Technically called the transcendental reduction, it suspends all empirical or naturalistic assumptions. If the first reduction achieved a rudimentary phenomenology, not totally demarcated from psychology, the second reduction attains what is called 'pure phenomenology'. Now Husserl admits a 'pure ego' as 'necessary and plainly indubitable'. The transcendental reduction could not suspend it, since it is found as given together with all the processes of consciousness. The epoche brackets the empirical elements, enabling one to focus exclusively on the transcendental elements of consciousness. A clear distinction thus emerges between the empirical and the transcendental ego. It now remains to understand what purpose this ego serves and in what sense it cannot be repudiated as a 'corrupt form of ego-metaphysics' which Husserl so consciously sought to avoid in his *Logical Investigations*. It is possible that Husserl was led to this because of his increasingly deep involvement with the analysis of time-consciousness. In any case, with the introduction of transcendental reduction in *Ideas*, a radically different picture emerges. The empirical ego and the phenomenological ego are now seen as intentional objects, as unities that are results of intentional constitution and 'over and beyond this nothing at all'. The idea of a pure ego that phenomenological inspection now reveals is 'neither experience nor a process', but 'the active and affected subject of consciousness'. Husserl describes it in his *Cartesian Meditations* as that which 'lives in all processes of consciousness and is related through them to all object poles'.[5] This is a description of the ego in its transcendental aspect, which does not involve any ontological commitment.

The third and final step is the eidetic reduction which aims at disclosing universal, a priori, necessary structures in the domain where this reduction is carried out. For an investigation into the nature of ego this implies the possibility for 'a study of those

5 E. Husserl, 1960, *Cartesian Meditations*, trans. D. Cairns (The Hague: Martin Nijhoff).

transcendental features of the ego and its acts that are universal and necessary'.[6] The eidos ego is the universal structure of any ego whatsoever. This structure would include (a) the mere subject pole of all intentional acts, (b) the genesis of an ego, i.e., an account of how an ego's life unfolds, and (c) the general form of time in which all experiences of an ego come together as one compossible world.

A clearer picture of Husserlian egology appears as one further considers the *Cartesian Meditations*. In the fourth meditation, the problem of the self-constitution of the ego is dealt with. The following is a brief summary of the principal ideas. Under the section 'the ego as the identical pole of subjective processes',[7] it is observed that the ego not only experiences itself as a flow of mental life but also as 'I'. The 'I' who lives that mental life and the 'I' whom I experience as myself are the same. The mental acts are unified not merely objectively, i.e., as directed to one and the same object, but also as belonging to an identical ego. The ego is the active and passive subject of consciousness.

Recall that in the section entitled, 'the ego as the substrate of habitualities', it is stated that the ego is not merely an empty pole of identity. Every intentional act which I perform generates in me a new property which lasts until it is cancelled. Every decision that I take, every belief that I acquire, leaves in me a corresponding property, which itself, however, is not a temporal process. In this manner the ego continuously constitutes itself as a personal ego with a relatively abiding style known as its personal character.

Husserl distinguishes the ego taken in its full concreteness from both the above conceptions of the ego and calls it the monad. As a monad the ego includes not only its flowing intentional life, but also the objects meant in that life. Thus the ego sets up its surrounding world consisting first of those objects with which it is acquainted and then of those which it anticipates as possible objects of acquaintance. Each of these conceptions of ego may be understood either as an empirical or as a transcendental concept—empirical if understood independently of the transcendental epoche, and transcendental if all the concepts involved are understood in the

6 *Ibid.*
7 *Ibid.*

context of the epoche. Thus, one arrives at the profound thesis that the empirical and the transcendental are not two numerically distinct entities, but rather one and the same entity regarded from two standpoints. Husserl is aware that this would give rise to such questions as: is the transcendental ego born and does it die?[8] Furthermore, there arises also the question: if every empirical predicate has a transcendental counterpart, can one ascribe gender predicates, e.g., 'male' or 'female' to a transcendental ego?

I will not further explore this line of thinking here. The main point of this discussion is to emphasize how a philosophical stance can seek to avoid metaphysics of the natural standpoint while creating its own theory and to look at the Husserlian explanation as well as the accounts that Advaita Vedanta presents as examples.

Indeed, in the philosophy of Advaita Vedanta consciousness is gradually disclosed to be the absolute ground whereas the world along with it all that is worldly, including the ego, is seen as superimposed (*adhyastha*), even as false (*mithya*). However, a phenomenological approach to the philosophical reading as projected in Advaita Vedanta, needs to emphasize that '*mithyatva*' (falsity) is very much a technical term, which is used in the Advaita description of the object or the objective on the empirical/conventional level and is not to be taken as an evaluation or as a judgement using the criterion of the natural attitude. Similarly, although the word '*sat*' (being) is used in connection with '*cit*' (consciousness), the Advaita position must not be confused with any form of metaphysic of consciousness in any naïve sense but has to be understood in the light of the fundamental Advaitic philosophical motivation seeking, in the long run, to lay bare the foundational consciousness as non-dual.

Now let us refer to an important text in order to depict how the various steps of superimpositions (adhyasa) which, according to the Advaita Vedanta, manifests in the constitution of I-consciousness. In Brahmananda's commentary on Madhusudana Sarasvati's significant work entitled *Siddhantabindu*, one comes across an insightful description showing the two important stages of superimposition that are pre-empirical, apriori and a condition

---

for the possibility of mundane experience. I-ness (*ahamkara*) is recognized as a principle to which no beginning can really be ascribed. However, it is said to be superimposed on 'primal ignorance' (*ajnana*), depicted as beginninglessly (*anadi adhyasa*) masking/covering the underlying ontological reality which is pure consciousness (cit), which is further identified as being (sat) and bliss (ananda). The absolute and foundational character of consciousness is thus conveyed as generally unknown (but not as unknowable). This precisely indicates why the notion of nescience (*avidya*) plays an important role in the philosophy of Advaita Vedanta, which makes room for what is metaphorically described in the Upanisads as a journey 'from darkness to light'.

Note that I-ness is explained in the text as the first of a series of 'finite superimpositions' (*sadi adhyasa*), which is followed by a whole series of adhyasa or superimposition. These latter show step by step the constitution and extension of I-ness in its psychological, corporeal, and social layers of subjectivity. All such psychological processes as desire, resolution, etc. (*kamasamkalpadi*) are seen as attributes of the ego/*antahkarana*—implying that these cannot take place unless the subjective pole is *already* there characterizing consciousness, i.e., unless consciousness is qualified by I-ness (ahamkara). Likewise, the attributes of the sense-organs (*indriyadharmani*) are also appropriated by the ego. This kind of *adhyasa* gives rise to such cognitions as 'I am blind', 'I am sighted', or 'I am deaf'. There is, however, no direct superimposition of the sense-organs on the ego, hence no such cognitions as 'I am the eye' or 'I am the ear'. Next in order is the appropriation of the properties of the gross body by the ego as expressed in such statements as 'I am fat', 'I am thin', etc. Besides, note that there is no such cognition as 'I am the body', but rather as 'I am human'—'being human' is in part a corporeal attribute. From this one may pass on to a series of *adhyasa* accounting for the constitution of the sense of 'mine' (what is called the '*mama-adhyasa*'). The ego now gradually appears in its social context, adding dimensions that extend its reach over a son (*putra*) and property (*vitta*). The order of the various levels of constitution of the ego is said to be manifest in the degree of closeness that each adhyasa has to the sense of 'I', accounting for the subtle differences of love and attachment (*prema-taratamya*) that one has for them. This claim is to vindicate the idea that 'pure consciousness alone is onto-logically real, all the rest are mere ascriptions (*upacara*). In other words, transcendental consciousness appears as 'human' (*jiva*), there are various stages of the constitution, at the root of which is the principle of nescience (*avidya*)'.[9]

Let me conclude this suggesting that a collaborative work by those who know the original texts in the phenomenological as well as the Vedantic tradition can, very likely, further enhance our understanding regarding the idea of the constitution of the 'I', highlighting this remarkable mode of philosophization where various levels of subjectivity become gradually transparent.

SELF-AWARENESS IN BUDDHISM AND EXISTENTIALISM

One of the challenging questions that any philosophical study of the large theme of consciousness has to deal with is how to account for the phenomenon of 'consciousness of consciousness' or self-awareness[10] A cross-cultural philosophical investigation discloses that in the history of Western philosophy, as it also has been in the case of Indian philosophy, there have been several attempts at theory-making in this regard. Indeed, this theme of self-awareness is so central to an exploration of the phenomenon of I-consciousness that a comprehensive study of the wide range of views on this topic could itself be a major undertaking in a cross-cultural philosophical context. Note that while engaging in such a venture, one can unexpectedly stumble upon striking parallels in the theory-making task with regard to this theme. In order to demonstrate a case where such overlaps are discernible, I will, on the one hand, refer to the treatment of the issue of self-awareness as recorded

9 cf. my paper, 1992, 'Analysis of I-Consciousness in the Transcendental Phenomenology and Indian Philosophy', in D.P. Chattopadhyaya, Lester Embree, and J.H. Mohanty (eds), *Phenomenology and Indian Philosophy* (New Delhi: Indian Council of Philosophical Research).

10 See my essay, 2010, *New Perspectives on Sartre*, Adrian Mirvish and Adrian van den Hoven (eds) (Newcastle: Cambridge Scholars Publishing).

in the literature of Yogacara Vijnanavada, a well-known school of Buddhism and, on the other hand, to Jean Paul Sartre's existential-istic philosophical account concerning this phenomenon. Despite the differences in the overall concerns in these specific philoso-phies which developed in pronouncedly dissimilar historical and cultural settings, these discourses bear witness to remarkable simi-larities in the theorizing endeavours with regard to the theme of 'consciousness of consciousness' that often go unnoticed.[11]

While recapitulating the salient ideas that are relevant in this connection, let me mention at the outset that the intention here is by no means to situate or evaluate Vijnanavada Buddhism or Sartrean existentialism in the framework of their respective philo-sophical traditions or to defend either of the two. The aim of this cross-cultural review is to focus on the steps in their respective argumentations in the venture of making theories about this phe-nomenon of self-awareness. Given that in both cases the episte-mological scenario is drawn against the metaphysical background where no notion of a stable self is advocated, note that these are exemplifications of different versions of a 'no-ownership theory of consciousness'—to borrow a phrase from Strawson.[12]

These theories of self-awareness are particularly interesting on the background of their philosophical conceptualizations which entail a thorough rejection of the idea of self as a spiritual/mental substance that has been claimed by some philosophers to be cru-cial for providing unity to consciousness. Abandoning in common a substance-view of self necessitates in the case of Vijnanavada to discard the classical stance of atmavada as advocated by the Nyaya-Mimamsa traditions and for Sartre to go against the Cartesian. Both, as will be seen in what follows, nevertheless attempt to account for the phenomenon of self-awareness with much philosophical ingenuity that knows of strikingly parallel strategies. However, it is of significance that although the investigations of the issue of

11 For a more comprehensive study, see my PhD thesis, 1968, 'Une Etude Comparee de Quelque themes Philosophique Proposees par le Bouddhisme et' Existentialisme' (University of Paris).

12 P.F. Strawson, 1959, *Individuals: An Essay in Descriptive Metaphysics* (London: Methuen).

self-awareness in both cases are carried out with reference to a philosophical premise where an egological structure of conscious-ness is discarded, it is still a matter for separate consideration whether there are deeper implications of such a position that touch upon other dimensions (e.g., moral and/or soteriological) of the human situation that can be read differently in each case.

As has been mentioned earlier, the idea of an abiding self received a severe challenge in the Indian philosophical context with the advent of Buddhism. Buddhism, it is important to recall, is not the name of a single but a matrix of systems. Despite the inter-nal divergences among the different schools of Indian Buddhism, nonetheless a fundamental characteristic of this Anatmavada tradition is its contention that the idea of an unchanging, abiding self is logically absurd, psychologically superfluous, ethically, and soteriological even a hindrance.[13] Indeed, it is with the help of the idea of 'causal efficacy' as a criterion, that distinguishes the real from the fictitious, that the Buddhist logicians demonstrated—as has been elaborated in Chapter 6—why all that is real must be of momentary character.[14] This argument holds true also in the case of consciousness. Thus, there is no room for any notion of an unchanging, persisting ego/self in the chain of the transitory, momentary conscious states.

It may be recapitulated here that already in an early phase in the development of Buddhist thought, the idea that the individual is nothing but an aggregate of momentary elements was common-place.[15] It has already been discussed before that the Buddhists came to interpret mental life in terms of a process, where the chain of conscious moments follow each other not arbitrarily but in accor-dance with the law of dependent origination (*pratityasamutpada*,

---

13 T.R.V. Murti, 1955, *The Central Philosophy of Buddhism* (London: Allen & Unwin).

14 For more, see Chapter 7 in this volume.

15 Milinda-Panha, 1923, *Les Question de Milinda*, trans. from Pali by Louis Finot (Paris-Bossard). Recall the brilliant conversation between the monk Nagasena and King Milinda and how the Buddhist argues that neither within the bodily nor mental phenomena can be found anything that in the ultimate sense can be regarded as a self-reliant ego.

formulated as 'that being, this is'). This reading, according to which no self can be said to inhabit in or stand behind consciousness, not only led to prolonged controversies with all those for whom the notion of atman or self was of fundamental importance but also made the issue of self-awareness a crucial one for the Buddhists.

Without further elaboration on this brief recapitulation of the Buddhist idea of *anatman* or no-self, let me focus on how the theme of self-awareness comes to occupy an important place in the philosophy of Yogacara Vijnanavada, regarded as the most influential school of the last phase of Indian Buddhism. The principal advocates of this school, like Vasubandhu,[16] Santaraksita, Kamalasila, and others had all attempted an elaborate study of consciousness. Evidently the Vijnanavadins, being upholders of the no-self theory, could not support the idea that a 'consciousness of something' is revealed to an abiding self as a theoretical explanatory option that was considered epistemologically possible and viable in the case of some non-Buddhist theoretical frameworks, such as by the Naiyayikas who accepted the ontological reality of self. Nor, could the Vijnanavadins propound a view that a 'consciousness of something' becomes aware of itself only in a *subsequent* moment for philosophical reasons that will be discussed shortly. However, for the purpose of this specific cross-cultural study let me first turn to the philosophical stand on this question as advocated by J.P. Sartre and then return to the view proposed by the Vijnanavadin Buddhists.

The aim of Sartre's first philosophical work, entitled *The Transcendence of the Ego*[17] is to show that, as he has himself put it, 'the ego is neither formally nor materially in consciousness'. In his major philosophical work, *Being and Nothingness*,[18] Sartre has

16 Vasubandhu, 1932[1925], *Vijnaptimatratasiddhi, Vimsatika et Trimsika*, Pub. et trad. par S. Levi, I. Text sanskrit, (Paris: Materiaux pour l'etude de systeme Vijnaptimatrata).

17 J.P. Sartre, 1988, *The Transcendence of the Ego: An Existentialist Theory of Consciousness* [1966], trans. Forrest Williams and Robert Kirkpatrick (New York: Farrar, Strauss, and Giroux).

18 J.P. Sartre, 1956, *Being and Nothingness: A Phenomenological Essay on Ontology* [1943], trans. Hazel Barnes (New York: Philosophical Library).

maintained this same stand without any essential modification. To recount briefly, Sartre, in *The Transcendence of the Ego*, attacks the Husserlian idea of 'the transcendental ego' as well as the primacy of the Cartesian cogito. It is important to examine on what grounds Sartre rejects these notions and how he advances his own idea of consciousness as 'being-for-itself' (*pour-soi*) and as 'nothingness' (*neant*). The idea of intentionality of consciousness (i.e., all consciousness is consciousness of something) that Sartre adopted following Husserl led him to hold an altogether different view than what Husserl advocated concerning the ego. Sartre maintains that an application of the phenomenological method to the analysis of consciousness does not lead to the disclosure of any such 'transcendental ego', as Husserl claims. In fact, an affirmation of the transcendental ego is seen by Sartre as a betrayal of the initial claim of phenomenology. With the help of the concept of intentionality, Sartre shows that consciousness has no contents of its own. It is precisely for this reason that consciousness is described by him emphatically as 'nothingness'. This is why he says, that to accept an 'I' as a necessary structure of consciousness is to deprive consciousness of 'that character which rendered it—absolute existence by virtue of non-existence'.[19]

Thus for Sartre, the intentionality of consciousness necessarily implies that consciousness is transparent and is pure spontaneity. The two important ideas that emerge here follow from Sartre's understanding of this central idea of intentionality. Firstly, the idea that to admit of an 'opaque I' is to deprive consciousness of its translucent, transparent character, since—in accordance with this theory—all contents are expelled from consciousness; secondly, the idea that a consciousness of something entails consciousness (of) consciousness. Both these ideas are crucially important and will be further elaborated in what follows.

Husserl accepted the transcendental ego as a principle of unification, constitution, and meaning, whereas he rejected the psychological ego in the process of phenomenological reduction. For Sartre, the very notion of the transcendental ego is superfluous

---

19 Sartre, *The Transcendence of the Ego*. Note here how the terms self, ego, and I are used interchangeably.

and cannot be justified. Moreover, he insists, that the admission of the transcendental ego leads to the idea that consciousness has contents. Consequently, such a contention would deprive consciousness of all that is absolutely essential for it from the phenomenological standpoint, viz. intentionality and transparency. It is for this reason that Sartre maintains that if 'the I' is not an *object* for consciousness, then 'all the results of phenomenology begin to crumble'.[20]

In the same essay, Sartre also rejects the premise of the Cartesian ego. He points out that Descartes is actually dealing with a secondary activity when he states 'I think, therefore I am'. For Sartre, the consciousness which thinks has no 'I' in it; 'I' or the ego appears only on the reflective level. It may be observed in this connection that Sartre actually offers a two-level theory of consciousness—pre-reflective and reflective level. Note that the core of his argument against Descartes consists in maintaining that Descartes confuses these two levels. According to Sartre, the doubting consciousness belongs to the pre-reflective consciousness whereas the cogito appears in reflection, which posits the doubting consciousness as its object. Sartre's view is that the pre-reflective cogito as a primary consciousness is the foundation of the Cartesian cogito. From this it is evident that Sartre denies the notion of ego as a substantial entity or as an agent that 'owns' consciousness. Thus, for Sartre the pre-reflective level of consciousness is impersonal, there is no ego in it. Ego is constituted only in reflection. From this network of ideas, it follows that the ego is a *construct of reflection*. In other words, the ego exists for consciousness; there is consciousness of ego but no ego in consciousness since an ego in consciousness would have been a centre of opacity in consciousness.

The consequences that follow from the denial of a transcendental ego and that of the premise of the Cartesian cogito are of great philosophical importance. Firstly, his reading leads to the recovery of the primary transparency of consciousness; the ego has no privileged status since like everything else it is just as much an object for consciousness. Sartre first seemed to have thought

20 *Ibid.*

that only such an analysis of consciousness, as he claimed in his *The Transcendence of the Ego*, makes refutation of solipsism possible. However, later he found this explanation not to be adequate and again took up the question in his *Being and Nothingness*, while discussing the issue of the existence of others—a matter into which I cannot delve here.

From the above exposition it is now possible to delineate some of the major fundamental points of agreement between the Vijnanavadin Buddhists and Sartre. Both deny the ego to be an essential structure of consciousness and maintain that consciousness is basically impersonal. In this connection, it is particularly significant to note that a denial of an egological structure of consciousness does not mean, as Hazel Barnes has observed in her introduction to the translation of *Being and Nothingness*, that 'consciousness is general, a universal pan-psyche'. She further points out very aptly,

> a consciousness is even at the start particular, for the objects of which it is conscious are particular objects, and not the whole universe. Thus the consciousnesses of two persons are always individual and always self-consciousness, but to be individual and to be self-conscious does not mean to be personal. Another way of putting it is to say that the Ego is 'on the side of the psychic'...Consciousness determines the state, and the states constitute the Ego'.[21]

We shall go into further details of this question in the section below on self-consciousness.

In accordance with their conception of consciousness as being basically impersonal, both the Vijnanavadins and Sartre consider the ego to be a construct. Naturally the question that poses itself at this point is that if the ego cannot be said to constitute an essential structure of consciousness, how does it arise at all?

For the Buddhists, the claim of the fundamental impersonality of consciousness implies the absence of ego. This is brought out very clearly in their exposition of the theory of anatman, which has been discussed before in the chapter on Buddhism. For the Vijnanavadins, to say that the ego is a construct simply implies

---

21 Hazel Barnes, 'Introduction', in Sartre, *Being and Nothingness*.

that it has no ontological reality. Ego is a fiction. Lest there arises any misunderstanding about the Buddhist position, Stcherbatsky emphasized that 'Buddhism never denied the existence of a personality...in the empirical sense, it only maintained that it was not the ultimate reality (not a Dharma)'.[22]

It is evident that the notion of an unchanging, abiding self/ego in the sense of there being a substantial entity of spiritual nature, will of course be an antipode, a literal contradiction to the modal view that the Buddhist metaphysics continuously highlight, despite all their internal differences. In consonance with that paradigm, the Vijnanavadins maintain that the ego arises because of *Avidya*, i.e., nescience—a technical term indicating ignorance par excellence, which is pre-empirical. This is an idea that plays a significant role in the Buddhist soteriology. Philosophically speaking, it may be said, that they were pioneers and at an early date advanced a Humean[23] explanation for the arising of the ego, proposing that this seemingly permanent element in the midst of a changing stream of consciousness is due to the *similarity* of the conscious units that gives rise to the *illusion of identity* (*atisadrsatadatmabhrama*).[24]

Sartre discusses this question in detail in his work, *The Transcendence of the Ego* in the section, entitled 'The Constitution of Ego'. For him, 'the ego is a transcendent pole of synthetic unity, like the object-pole of the unreflected attitude, except that this pole appears solely in the world of reflection'. This signifies that the ego is intended by consciousness, like all other objects. It is,

22 F. Stcherbatsky, 1962, *Buddhist Logic*, vol.1 (New York, Dover Publications).

23 David Hume, 1978, *A Treatise of Human Nature*, ed. J.A. Selby-Bigge (Oxford: Oxford University Press; New York: Clarendon Press). Hume says: 'The passage of thought from the object before the change to the object after it, is so smooth and easy, that we scarce perceive the transition, and are apt to imagine, that 'tis nothing but a continu'd survey of the same object' p. 256.

24 S. Radhakrishnan, 1962, *Indian Philosophy*, vols 1 and 2 (London: George Allen & Unwin).

however, important to notice that consciousness intuits it in a special manner. The crucial point that Sartre makes in this connection is that the ego cannot be intuited either apodictically or adequately. He further argues that the ego, despite the fact that it has a dubious character, is not hypothetical (No one says 'perhaps I have an ego'). Thus for Sartre, the 'I' is not a hypothesis but as he says quite clearly 'the ego is the spontaneous, transcendental unification to/of our states and actions. In this capacity it is not hypothesis'.[25]

However, a critical question that may be raised here is how clear is really the status of the ego in the frame of this analysis? For Sartre, as has been noted before, the pre-reflective level of consciousness is impersonal. The ego appears only in the reflective level but for that reason it is not by any means illusory. However, for the Vijnanavadins to say that the ego is a construct implies that it has no ontological status. They would not hesitate to go so far as to call it a fiction. It may be observed here that in the case of Sartre it is not really clear in what sense both the pre-reflective and the reflective level can be said to have the same order of ontological reality, since for him the former is impersonal and the latter personal.

A review of the main ideas can now be attempted. Given that in both the philosophies consciousness is basically held to be impersonal, that is, not owned by any agent, this implies that for both the 'I' is a construct, although they differ with regard to the status of the 'I' and how it arises or is constituted. It is of great interest to observe, especially with reference to the issue of self-awareness, that the common assumption of a non-egological structure of consciousness immediately leads to the query how then consciousness becomes aware of itself, a challenge which is central to both. Let me first summarize the accounts that are given in each case.

In his work *Being and Nothingness*, Sartre discusses this issue with much ingenuity. For Sartre, intentionality is the defining character of consciousness. In other words, all consciousness is

25 Sartre, *The Transcendence of the Ego.*

consciousness of something. As has been noted previously, an immediate consequence of the idea of intentionality of consciousness—according to Sartre—is that consciousness is devoid of all contents and it directs itself towards an 'other' by transcending itself. Another very important implication of the notion of intentionality that he makes explicit is that 'the necessary and sufficient condition for a knowing consciousness to be knowledge of itself is that it be conscious of itself as being that knowledge'.[26] This, in brief, contains the essential idea pertaining to Sartre's account of how consciousness knows itself.

Besides, Sartre further points out in the same text that knowledge would be impossible if consciousness were not aware of itself. It is not possible for me to be conscious of the table if 'my consciousness were not conscious of being consciousness of the table'. Thus for Sartre 'every positional consciousness of an object is at the same time a non-positional consciousness of itself'. This is what Sartre expresses by saying that consciousness of something is consciousness (of) consciousness. If that were not the case, this would mean that consciousness of an object is not conscious of being so. Moreover, as Sartre argues, a consciousness that is not conscious of itself, that is, a consciousness ignorant of itself is an absurdity. To say that consciousness is transparent implies that it is present to itself, although the only mode of existence that is possible for consciousness is to be conscious of something. For Sartre, as he puts it in his *The Transcendence of the Ego*, 'to be and to be aware of itself are one and the same thing for consciousness'.[27]

It is important to emphasize that the subject-object dualism, which is so typical of the knowledge situation, does not hold good of consciousness knowing itself. On the pre-reflective level, while consciousness posits its object, it is aware of itself in the non-positional mode. This means that consciousness does not posit itself as its own object. There is no subject–object dualism to be found here. If that were the case, it would mean that another consciousness would be required to make consciousness known to itself and thus one cannot avoid the fallacy of infinite regress.

---

26 Sartre, *Being and Nothingness*.
27 Sartre, *The Transcendence of the Ego*.

Sartre expresses these ideas vividly in the introduction of *Being and Nothingness*:

> The reduction of consciousness to knowledge in fact involves our introducing into consciousness the subject-object dualism which is typical of knowledge. But if we accept the law of the knower-known dyad, then a third term will be necessary in order for the knower to become known in turn, and we will be faced with this dilemma: Either we stop at any one term of the series – the known, the knower known, the knower known by the knower, etc. In this case the totality of the phenomenon falls into the unknown; that is, we always bump up against a non-self-conscious reflection and a final term. Or else we affirm the necessity of an infinite regress...which is absurd.[28]

Hence, it is argued that all reflection presupposes this non-dual awareness on the part of consciousness. On the reflective level, however, consciousness turns back upon itself and posits itself as its object. In other words, consciousness becomes conscious of itself in the positional mode. The reflective operation, for Sartre, is an operation of the second degree—a consciousness directed upon consciousness, a consciousness that takes consciousness (of something) as an object. On the pre-reflective level, Sartre emphasizes, 'consciousness of consciousness is not positional; it is because it *is one with the* consciousness of which it is consciousness'.[29] There is an indissoluble unity between the two, as it is not possible for the reflecting consciousness to exist without the reflected one. Thus, in reflection, consciousness is conscious

---

28 Trans. Hazel Barnes, 1956, cf. section liv, 'The Pursuit of Being'. The original in French in '*L'Etre et le Neant*' is as follows:

> *La reduction de la conscience a la connaissance, en effet, implique qu'on introduit dans la conscience la dualite sujet-objet, qui est typique de la connaissance. Mais si nous acceptons la loi du couple connaissant-connu, un troisieme terme sera necessaire pour que le connaissant devienne connu a son tour et nous serons place devant ce dilemme: ou nous arreter a un terme quelconque de la serie: connu-connaissant connu—connaissant connu du connaissant, etc. Alors c'est la totalite du phenomene qui tombe dans l'inconnu c'est-a-dire que nous butons toujours contre une reflexion non-consciente de soi et terme dernier—ou bien nous affirmons la necessite d'une regression a l'infini..., ce qui est absurde.*

29 Sartre, *Being and Nothingness*.

of itself, whereas on the pre-reflective level there is consciousness *of* object. It is in this way that Sartre shows that consciousness knows itself only as absolute inwardness and that it is not necessary to introduce the dichotomy of subject–object to explain that 'consciousness has no need at all of a reflecting consciousness in order to be conscious of itself'.[30]

Let us now turn to the analysis offered by the Vijnanavadins. They maintain that consciousness' awareness of itself is not a judgemental knowledge. In other words, for consciousness to know itself it is not necessary that there be any subject–object dualism. Consciousness does not know itself as an external object, as consciousness is not an 'other' to itself. This is precisely what is expressed in the well-known statement—'It reveals itself, being free from the subject-object dualism'.[31] Consciousness of consciousness does not involve any duality. It is not a relation between two terms. It is not a discursive knowledge. The Vijnanavadins compare consciousness with light. As light reveals and is self-revealing, so is consciousness. 'Consciousness does not require any other consciousness to make itself known'.[32] The cognized object and the cognition are invariably apprehended together. The precise meaning of the technical term '*sahopalambha*' is co-apprehension. In other words, the claim is that for consciousness to be aware of its object is to be conscious of itself. 'Consciousness and self-consciousness, therefore are interchangeable terms'.[33] This is the very presupposition of all knowledge. The idea of '*svasamvedana*' or co-apprehension has been used repeatedly in order to emphasize the phenomenon of self-awareness as immediate, non-positional awareness. As has been said before, this is a theoretical move in order to avoid the fallacy of infinite regress (*anavastha*) which would be inevitable if consciousness required another consciousness to make itself known to itself. This is how the Vijnanavadins argue that if consciousness is not self-revealing (*svayamprakasa*),

30 Sartre, *The Transcendence of the Ego*.

31 '*Grahya-grahaka vaidhuryat svayamsaiva prakasyate*'.

32 See Ashok Chatterji, 1962, *Yogacara Idealism* (Varanasi: B.H.U.).

33 cf. Satkari Mukherji, 1935, *Buddhist Philosophy of Universal Flux* (Calcutta).

knowledge is not possible and claim that 'all cognition and feelings are known by themselves'.[34]

Finally, let me observe that in spite of all the differences that separate these two schools of thought—not only with reference to their cultural and historical settings but also in their overall concerns that may be expressed in metaphysical or methodological terms—it is not possible to ignore the striking similarity of the epistemological formulations of the specific answers that these provide with regard to the question of how consciousness knows itself. This problem is of acute interest to both, as for neither there is any primordial entity, viz. the ego, I, or an abiding self in or behind consciousness.

While concluding this discussion, it may be further observed that the ethical context is also particularly challenging for theoreticians who seek to deny the idea of an abiding self, as is the case with the two positions studied here. In his *Notebooks for an Ethics*, Sartre projects forcefully the view that a Platonic idea of good is self-contradictory, it is 'an aberrant synthesis of being and ought-to-be'.[35] The notion of agency comes to play a crucial role in his existentialist interpretive strategy. In the chapter entitled 'The Good and Subjectivity', he writes that 'the Good has to be Done', since for him 'the Good presents itself as what has to be posited as an objective reality through the effort of a subjectivity' and that 'the relation between acting subjectivity and the Good is as tight as the intentional relation that links consciousness to its object, or the one that binds man to the world in being-in-the world'.[36]

All these stances are of course intimately tied to the view that 'human reality is a project', as opposed to all those ideas which assume that 'man is initially fully made and that afterward he enters into a centripetal or centrifugal relation with the Good'. In brief, while analysing the universal structure of good, Sartre resents the idea that the good is 'pre-established', consequently, the universality of the good is to be treated as 'not de facto but

---

34 '*Sarvam citta-caittanam atmasamvedanam*'.

35 Sartre, 1992, *Notebooks for an Ethics*, trans. David Pellauer (Chicago).

36 *Ibid.*

de jure'. This view is evidently allied to the reading that 'I exist as a choice'. For Sartre, 'this choice is precisely the positing of a transcendent, it takes place on the unreflective plane'. In other words, here comes in once again his two level theory of consciousness which is indispensable for his account of moral choice along with an anti-Cartesian rendition of what the 'I' stands for—'I am free and responsible for my project with the reservation that it is precisely as having been there first'.

A deeper analysis of the structure and the constitution of the ego in interpersonal context with reference to these two modes of thinking—the Vijnanavada version of Buddhism and Sartre's interpretation of existentialism—is a matter of a separate study. However, what will be interesting to watch in such an undertaking is firstly the steps in their respective argumentations in support of their theories of no-self views along with the accounts of self-awareness. After that it will be crucial to examine the manner in which each position reflects the conventional understanding of the ethical demand in terms of overcoming the limitations of the ego and thereby bridging the gulf between itself and the 'other'. In brief, the point of such a study will be to note the extent to which such networks of ideas can be said to be coherently woven into their respective egology. In Sartre's analysis, it seems to me, the tension between the two levels (pre-reflective and reflective) of consciousness and the constitution of ego lay bare his deep struggle to make emerge a concept of personhood that is viable in an existentialist framework for ethics. Some of his critics think such an attempt to be cohesive whereas others find it to be incoherent and unconvincing.

In the case of Buddhism, ethical concerns do play a crucial role. Although Buddhist thought is not theistic, one does encounter nevertheless clear soteriological leanings. The practice of ethical precepts such as compassion (*karuna*) has been strongly recommended. This has provoked the Vijnanavadins to undertake a profound search that led to the idea of 'equality of all beings' (*samata-jnana*). It is noteworthy that the idea of a foundational consciousness as non-dual[37] goes hand in hand with the

37 The theory is called *advayavada*.

understanding that wisdom and compassion are two sides of the same coin. In their empirical accounts the no-substance/no-self theory, as has been discussed above, draws heavily from the idea of causal efficiency as the criterion of reality (*arthakriyakaritva*) whereas the phenomena of continuity and unity of consciousness are explained with the help of the theory of dependent origination (pratityasamutpada). This latter idea is said to be able to explain the psychological phenomena of memory, recognition, etc., without the postulation of any notion of self as a substance. The Buddhist philosophers have claimed through centuries that the no-self theory has full explanatory power in the ethical as well as in the soteriological contexts.

At the end of this chapter, the main points to observe is that the possibility that consciousness reveals itself to a 'self' or ego (as can be seen in the case of some expositions that directly deal with ownership-theories of consciousness), is ruled out. Both are therefore faced with the task of accounting for how consciousness knows itself. Again, it is worth noting in this connection that they equally reject the possibility that 'consciousness of something' may be or does become aware of itself only in a subsequent moment on the same ground that such a conceptual move would inevitably lead to the fallacy of regressus ad infinitum (anavastha). Thus, they are led to the same conclusion that consciousness of something knows itself as being that consciousness. Both claim that this is not positing knowledge as there is no dichotomy of subject and object which characterizes the usual knowledge situation. Moreover, they both insist that it is an immediate non-cognitive awareness and say that this is the presupposition of all knowledge. As Sartre says, 'consciousness must be present to itself, not as a thing, but as an operative intention, which can exist only as the revealing-revealed', laying emphasis that 'the only mode of existence which is possible for a consciousness of something'.[38]

In the Vijnanavadin formulation, taken once more from the well-known work by Santaraksita, entitled *Tattvasamgraha*, the idea sounds as follows: 'It is because consciousness is self-evident,

---

38 Sartre, *Being and Nothingness*.

that it can make other things evident'.[39] The insistence is on the idea that that which does not know itself cannot know anything else.

It is also relevant to observe here once more that the idea that consciousness is basically impersonal and that the ego is a construct is also of vital importance in the overall philosophical perception that freedom of choice and action are integral to the human situation as such.

The idea that all actions are chosen in and through freedom— from which there is no escape —is a human predicament that has been discussed at length by Sartre. It is through action that 'man makes himself'. The theme that by choosing a particular course of action one chooses oneself appears and reappears in existentialist literature. Sartre repeats throughout his major work *Being and Nothingness* that consciousness is the other name of freedom. In fact, 'nothingness' for him means nothing but this absolute freedom on the part of consciousness to choose its own being. Thus, it seems that the idea that consciousness is basically impersonal or pre-personal—as emphasized by Sartre time without number—is not without significance for the existential theory that he offers concerning choice, action, and responsibility. In this connection it is also relevant to observe that the idea that consciousness is basically impersonal and that the ego is a construct are also of vital importance in the overall philosophical perception that freedom of choice and action are integral to the human situation as such— especially there being no idea of a God either in Buddhism or in Sartrean existentialism. One fundamental implication of it which seems to be shared by both is that an individual is free (to do), his/her destiny, so to speak is determined by his/her actions—since no other external factor, no one else, no God can be held responsible for it. This moral thrust brings out the basic human freedom to make one's own decisions and to choose one's own actions and through that one's own destiny. Even if a soteriology operates in the case of Buddhist thought, this description of the human situation is indeed closely connected with the anatman or no-self view.

39 Santaraksita, 1968, *Tattvasamgraha*, with the commentary *Panjika* of Kamalasila, ed. Swami Dwarakanath Shastri, Varanasi. The words are: '*Apratyaksopalambhasya narthadrstih prasajyate*'.

Murti analyses the Buddhist motivation for discarding the notion of atman as follows:

> As the permanent is of one uniform, immutable nature ... It is neither the worse nor the better for the actions performed. It is impervious to any reform or progress. Precisely to avoid this insuperable difficulty did Buddha, taking his stand on the efficacy of Karma (act) as the sole arbiter of an individual's destiny, refuse to accept the permanent soul.[40]

From this it is clear that the denial of an ego as a substantive entity residing in or behind consciousness is of basic importance for the Buddhists so that our moral life can be at all meaningful. If the Buddhists replaced the idea of an abiding, immutable self 'by the theory of a mind-continuum', it is because 'this alone provides for progress (change, efficacy) and continuity (responsibility), as each succeeding state (good or bad) is the result of the previous state'.[41]

The idea, that all actions are chosen in and through freedom—from which there is no escape—is a human predicament, has been discussed at length by Sartre. It is through action that 'man makes himself'. The theme that by choosing a particular course of action one chooses oneself appears and reappears in existentialist literature. Sartre repeats throughout in his major work *Being and Nothingness* that consciousness is the other name of freedom. In fact, 'nothingness' for him means nothing but this absolute freedom on the part of consciousness to choose its own being.

In brief, what seems of a deep philosophical relevance is the focus on understanding an individual, above everything else, in terms of an individual conscious process which is fundamentally impersonal but self-conscious. This in both cases is related to the idea that the individuals makes their choice in and through absolute freedom and thus has to bear full responsibility for all the actions committed.

40 Murti, *The Central Philosophy of Buddhism.*
41 *Ibid.*

Epilogue

A review of the range of readings from diverse philosophical perspectives and a critical evaluation of significant polemical discussions—undertaken in this monograph—clearly shows the formidable challenge of the phenomenon of I-consciousness. To those who have pondered over the mystery of this phenomenon, this intellectual journey provides a breathtaking philosophical scenario. Given that the presence of I-consciousness in our mental life is universally recognized—some thinkers have gone even so far as to claim that no living being is without this I-sense—there are indeed many questions and concerns related to this multifaceted theme of I-consciousness, some of which have been addressed in this work. The variety of treatment that these have received at the hands of the philosophers—Indian and Western—leaves one awestruck. In some ways one is likely to assume that this is a theme that stands out among the long range of really difficult topics for philosophical deliberations because of its unique features, yet perhaps it is not unlike a number of other fundamental questions. There is no simple solution in sight for any of these basic questions and it seems that many of the contending views on all such topics are here to stay. It is indeed tempting to observe that the most profound problems that keep on pressing for our attention are precisely those that we are neither able to resolve to the satisfaction of all enquirers nor to dissolve as being irrelevant or trivial. I-consciousness is certainly one of such perennial questions with regard to which our fascination seems to remain unimpeded. As one gazes at the wide cross-cultural conceptual canvas where relevant documents reflect the debates and controversies spanning through the centuries, one cannot help but take note of the distinctly visible dimensions of I-consciousness, seen from epistemological, metaphysical, linguistic, as well as ethical and soteriological points of view.

Let me dwell here briefly on a few high points of this fascinating philosophical adventure. Being open to both the Indian traditions of philosophical thinking and the Western, it has been possible to gain access to a wide vista of ideas across the cultural and geographical boundaries. It is my hope that this work will be seen as partly fulfilling the task of setting up a common frame of enquiry that is still missing but is needed for a careful scrutiny of views, especially concerning those central questions that no articulate thought-tradition can bypass. I have found it to be immensely worthwhile to explore a range of read ngs that the history of ideas in India and the West contain on this topic and to come across several similar paradigms for interpreting I-consciousness, in spite of many overt and covert differences. Most remarkable is the fact that we are confronted here with a phenomenon considered unanimously to be indubitable but which nevertheless keeps resisting disclosure. Despite repeated intellectual probes to unveil its mystery, it seems that no account that has been so far documented could be to every enquirer's satisfaction.

To the question whether 'I-consciousness' presupposes an abiding self, we have seen two principal kinds of responses—one affirming and the other denying it to be so. A host of possible variants that can be classified under each of these two principal theoretical modes of handling the question are carefully recorded in the history of philosophy. The Vaisesika philosophers and the Buddhists typically represent these two major alternative standpoints in the Indian context, just as the Cartesian and the Humean do in the Western.

For the Vaisesika philosophers the self is the very basis of I-consciousness. Linguistically, this self is the referent of the word 'I'; metaphysically, it is a homogenous, indivisible entity. In tune with other Atmavadins they firmly hold the view that the self can never be reduced to a stream of consciousness, understood in terms of a chain of mental episodes, or explained simply as an aggregate of various factors. The Buddhists, on the other hand, radically oppose the idea of an identical, unchanging self, emphasizing that mental life is a flow where nothing abides, nothing ever remains identical.

As has been discussed earlier, the Buddhists urge that the confusion between similarity and sameness needs to be removed both for theoretical and practical purposes.

However, the view that thought is the essence of self, designated as an immaterial substance, can be seen in the philosophy of René Descartes. This claim that thought must have a thinker gave rise to polemics. As it has been noted in the course of this study, there have been several attacks on this Cartesian rendition of the self from both analytical and phenomenological traditions. One typical reaction sounds similar to that of Lichtenberg. To Descartes' statement 'I think, therefore I am', Lichtenberg's response was that instead of making such an observation regarding the subject of experience, Descartes could have claimed that 'This is a thought, therefore at least one thought is being thought'.[1] It is possible to multiply several such philosophical observations that are intended to question the Cartesian reading. Nevertheless, many still argue along the Cartesian line, as Reid's remark demonstrates: 'I am not thought, I am not action, I am not feeling; I am something that thinks, and acts, and suffers'. Indeed, history of philosophy shows that repeated attempts have been made to challenge the idea of an identical self as the basis of I-consciousness and even to demonstrate the very idea of an abiding, indivisible self to be a mistake.

Within the Vedantic tradition itself, the question that eventually comes up is whether self and consciousness are equivocal terms. It has been discussed earlier that the Advaitins hold the view that there is ultimately no difference, while defending the thesis of the ontological reality of non-dual consciousness. They said repeatedly that there is no room for difference (bheda) in this foundational consciousness. The Dvaitins and the Visistadvaitins oppose that idea and maintain the I to be the self. As all of them participated in this battle of ideas, deeper issues kept surfacing, and we find them struggling to answer the question what forms the basis of I-consciousness.

On the other hand the Buddhists, perhaps the pioneers in the direction of repudiating any notion of an identical self, had

1 Lichtenberg.

introduced already around 500 BC a conceptual strategy for looking at ourselves as composites (*sanghata*), as a stream (*santana*) rather than as indivisible, identical entities. Cogent arguments were formulated in support of the no-self view.

However, abandoning the notion of self is no easy task. We know how centuries of controversies followed where not only a chain of Atmavadins kept insisting on the indispensability of the idea of an abiding self on epistemological, metaphysical, and ethico-religious grounds. Even the Vatsiputriyas from within the Buddhist tradition see the no-self position as falling short of the explanatory power while accounting for unity of consciousness or while seeking to provide justifications for moral and soteriological pursuits. This is why even though the Vatsiputriyas were no supporters of *atmavada*, they proposed '*pudgalavada*' instead of adhering to the existing interpretation of *anatmavada* of the first phase of Indian Buddhism.

It may be observed here that once the idea of self is accepted as the basis of I-consciousness, some philosophers begin to ponder further over a few metaphysical implications of that premise. Some of them, for example, put forward the notion of the immortality of the self as one such implication. In this connection, it is very interesting to observe that in the Indian context even philosophers who propounded the no-self theory did not abandon the possibility of conceiving consciousness as a continuing process beyond death. The Buddhist thinkers, for example, do not consider the event of death as annihilation of consciousness.

In ancient as well as contemporary Western thought, one finds instances where philosophers are seen struggling with these issues. Descartes, for example, viewed the self to be indivisible, hence as indestructible. However, Parfit in his study—which is geared toward an abandonment of the Cartesian idea of self—concludes after a long analysis that Lichtenberg's objections to Descartes still hold since it is possible for us to 'refer to and describe different thoughts, and describe the relations between them, without ascribing these thoughts to thinkers'. Moreover, Parfit's additional comment which follows is that indeed 'we do ascribe thoughts to thinkers. Because we talk in this way. Descartes could truly claim. 'I think, therefore I am'. But Descartes did not show that a thinker must be a separately existing entity, distinct from a brain and body'. What lies at the core of his objection becomes clear when Parfit says that 'besides assuming that every thought must have a thinker, Descartes argued that a thinker must be a pure Ego, or spiritual substance. A Cartesian Pure Ego is the clearest case of a separately existing entity, distinct from the brain and the body'.[2] There is indeed such a philosophical demand to which some philosophers across cultures felt obliged to answer. This is precisely why, for example, the Vaisesika philosophers were taking pains to argue elaborately in support of the view that the self must be regarded as something over and above body, mind and the sense-organs (*deha-mana-indriyatirikta*). These arguments have been discussed earlier.

Is there a possible resolution to this debate concerning the idea of self? Or are we to keep on hearing the echoes that resounded through the corridors of several centuries, confronting us repeatedly with all these familiar strategies that persuade us to sway from one to the other of a finite number of alternatives in each camp? As it is, we are either persuaded to perceive the self as that which remains unchanged in the midst of change or are told emphatically that nothing whatsoever can be said to be exempt from change and thereby seeking to seal the fate of any notion of an unchanging, abiding, and identical self. In the Indian scene, one hears the thunderous voice which keeps declaring that the unchanging, abiding self is an ontological reality and that this self is undeniably distinct from all that is changing, just as 'the thread in a garland is different from the flowers'. The adherents of the no-self view, on the other hand, insist that this self (so-called) that some so vehemently hold to be the very basis of I-consciousness, is no more than 'just an appellation, a form of speech, a description, a conventional usage'. Readings with similar intents that come in different versions can also be seen in Western thought.

However, it may be briefly mentioned here that both the Atmavada and the Anatmavada traditions are ultimately bearers not only of logical, epistemological, linguistic, or metaphysical

2 D. Parfit, 1984, *Reasons and Persons* (Oxford: Oxford University Press).

ideas, they are also seen in due course as striving to seek the path to freedom. Keeping in mind the goal of *nirvana* as the final aim of the teaching of the Buddha, the reputed Buddhist scholar Chandrakirti made an astounding observation that is absolutely worthwhile recalling in the context of the philosophical tensions between the self and no-self paradigms. He made a remarkable attempt to bridge the conceptual opposition of the ideas of self and no-self by emphasizing that these are nothing but skilful means or devices (*upaya-kausalya*) with a definite aim of pursuing Freedom. He pointed out that for those who are inclined toward nihilism the idea of self is useful for pointing out that Karma continues, whereas for those who are dogmatically attached to the self, the no-self view must be taught in order to liberate themselves from such attachments.

It is crucial to note here that in the unfolding of the Upanisadic and Buddhist traditions, neither of the two contending traditions did ever succumb to any form of naturalistic explanation with regard to the general theme of consciousness. This holds true irrespective of whether their advocates accounted for I-consciousness with or without postulating the notion of an abiding self. In this connection, recall that the well-known Buddhist philosopher Kamalasila, while commenting on Santaraksita's renowned work entitled *Tattva-samgraha*, has recorded in detail an exchange between the Carvakas and the Buddhists. The Carvakas argue that since the Buddhists champion *anatmavada*/no-self theory, in principle they ought to join forces with the Carvakas. To this the Buddhists retort by saying that *anatmavada* is not tantamount to accepting the naturalistic position on consciousness. Note that despite the differences in the metaphysical commitments by different schools of Buddhist philosophy, there are important overlaps with the ethos of the Upanisadic tradition in so far as the ideas of karma (a complex version of moral retribution), *punarjanma* (rebirth), and nirvana (ultimate freedom) are concerned. These ideas do remain intact in all the phases of Indian Buddhism.

It is remarkable that in the Indian context, all the proponents—no matter of which version of the self or no-self theories—had to face the challenge of the sceptics, the agnostics, as well as that of the naturalists. The records of these debates are available.

A proper appreciation of these conceptual battles leads one to a deeper understanding of the Indian philosophical discourse. The main thrust of the Carvaka philosophical enterprise, despite the internal differences among them, is on their common repudiation of the idea of consciousness as a distinct principle, that is as being independent of the material (the elements) or biological (living body) processes. Today, however incomplete may be our knowledge of their extant texts, it is evident that the objections that were raised by these Indian naturalists were taken seriously by the philosophers of the Upanisadic, Buddhist, and the Jaina traditions who, in turn, critically questioned the legitimacy of the naturalistic interpretation.

At present one encounters in the West a bold return of the naturalists in full force, equipped with sophisticated tools for questioning all forms of philosophical explanations that cannot be appropriately labelled as 'naturalistic'. However, as I have observed earlier, a survey of these contemporary theories provoke more questions than answers. An explanation of the connection between the brain and the conscious processes still remains, as was said by William James, 'the ultimate of ultimate problems'. Like many others, I am inclined to think that the possibility for a cogent and consistent form of naturalistic explanation for the emergence of consciousness is still far away. The contemporary neuro-philosophers seem to be trying their best to incorporate the latest developments in the field of neuro-sciences in their speculations and to keep the doors open for a naturalistic philosophical explanation.

However, for many philosophers, a naturalistic explanation of consciousness is a well-nigh impossibility, as it seemed to Sankara, the great exponent of Advaita Vedanta. In his well-known commentary on *Brahma Sutra*, while confronting the Indian naturalists who did not accept the idea of the ontological primacy of consciousness and treated consciousness only as a derived phenomenon, Sankara remarked that to postulate consciousness as being dependent on that which is revealed by consciousness is like claiming that an acrobat is so skilled that he can climb upon his own shoulder.

It has been mentioned earlier that Sankara's own position is significantly much more than a simple claim for the epistemic primacy of consciousness. In the Advaitic discourse one comes across a series of arguments that repudiate any form of pluralistic metaphysics. The attempt has been to construe a form of ontology which is in harmony with the idea of an undivided unity—rather non-duality—of consciousness as ultimate. A colossal amount of material is available within the context of the Advaita Vedantic discourse, mapping an intricate journey beginning from such observations as that all living beings have I-sense to the moment of the culminating salvatory knowledge expressed as 'I am Brahman' (*aham Brahmasmi*)—one of the great sayings (Mahavakya) on which a band of Advaitin scholars have commented over centuries. Indeed, it is said that the fruition of the Upanisadic tradition is seen with the rise of the school of Advaita Vedanta.

It is worth noting that in the various philosophical systems in the Indian context the notions of space, time, and causality are woven into different conceptual structures that are non-dualistic, dualistic, and pluralistic. While construing a cogent view of being as non-dual, immutable, and impartite, one finds that in the non-dualistic reading of Advaita Vedanta, space–time–causality are seen as part and parcel of the mundane, empirical experience of change and plurality to which no ontological status is granted. This notion of 'empirical'/'conventional' (*vyavaharika*) neverthe-less remain crucially important for construing the idea of the absolute foundational consciousness.[3]

This is also why Advaita Vedanta grants the world the status of 'empirical reality' and regards Brahman as reality per se; the former has only epistemic whereas the latter has ontological status, it is being par excellence. This is a theoretical move that allows for a classification of levels of 'reality' (*sat*). These are as follows: (a) '*paramarthika*', i.e., the ultimate as the unsublatable; (b) '*vyavaha-rika*', i.e., the empirical; and (c) '*pratibhasika*', i.e., the illusory. The last two are described as eventually sublatable. There is evidently a soteriological dimension to this way of formulating the categories of being/reality, which however, by no means indicates any lack of rational stringency.

---

3 For a deeper comprehension of the Advaitic stand, further explore the concepts of '*vivartavada*' and '*satkaranavada*'.

It is indeed illuminating that similar readings, disclosing the entirely dependent status of the world in the face of God-experience, are present in the literature of other philosophical and theological traditions across the boundaries of cultures. Consider, for example, the following statement of St. Augustine: 'and I beheld the other things below Thee, and I perceived that they neither altogether are, nor altogether are not, for they are since they are from Thee, but are not, because they are not what Thou art. For that truly is, that remains unchangeably'.[4]

While summing up all these diverse views and interpretations of self and consciousness, it is worth recapitulating the careful review made by the American philosopher William James. Drawing from his knowledge of philosophical views held by notable Western philosophers who preceded him, James classifies all these theories under three categories, viz. the soul-substance, the associationist, and the transcendentalist theories of the self. These are of course exemplified by the Cartesian, the Humean, and the Kantian views. Despite significant differences, one could refer to similar paradigmatic structures from the Indian sources as exhibited in such philosophical models as those of the Vaisesika, the Buddhist, and Advaita Vedanta, which have been already discussed.

James formulated his own views cautiously distinguishing his position from his predecessors. He noted that the I, or 'pure ego' is a much more difficult subject of inquiry than the 'me'. It is that which at any given moment is conscious, whereas the me is only one of the things which it is conscious of. [The I] is the thinker; and the question immediately comes up *what* is the thinker? Is it the passing state of consciousness itself, or is it something deeper and less mutable? The passing state we have seen to be the very embodiment of change. Yet each one of us spontaneously considers that by 'I', he means something which is always the same. The currents of ideas that are present in James's writings have undoubtedly inspired much of the contemporary western thinking in this area. Flanagan has remarked that James's reading of personal identity is more in tune with Lockean tradition and

4 Augustine, 1957, *The Confessions*, trans. by E.B. Pusey, New York.

exhibits a clear rejection of Descartes' as well as Kant's views. It may also be observed that actually there are many passages where James's rejection of transcendental self reminds one of Buddhist philosophical accounts explaining the difficulties ingrained in the idea of an identical, abiding self, especially when he makes such observations as, there is no such thing as a person or that 'the sense of our personal identity is exactly like any one of our other perceptions of sameness among phenomena. It is a conclusion grounded on the resemblance in a fundamental respect'. What is remarkable about James is that his boundless curiosity and his professional knowledge of medical science led him to look into the scientific findings of his time. Already around 1890, James attempted to bring in the scientific knowledge of the brain of his day while exploring consciousness but he did not ignore the conceptual resources from philosophical traditions, both secular and religious.

It is striking that with the advancement of neuro-biology and brain research, there is a tremendous zeal for a science of mind/consciousness at present. However, many theoreticians in their overall framework of research seem to outright exclude the ideas and concerns embedded in religious traditions. Some brand religious ideas as 'opinions...that cannot be taken seriously'. Moreover, there are also others who firmly reject dualism as 'unscientific'. However, caution needs to be exercised with regard to what is made to pass as 'scientific view'.

As examples of scientists who have been deeply involved with the problem of brain and consciousness in their own work and came to adopt a clear dualistic view, mention may be made of Wilder Penfield, a pioneering neuro-surgeon and John Eccles, a leading neuro-physiologist. Their views may be described as non-naturalistic. Clearly, they are in favour of dualism. Eccles[5] held consciousness to be a power of a non-physical substance or as composed of non-physical properties. Penfield, as he writes himself, struggled in the beginning of his career to prove that the brain accounts for the mind but 'in the end' concludes 'that there is no

5 Karl Popper and John Eccles, 1977, *The Self and its Brain* (New York: Routledge).

good evidence, in spite of new methods, such as the employment of stimulating electrodes, the study of conscious patients and the analysis of epileptic attacks, that the brain alone can carry out the work that the mind does'. He comes to conclude that 'it is easier to rationalize man's being on the basis of two elements than on the basis of one'. At the end, Penfield has a word of warning for his readers, viz. that granted research is still going on, 'one should not pretend to draw a final scientific conclusion'.[6]

Before annulling the non-naturalistic views in the name of science, we need then to consider the question whether there is any such thing as a rigid, static scientific world view? From what we know, it seems to evolve all the time in surprising ways, often a real breakthrough is achieved by discarding presuppositions that were central to the previously accepted scientific picture of the world.

Given that in multiple disciplines today the one key concern that keeps appearing across the board is how to account for and explain the emergence and the presence of consciousness in the natural world, the practice of open-mindedness is crucial. This is important if we are to remove gradually the stance of incompatibility between the scientific and the philosophico-religious undertakings in the pursuit of knowledge. The cognitive claims associated with the world-religions need to be looked at with the same critical acumen and intellectual veneration as any secular, scientific theory. The possibility of creating a broader and richer frame, drawing on multidisciplinary resources, has only recently begun to be seen as a legitimate and a worthwhile endeavour. To foster a spirit of a common enquiry, especially with regard to ultimate questions, calls for a construction of a cognitive setting where it is possible to accommodate, integrate, and order our experiences focusing not only on what is experienced but also on the experiencer.

No doubt the wonder about the world as our habitat—when clearly recognized as a transitory abode for each one of us—leads to the whither and whence questions. These have been repeatedly raised since time immemorial and still have not lost their pertinence or fervour in any way. The questions that confront us most

6 Wilder Penfield, 1975, *The Mystery of the Mind* (New Jersey: Princeton University Press).

poignantly are not exclusively regarding what surrounds us but are also related to the phenomenon of subjectivity. It is incredible that a phenomenon like I-consciousness which is so intimate can yet remain inaccessible to our cognitive grasp. It is not only a quest for the religious or the mystic. It is also, as Schrödinger puts it, 'not only one of the tasks, but the task, of science, the only one that really counts....to answer the one great philosophical question which embraces all others, the one that Plotinus expressed by his brief: who are we'?[7]

Indeed, it is both a fascinating and a disconcerting task to gradually uncover before one's own critical gaze theory after theory regarding I-consciousness and recognize the unfathomable depth of the 'mystery' of our own being. What is known seems insignificant when compared to what remains to be known. Cognitively speaking, in more than one way, it seems like confronting an unknown territory. I-consciousness is indeed an enigma. It is existentially the closest but nevertheless remains farthest from our understanding.

7 Erwin Schrödinger, 1983, *My View of the World* (Connecticut: Ox Bow Press).

Glossary

abheda	non-different
abhideya	nameable
abhinivesa	fear, especially of death
abhyasa	practice
acit	non-conscious
adhikara	eligible
adhisthana	ground, basis
adhyasa	superimposition
adhyastha	constituted/superimposed
aguntaka dharma	adventitious property
ahamkara	ego/I-ness
aham-pratyaya	I-consciousness
ajnana	ignorance
akhanda	indivisible
alaya	store-house consciousness
amurta	formless
ananda	bliss
anatman	not-self
anatmavadins	no-self theory proponents
anavabhasat	not experienced
anavastha	fallacy of infinite regress
anidam	not-this
anityam	impermanent
antahkarana	mind

antarendriya	internal sense-organ
antim	ultimate
anumana	inference
anuvyavasaya	cognition of cognition/mental perception
aparinami	unchanging
apavarga	ultimate freedom
aropya	superimposed
artha	referent
arthakriyakaritva	criterion of reality as causal efficiency
asmad-pada	the word 'I'
asmita	am-ness
astanga Yoga	eightfold Yoga practices
atisadrsatadatmabhrama	similarity generating illusion of identity
atma saksatkara	self-realization
atma-drsti	false notion of ego
atma-mana	conceit of egoity
atma-moha	ignorance about ego
atman	self
atma-prema	attachment to ego
Atmavada	other name of the Upanisadic tradition that supports the ontological reality of atman or self
atma-vidya	knowledge of the self
avartana	regular rotation
avedyatva	unknowability
avidya	nescience
avinasi	indestructible
avisaya	non-object
badhira	deaf

bahya	external
bahya-padartha	external entity
bhasya	revealed
bhokta	enjoyer/experiencer
bhrama	fallacious
bhuta-pratyaveksa	free from all standpoints
bodha	awareness, feeling
buddhi	mental faculty
caitanya	consciousness
cetana dravya	substance which is conscious
cid-acidgranthi	knot of self and not-self
cidgunaka	quality of being conscious
cidrupa	essence of consciousness
cit	consciousness
darsana-sakti	principle of cognition
deha	body
dehadi-atirikta	over and above the body etc.
dehadi-samghatamatra	aggregate of body, sense organs, etc.
dehatmavada	physicalism
dehatmavadins	physicalists
dharma	characteristics
dhurta	sly
drastrtva	seer-function
dravya	substance
drk-sakti	pure awareness
drasta	seer
drsya	seen or witnessed
duhkha	suffering
dvesa	hatred
eka-kartrkatava	singular agency
gauna	secondary

granthi	knot
guna	attribute
iccha	desire
idam	this
indriya	sense-organs
indriyatmavada	view of sense-organs as the seat of selfhood
jada dravya	substance which is material/ non-conscious
jada	insentient
jada prakrti	non-conscious nature
jagadandhya-prasanga	context of darkness of the world
jagat-satyatavadi	proponents of the idea of reality of the world
jagrata	waking
jiva	creature, living being
jnana	knowledge
jnata	knower
jnata-aham	I as the knower, subject-ego
jneya	knowable
jneya-aham	I as known, object-ego
jyotisam jyotih	light of all lights
kaivalya	Freedom as a soteriological goal
kalaprabhavamukta	free from the influence of time
kama	desire, passion
kamasamkalpadi	psychological processes as desire, resolution, etc.
karana	cause/instrument : (ask me, without a diacritical mark, there is a slight problem)
karta	agent/doer
karuna	compassion

klesa	affliction
krsa	thin
krti	performance, accomplishment
ksanabhangavada	theory of universal momentariness
kutastha	unchangeable
laukika vyavahara	conventional usage
linga	marks
lokayata darsana	philosophy of the common/ unsophisticated man
mahavakya	great saying
mamakara	my-ness
manana	process of intellection
manas	mind
manasa pratyaksa	mental perception
manatmavada	theory of the mind as the self
maranaeva pavarga	death is salvation
mayic	illusory
mithya	false
mithyatva	falsity
moksa	liberation
mukhya	primary
mukhya-siddhanta	fundamental tenet
mukti	liberation/salvation
naiyayikas	Indian realists of the Nyaya school
nama-rupa	psychophysical complex
nana-kartrk	plurality of subjects
nanatmavada	plurality of selves
neant	nothingness
nihsvabhavada	theory that denies essentialism
nirasraya	without substrate

nirvisaya caitanya	objectless mental state
nirvisaya	non-intentional
nirvisayaka	objectless
nirvisesa	indeterminate
nitya	eternal
pada	word
panca-klesa	five forms of affliction
panca-skandha	five aggregates
panca-viparyaya	five forms of error
paramarthika	ontologically real/transcendental level/unsublatable
parama-vidya	highest knowledge
parinami	changing
parinispanna-vijnana	foundational consciousness
pour-soi	being-for-itself
prakrti	nature/dynamic matter
pramana	evidence
pramana-nirapeksa	independent of evidence
pramanasiddha	established by evidence
prameya	demonstrable
prasthana	departure
prasupta	dormant
pratibhasika	illusory
pratiti	awareness/sense
pratityasamutpada	law of dependent origination
pratyabhijna	phenomenon of recognition
pratyagatma	self
pratyaksa	perception
pratyakta	quality of inwardness
prayatna	effort

prema-taratamya	subtle difference in love and attachment
Pudgalavada	a theory advocated by the Vatsiputriyas, that there is a principle of individuality which is neither identical with nor different from the Skandhas or aggregates
punarjanma	rebirth
purusa	self
putra	son
qualia	technical term for the quality of subjectivity
raga	desire, attachment
rupa	physical
sabda	verbal testimony
sabda vyavahara	linguistic usage
sadajnata	constantly aware
sadi adhyasa	finite superimpositions
sahopalambha co-apprehension	
svasamvedana	awareness being aware of itself
sajatiya	pertaining to the same class/ genus
sakhanda	composite/divisible
saksi	witness
saksisiddha	established by witness con- sciousness
samata-jnana	equality of all beings
sambit	awareness
samjna	designation
samkalpa	resolution
samsara	world-process

samskara	mental disposition/trace
sannikarsa	contact
santana	stream/flow
sarira/deha	body
sarvam anityam	universal impermanence
sarvanama	pronoun
sarvanubhavasiddha	witnessed/testified by all
sasmita-samadhi	technical term for a specific state of concentration
sasvatavada	eternalism
sat	being
siddhanta	established thesis
sruti	revealed scriptures
sthira	static
sukha	happiness
sukhi	happy
sunya	void
sunyasya'pi saksitvat	even voidness calls for the witness consciousness
sunyata	lack of essence
susiksita	sophisticated
sususpti	deep sleep
sutras	aphorisms
svabhavavada	naturalism
svabhavavadin	naturalist
svagata	pertaining to itself
svapna	dream
sva-prakasa	self-luminous
svarupa	essence of the self
svayam-prakasa	self-revealing
svayamsiddha	self-established/self-evident

tanu	attenuated
tika, varttika	glosses, sub-commentaries
trilaksana	three fundamental characteristics
ucchedavada	nihilism
udara	active
upacara	fallacious attribution
upamana	comparison/analogy
upaya-kausalya	conceptual devices
vahirindriyagrahya	graspable by external sense-organs
bahu-purusavada	theory of plurality of selves
vairagya	detachment
vasana	propensities
vastu-sat	having basis in reality
vedana	feeling
vedya	knowable
vibhu	all-pervasive
vicchinna	interrupted
vijatiya	of a different class/genus/species
vijnana	cognition
vikalpa-pratyaya	conceptual construction
vinasa	total destruction
viparyaya	error
visaya	object/contents
visayanubhava	awareness of object
visesa guna	special qualities
vithi	series
vitta	property
vivartavada	*the view propounded by Advaita Vedanta according*

	to which that which underlies all change remains itself unmodified
viveka-jnana	discriminatory knowledge
vyavahara conventional	experience
vyavaharika	empirical

Select Bibliography

Anscombe, G.E.M., 1975, 'The First Person', in S. Guttenplan (ed.), *Mind and Language* (Oxford: Clarendon Press) pp. 45–65.

Ayer, A.J., 2000, *Hume: A Very Short Introduction* (USA: Oxford University Press).

Balslev, Anindita Niyogi, 2010, 'Philosophical Explanations of self-awareness in Vijnavada Buddhism and Sartre's Existentialism', in Adrian Mirvish and Adrian van den Hoven (eds), *New Perspectives on Sartre* (Newcastle: Cambridge Scholars Publishing).

———, 2009, *A Study of Time in Indian Philosophy*, 3rd ed. (New Delhi: Motilal Banarsidass Publishers).

———, 2008, 'The Idea of Abhyasa', *Visual* (The India Habit Centre's Art Journal).

———, 1997, 'Philosophy and Cross Cultural Conversation: Some Comments on the Project of Comparative Philosophy', *Metaphilosophy*, Vol. 28, No. 4, pp. 359–70.

———, 1993, 'Time and the Hindu Experience', in Anindita Niyogi Balslev and Jitendranath Mohanty (eds), *Religion and Time* (The Netherlands: E.J. Brill).

———, 1992, 'Analysis of I-Consciousness in the Transcendental Phenomenology and Indian Philosophy', in D.P. Chattopadhyaya, Lester Embree, and J.H. Mohanty (eds), *Phenomenology and Indian Philosophy* (New Delhi: Indian Council of Philosophical Research).

———, 1991, 'The Notion of *Kleśa* and Its Bearing on the Yoga Analysis of Mind', *Philosophy East and West*, Vol. 41, No. 1, pp. 77–81.

———, 1988, 'An Appraisal of I-consciousness in the Context of the Controversies Centering around the No-self Doctrine of Buddhism', *Journal of Indian Philosophy*, Vol. 16.

———, 1987, 'Time, Self and Consciousness: Some Conceptual Patterns in the Context of Indian Thought', *Journal of Indian Council of Philosophical Research*, Vol. 5, No. 1, pp. 111–20.

———, 1968, 'Une Etude Comparee de Quelque themes Philosophique Proposees par le Bouddhisme et' Existentialisme', PhD thesis, University of Paris.

Balslev, Anindita Niyogi, ed., 2000, *Cultural Otherness*, Correspondence with Richard Rorty, 2nd ed. (USA: Oxford University Press).

———, and Dirk Evers, eds, 2010, *Compassion in the Religions of the World* (Germany: Udo Keller Stiftung Forum Humanum and Cross Cultural Conversation).

Bhattacharya, Gadadhara, 1929, *Saktivada*, ed. D. Shastri (Kashi Sanskrit Series).

Bhattacharya, K.C., 1932, 'The False and the Subjective', *Studies in Philosophy*, Vol. 2, edited by Gopinath Bhattacharya (Calcutta: Progressive Publishers).

———, 1930, *The Subject as Freedom* (Bombay: Indian Institute of Philosophy).

Bhattacharya, Sibajiban, 2001, 'The Emergence of the Person: Some Indian Themes and Theories', *Sandhana*, Vol. 1, No. 1.

Bhattacharya Srimohan and Dinesh Chandra Bhattachrya Sastri, eds, 1979, *Bharatiya Darsana Kosa* (Calcutta: Sanskrit College).

Butler, J., 1736, *The Analogy of Religion* (London: Knapton).

Cary, Phillip, 2000, *Augustine's Invention of the Inner Self: The Legacy of a Christian Platonist* (Oxford: Oxford University Press).

Candrakirti, 1960, *Prasannapada* (Darbhanga: Mithila Institute of Postgraduate Studies).

Chatterji, Ashok, 1962, *Yogacara Idealism* (Varanasi: Banaras Hindu University).

Chattopadhya, D.P., 1973, *Lokayata: A Study in Ancient Indian Materialism* [1959] (New Delhi: People's Publishing House).

Chisholm, Roderick M., 1969, 'On the Observability of the Self', *Philosophy and Phenomenological Research*, Vol. 30, pp. 7–21.

Churchland, Patricia, 1994, *Can Neurobiology Teach Us Anything About Consciousness?* (Lancaster: Lancaster Press).

Descartes, René, 1993, *Meditations on First Philosophy* [1641], 3rd ed., trans. Donald A. Cress (Indianapolis: Hackett).

Einstien, *My View of The World* [Mein Weltbild].

Erwin Schrödinger, 1983, *My View of the World* (Connecticut: Ox Bow Press).

———, 1958, *Mind and Matter* (Cambridge: Cambridge University Press).

Flanagan, Owen, 1993, *Consciousness Reconsidered* (Cambridge: MIT Press).

Flew, Antony, 1951, 'Locke and the Problem of Personal Identity', *Journal of the Royal Institute of Philosophy*, Vol. xxvi.

Fodor, Jerry A., 1994, 'The Mind-Body Problem', Richard Warner and Tadeusz Szubka (eds), *The Mind-Body Problem: A Guide to the Current Debate* (USA: Blackwell).

Gurwitsch, Aron, 1974, *Phenomenology and Theory of Science*, ed. L. Embree (Evanston: Northwestern University Press).

Hendel, Charles W., ed., 1955, *Hume: An Enquiry Concerning Human Understanding* (New York: Pearson).

Hume, David, 1978, *A Treatise of Human Nature*, ed. J.A. Selby-Bigge (Oxford: Oxford University Press; New York : Clarendon Press).

Husserl E., 1970, *Logical Investigations*, trans. J.N. Findlay (New York: Humanities press).

——, 1960, *Cartesian Meditations*, trans. D. Cairns (The Hague: Martin Nijhoff).

The Husserlian volumes XIII, XIV, and XV.

James, William, 1950, 'On Consciousness of Self', *The Principles of Psychology* [1897] (New York: Courier Dover Publications).

Kenny, A. 1988, *The Self* (Milwaukee: Marquette University Press).

Locke, John, 1690, *Essay on Human Understanding.*

Madhavacarya, 1904, *The Sarvadarsanasamgraha of Madhavacharya* [1924], Gaekwad Oriental series, trans. E.F. Cowell and E.E. Gough (London).

Mahadevan, T.M.P, 1938, *The Philosophy of Advaita* (London: Luzac & Co).

Marcel, Gabriel, *L'Etre et L'Avoir.*

Matilal, B.K., 1985, *Language, Truth, and Reality* (Delhi: Matilal Banarsidas).

McGinn, Collin, 1991, *The Problem of Consciousness* (Oxford: Blackwell).

Milinda-Panha, 1923, *Les questions de Milinda*, trans. by Louis Finot (Paris-Bossard).

Misra, Parthasarathi, 1915, *Sastradipika* (Bombay: Nirnayasagar Press).

Mukherji, A.C., 1943, *The Nature of Self* (Allahabad: The Indian Press).

Mukherji, Satkari, 1935, *Buddhist Philosophy of Univeral Flux* (Calcutta: University of Calcutta).

Murti, T.R.V., 1955, *The Central Philosophy of Buddhism* (London: Allen & Unwin).

——, 1963, presidential address, Indian Philosophical Congress, 37th session, Chandigarh.

——, 1935, 'Illusion as Confusion of Subjective Functions', *Philosophical Quarterly*, April.

Nagel, Thomas, 1989, *The View from Nowhere* (USA: Oxford University Press).

Nozick, Robert, 1981, *Philosophical Explanations* (Oxford: Clarendon).

Pande, G.C., 1993, *Studies in Mahayana*, Sarnath: Varanasi.

———, 1974, *The Origins of Buddhism*, 2nd ed. (Delhi: Motilal Banarsidas).

Parfit, D., 1984, *Reasons and Persons* (Oxford: Oxford University Press).

Penfield, Wilder, 1975, *The Mystery of the Mind* (New Jersey: Princeton University Press).

Popper Karl, and John Eccles, 1977, *The Self and its Brain* (New York: Routledge).

Radhakrishnan, S., 1962, *Indian Philosophy*, vols 1 and 2 (London: George Allen & Unwin).

Reid, T., 1785, *Essays on the Intellectual Powers of Man*.

Ryle, Gilbert, 1949, *The Concept of Mind* (Chicago: University of Chicago Press).

Santaraksita, 1968, *Tattvasamgraha*, with the commentary *Panjika* of Kamalasila, Swami Dwarakidas Shastri (ed.) (Benaras: Bauddha Bharati).

Sarasvati, Madhusudana, 1937, *Advaita-Siddhi*, 2nd ed., Ananta Krishna Shastri (ed.) (Bombay: Nirnaya-Sagar Press).

Sartre, Jean-Paul, 1992, *Notebooks for an Ethics*, trans. David Pellauer (Chicago: University of Chicago Press).

———, 1988, *The Transcendence of the Ego: An Existentialist Theory of Consciousness* [1966], trans. Forrest Williams and Robert Kirkpatrick (New York: Farrar, Strauss, and Giroux).

———, 1960, *The Transcendence of the Ego* [1957] (New York: Farrar, Straus and Giroux).

———, 1956, *Being and Nothingness: A Phenomenological Essay on Ontology* [1943], trans. Hazel Barnes (New York: Philosophical Library).

Sherover, Charles, 1975, *The Human Experience of Time* (New York: New York University Press).

Shastri, Daksinaranjan, 1982, *Charvaka Darshana* (Calcutta: Rajya Pustak Parsat).

Searle, John, 2003, *Rationality in Action* (Cambridge, MA: MIT Press).

———, 2001, 'Consciousness, Free Action and the Brain', *Rationality in Action* (Cambridge MA: MIT Press).

———, 2000, 'Consciousness', *Annual Review of Neuro-science*, Vol. 23, No. 1.

———, 1997, *The Mystery of Consciousness* (New York: New York Review of Books).

———, 1992, *The Rediscovery of the Mind* (Cambridge, MA: MIT Press).

Stcherbatsky, F., 1962, *Buddhist Logic*, Vol. 1 (New York: Dover Publications).

Strawson, Galen, 1997, 'The Self', *Journal of Consciousness Studies*, Vol. 4, Nos 5/6, pp. 405–28.

Strawson, P.F., 1959, *Individuals: An Essay in Descriptive Metaphysics* (London: Methuen).

Taylor, Charles, 1981, *The Sources of the Self* (Cambridge, MA: Cambridge University Press).

Udayanacarya, 1940, *Atmatattvaviveka* (Varanasi: Chowkhamba Sanskrit Series Office).

Vaidya, P. L., ed., 1960, *The Madhyamakasastra of Nagarjuna* (Darbhanga: Mithila Institute).

Vasubandhu, 1925, *Vijnaptimatratasiddhi, Vimsatika et Trimsika*, Pub. et trad. par S. Levi, I. Text sanskrit, Paris: Materiaux pour l'etude de systeme Vijnaptimatrata, 1932.

Wilber, Ken, 1997, 'An Integral Theory of Consciousness', *Journal of Consciousness Studies*, Vol. 4, No. 1.

Brahma Sutra.

Brhadaranyaka Upanisad.

Brhaspati Sutra.

Jayarasi, *Tattvopaplava Simha.*

Kanada Sutra.

Nyay Sutra.

Ramanujacarya, *Sribhasya* (Nirnayasagar edition).

Ratnakuta Sutra.

Srinivasa, *Yatindramatadipika* (Anandaasrama edition).

Sadananda, *Vedantasara.*

Vacaspati Misra, *Tattvakaumudi.*

Yoga Sutra.

Index

About the Author

Anindita Niyogi Balslev is a philosopher and the initiator of the forum 'Cross-Cultural Conversation' (CCC). She graduated from the University of Calcutta and received her doctorate from the University of Paris. Her educational, research and teaching experience span over India, France, Denmark, and USA. She has published widely in the areas of Indian and Western thought, culture and religion. She has organized several important international CCC conferences focusing on concerns relevant for meeting of cultures and encounter of world religions. She has published widely in the areas of Indian and Western thought, culture, and religion. Apart from numerous articles in professional journals, her publications include *A Study of Time in Indian Philosophy, Cultural Otherness: Correspondence with Richard Rorty, Indian conceptual World*, and the edited volumes, *Cross Cultural Conversation, Toward Greater Human Solidarity*, and *On India:Self-image and Counter-image*. She is also the co-editor of the volumes, *Compassion in the World's Religions* and *Religion and Time*.